To Faith,
I look forward
to working with
you soon.

Sincerely,
Marty Redish

The Adversary First Amendment

FREE EXPRESSION AND THE
FOUNDATIONS OF AMERICAN
DEMOCRACY

Martin H. Redish

STANFORD LAW BOOKS

An Imprint of Stanford University Press

Stanford, California

Stanford University Press
Stanford, California

Printed in the United States of America on acid-free, archival-quality
paper

Library of Congress Cataloging-in-Publication Data

Redish, Martin H., author.
    The adversary First Amendment : free expression and the
foundations of American democracy / Martin H. Redish.
        pages cm
    Includes bibliographical references and index.
    ISBN 978-0-8047-7215-0 (cloth : alk. paper)
    1. Freedom of expression—United States. 2. United States.
Constitution. 1st Amendment. 3. Democracy—United States.
I. Title.
        KF4770.R428 2013
        323.440973—dc23   2012049540

ISBN 978-0-8047-8634-8 (electronic)

Typeset by Thompson Type in 10/13 Galliard

For Caren

Contents

Preface

This book is the outgrowth of the last five years of my scholarship on the theory of free expression. In a certain sense, however, it is designed to serve as a prequel to much of my scholarly work on the First Amendment over the last forty years. It is in this book that I have, I believe, finally located the core first principles of political theory that have always provided the implicit framework for my writings on the First Amendment.

Many of the chapters find their origins in articles I have authored or coauthored in recent years, though in each case the final chapter represents a revised version of the prior works. In some cases, the individual chapters represent a synthesis of one or more articles with earlier scholarship. More important, the articles have been modified to bring them together as a coherent statement of the political foundations of the theory of free expression.

Portions of Chapters Two and Four grew out of my article, "Understanding Post's and Meiklejohn's Mistakes: The Central Role of Adversary Democracy in the Theory of Free Expression," 103 *Northwestern University Law Review* 1303 (2009), coauthored with former student Abby Marie Mollen. Chapter Three is based on my article, "Commercial Speech, First Amendment Intuitionism and the Twilight Zone of Viewpoint Discrimination," 41 *Loyola Los Angeles Law Review* 67 (2007). Chapter Five derives from my article, "'Worse than the Disease': The Anti-Corruption Principle, Free Expression, and the Democratic Process," 20 *William & Mary Bill of Rights Journal* 1053 (2011), coauthored with former student Elana Nightingale Dawson. Finally, Chapter Six finds its origins in my essay, "Freedom of Expression, Political Fraud, and the Dilemma of Anonymity," which first appeared in a volume entitled *Speech and Silence in*

American Law, edited by Austin Sarat and published by Cambridge University Press in 2010. These articles have been reproduced with the permission of the publishers.

Both of my coauthors, Abby Mollen and Elana Nightingale-Dawson, deserve significant credit for shaping the articles on which we collaborated. In addition, I would like to thank Matthew Arnould, Kerry Slade, and Vanessa Szalapski, all current or former students at Northwestern University School of Law, for their invaluable research assistance on different portions of the book.

This book would not have been possible without the support—both moral and financial—of Northwestern University School of Law and both its current dean, Daniel Rodriguez, and its former dean, David Van Zandt. I am forever in their debt for the way in which both did all they could to facilitate my research on this book. I also appreciate the thoughtful and insightful challenges of my Northwestern colleague Andy Koppleman, who constantly forced me to refine and rethink the positions I take in this book—thereby making them stronger—through his powerful intellectual critiques of my theories.

In addition, my sincere thanks go out to Marcia Lehr, librarian at Northwestern Law, for her resourcefulness in helping me track down books and articles, and Juana Haskin, my assistant, for her tireless efforts in revising draft after draft of the manuscript. Both played a vital role in the preparation of this book.

Finally, deserving of special appreciation are the members of my family—my wife, Caren, and my daughters, Jessica and Elisa. Without their unwavering love and support, none of this would matter.

THE ADVERSARY FIRST AMENDMENT

CHAPTER ONE

Introduction: The First Amendment and American Democracy

The assertion that democracy and free expression are inextricably inter-twined in a symbiotic relationship should hardly be controversial. Democracy could not exist in any meaningful sense absent a societal commitment to basic notions of free expression, nor could free expression flourish in a society uncommitted to democracy. It is therefore not surprising that among the most prominent and widely accepted theories of the First Amendment are those that explain the Free Speech Clause as either catalyst for or protection of democracy itself.[1] These democratic theories of the First Amendment posit that speech receives constitutional protection because it is essential to a functioning and legitimate democracy. Different democratic theories of the First Amendment suggest competing explanations of exactly how free speech advances or defends democracy. Some suggest that free speech facilitates the informed decision making that self-rule requires.[2] Others argue that free speech furthers democracy by allowing individuals to recognize themselves as self-governing.[3] Still others simply conclude, without elaboration, that democracy would be "meaningless" without the freedom to discuss government and its policies.[4] Every democratic theory of the First Amendment, though, in one way or another views free speech as a means to a democratic end.

Of course, democracy itself is an amorphous concept, both historically and theoretically.[5] Despite the concept's simple translation to "rule by the people," political theorists since Aristotle have advanced competing theories of democracy that are inconsistent, if not contradictory.[6] To say that the First Amendment advances "democracy" without more, then, is to say much less than First Amendment scholars often assume.[7] Still, "democracy" is not so empty a referent that it is impossible to evaluate whether so-called democratic theories of the First Amendment are indeed democratic.

The goals of this book are threefold: first, to demonstrate that the form of democratic theory that appropriately characterizes the American governmental system—both normatively and descriptively—is adversary democracy; second, to establish the inescapable linkage between that form of democracy and the philosophical foundations of the First Amendment right of free expression; and third, to explore the implications of the framework for specific issues of free expression of current importance. Specifically, doctrinal issues to be examined include the protection of commercial speech, the constitutional right to anonymity, and the validity of the so-called anticorruption principle as a limitation on the constitutional right of free expression in the context of the electoral process.

Any democratic theory must encompass two principles. First, democratic theories must respect the principle of self-rule. They may differ about what it means, precisely, for the people to govern themselves, but they must at least accept the basic premise that democracy requires self-government.[8] Otherwise, democracy would incoherently collapse into authoritarianism. Democratic theories, as a result, must respect the principle of epistemological humility. In other words, they must assume that no determinate "truth" or "good" exists, apart from what the electorate or those accountable to it determine. Democratic theories must therefore commit such substantive valuations to the people to decide through democratic procedures.[9] Epistemological humility is a direct outgrowth of the principle of self-rule: The people cannot be self-governing if some external concept of truth or goodness coercively determines their decisions.

Second, democracy must mean that government follows the self-governing decisions of the people—either because the people themselves make and implement their decisions or because the people's elected representatives are accountable for doing so. Again, democratic theories can differ over how exactly this occurs, particularly in a representative democracy. The point, though, is that democracy must at least assume that authority is "controlled by public opinion, not public opinion by authority."[10] This second principle overlaps with the first: Public opinion must be autonomous from government to check government. As a result, any democratic theory must prohibit the government from managing public opinion, whether by overt coercion or by the indirect manipulation that comes with forcing a people to be ignorant. In the words of Thomas Jefferson, "If a nation expects to be ignorant and free . . . it expects what never was and never will be."[11]

A number of respected free speech theorists have understood democratic autonomy in its collective sense. Alexander Meiklejohn, for example, believed that democracy is simply a "compact" among individuals to govern in pursuit of the common good.[12] Robert Post likewise begins with the premise that "democracy is not about individual self-government, but about collective self-determination"[13] and ends with the conclusion that "democracy requires individual autonomy only to the extent that citizens seek to forge 'a common will, communicatively shaped and discursively clarified in the political public sphere.'"[14] Thus, both theorists ultimately understand democracy largely as a cooperative pursuit in which individuals collectively "plan[] for the general welfare"[15] or "forge a common will."[16] It is therefore appropriate to characterize each theory as positing a "cooperative" ideal of democracy.

Yet, as much as democracy includes this potential for societal cooperation, it must also embrace the inevitability of competition, among both competing ideologies and competing interests. For democracy to reflect both the political realities of a large, heterogenous, and pluralistic society and the normative values that underlie the precept of self-government, it must be grounded in the centrality of diversity and potential competition among the backgrounds, statuses, values, needs, and interests of the citizens. The assumption that all of these competing backgrounds, values, needs, and interests may be forged into a cooperative pursuit of some notion of the common good is quixotic at best and disingenuously manipulative at worst.

In contrast to these collectivist theories of democracy, the theory of adversary democracy both acknowledges the inevitable existence of conflict among competing interests as a descriptive matter and embraces its pluralism and diversity as a normative matter. This does not necessarily mean that adversary democracy categorically rejects the value of cooperation. The key cooperative element inherent in adversary democracy recognizes the need for peaceful and orderly processes by which these often competing needs, values, and interests may be resolved. Indeed, to deny or ignore these individual needs, interests, and values would be to deny the individuality and integrity of the citizens, thereby rendering the democratic process a counterproductive exercise. At its core, then, American democracy involves an ordered form of adversary process, in which citizens must be allowed to determine for themselves what governmental choices will improve their lives or implement values they hold dear and then to seek to persuade others to accept their views.

Contrary to the cooperative ideal of democracy, this book adopts a notion of representative government built on the concept of adversary democracy, drawn from modern political theory. Based on the premise that democracy at its core involves a competition among adverse interests, this book argues that the purpose of democracy is to guarantee individuals the opportunity to seek to affect the outcomes of collective decision making according to their own values and interests as they understand them. The book therefore concludes that a valid democratic theory of the First Amendment must be construed to reach all speech that allows individuals to discover their personal needs, interests, and goals—in government and in society at large—and to advocate and vote accordingly.[17] Individuals' free speech rights may therefore not be limited or excluded from the scope of the constitutional guarantee either because the speaker seeks to advance her own personal interests rather than those of the public at large or because the speaker seeks to exercise her right in a competitive, rather than a cooperative, manner. It is true, of course, that no First Amendment theorist would actually exclude from the constitutional guarantee *all* expression that fits this description. Many scholars who would exclude from the First Amendment's reach certain expression because of its selfish motivation readily extend protection to equally self-promoting expression in other contexts.[18] But that fact is itself a symptom of the pathology that inescapably flows from theorists' failure to recognize the universality of adversary democracy as the foundation of the constitutional protection for free expression.[19] It is the *selective* exclusion of categories of expression because of their adversary or self-promotional nature that underscores the inherently irrational (or on occasion, ideologically manipulative) nature of the more communitarian or cooperative theories of free expression.[20]

Those free speech scholars who have shaped democratic theories of free expression have almost universally viewed democracy in the cooperative or collectivist sense. In contrast, this book seeks to provide a global alternative to the collectivist democratic visions of these scholars. The position taken here is that to provide expression with the necessary level of protection, free speech theory must be shaped in accordance with the precepts of adversary democracy. The common linkage in the mistakes of prior theorists of democratic free speech is their failure to recognize the central role that adversary democracy both should and does play in the American political and constitutional structures. The adversary theory of democracy emphasizes individual autonomy as theoretically and practically interwoven into the processes of collective self-government. Based on the adversary theory of democracy, this book proposes a new democratic theory of the First Amendment—one very different from those proposed to date by leading free speech theorists.

In the chapter that follows, the book explores the theoretical underpinnings of the concept of adversary democracy, explains its centrality to American democratic theory, and asserts the inherent symbiotic intersection of adversary democracy and the theory of free expression.[21] Chapter Three critically examines the free speech theories of the two leading cooperative democratic theorists of free expression, Robert Post and Alexander Meiklejohn. The chapter explores the significant flaws in both of their theories flowing from their failure to recognize the centrality of adversary democracy in the modern theory of free expression.[22] In Chapter Four the book applies the First Amendment theory of adversary democracy to commercial speech. The chapter argues that free speech theorists' opposition to the extension of full First Amendment protection to commercial speech because of its inherently selfish motivation improperly ignores the inherently adversary and self-promotional nature of much noncommercial expression, which has traditionally been extended full constitutional protection.[23] Chapter Five critically examines the so-called anticorruption principle, which seeks to rationalize wide-ranging restrictions on self-interested political activities. The chapter argues that the core premises underlying the anticorruption principle are fundamentally inconsistent with both the normative foundations of the American democratic system and well-accepted political practice. Chapter Six recognizes the need for qualifications on the First Amendment right in an effort to avoid the potential pathologies that potentially flow from a commitment to adversary democracy as the political foundation of free expression. The chapter proposes imposition of strict limitations on any First Amendment–based right of speaker anonymity, so that recipients of the expression will be able to discount appropriately for speaker bias or interest.[24] All of the chapters are linked by their ultimate reliance on the concept of adversary democracy and the democratic theory of free expression that grows out of it.[25]

CHAPTER TWO

Adversary Democracy and American Political Theory

DEFINING ADVERSARY DEMOCRACY

"Adversary democracy" is a democratic theory that acknowledges that disagreement characterizes collective self-government in a heterogeneous society and that values democracy precisely for the autonomy it provides the individual in this setting of conflict.[1] It is adversarial in the *descriptive* sense because it recognizes that individuals' conflicting interests will always divide a heterogeneous society and, to varying degrees, affect individuals' participation in self-government.[2] Adversary democracy recognizes that, in a large and diverse society, the notion of a consensus form of democratic decision making in which the collective cooperatively seeks to advance the "common good" is unrealistic at best and manipulative at worst. This form of democracy is adversarial in the *normative* sense because it recognizes democracy as a system of collective self-government that manages conflict—and thus protects and facilitates individual autonomy—by institutionalizing it as a normal part of democratic life.[3]

The word *conflict*, as used here, refers to the competing interests and ideologies that motivate individuals and that may foreclose the existence of, or collective agreement on, a singular vision of a substantive common good.[4] Cooperative theories of democracy either unrealistically assume individuals will ignore their own self-interest or personal ideology to pursue a common good or assume that democratic processes can resolve conflict by somehow forging a common will. By sublimating conflict, cooperative theories invite it to take a pathological form. In other words, they have the effect of inviting democracy to deteriorate into a "tyranny of the majority" in which conflict is resolved by exclusion, marginalization of minority interests, and ultimately domination.[5]

Adversary democracy institutionalizes and thus tempers conflict in two ways. First, it grants individuals equal power to affect the outcome of collective decision making by virtue of their power to vote.[6] In this sense, adversary democracy understands democracy as an *ex ante* agreement among potential opponents to resolve disputes as merely adversaries, rather than mortal enemies.[7] The value of democracy from this perspective is simultaneously individuals' power to seek to implement their preferences and their security from domination even when they are in the minority. As such, adversary democracy is a theory of democratic equality: In the words of the scholar who first recognized this form of democracy, the central egalitarian ideal in an adversary democracy becomes "the equal protection of interests, guaranteed by the equal distribution of power through the vote."[8] In this sense, the theory is "adversarial" because it recognizes that democratic decision making involves a contest between individuals who each possess power to affect its outcome. The individual's power to vote, in and of itself, does not automatically constitute the power to institutionalize and enforce his preferences. Nevertheless, he possesses the ability to join with others having shared interests and ideologies to influence public opinion and shape the outcome of collective decisions by influencing the votes of other individuals. The relationship is adversarial, rather than cooperative, because it acknowledges that collective decision making will inevitably produce winners and losers.

Although adversary democracy requires the losers to consent to majority rule, it does not force losers to adopt majority preferences as their own.[9] In this sense, the theory is adversarial because it rejects Aristotelian harmony as the normative goal of politics, instead accepting ongoing adversarial conflict and dissent as normal—indeed, expected—aspects of political life. The value of democracy under this principle is individuals' abiding liberty to engage in an adversarial critique of the existing political order itself and, in doing so, to convince others to join them. As philosopher Stuart Hampshire has argued, because individuality depends on the individual's ability to "resist the invasion and dominance of the active things around it," diversity and conflict are "not a superficial but an essential and deep feature of human nature—both unavoidable and desirable."[10] The associative value of democracy under this principle, then, is its respect for individual autonomy.[11]

THE TWO VERSIONS OF ADVERSARY
DEMOCRATIC THEORY

Adversary democracy can be grounded in liberal democratic theory, as well as in the far more cynical pluralistic version of democratic theory sometimes referred to as "possessive individualism," a branch of public choice theory. Though in a certain sense the two theories appear to begin from very different assumptions about human nature, ultimately the two rationales coexist. Both the pluralistic and liberal versions of adversary theory have long and partially intersecting philosophical traditions. Pluralistic adversary theory finds its origins in the writings of Thomas Hobbes, who "developed a political theory based on self-interest alone."[12] The theory corresponded with the free market capitalistic marketplace of Adam Smith.[13] Such pluralistic, self-interest based theories, as previously noted, can be described as "possessive individualism."[14] According to one scholar, "In the political theory of possessive individualism society is presumed to consist of relations among independent owners, and the primary task of government is to protect owners against illegitimate incursions upon their property and to maintain conditions of orderly exchange."[15] This exposition of adversary theory may be characterized as a kind of skeptical, "self-protective" version of liberal political theory that effectively allows each individual to "watch his back" because someone inevitably will attempt to insert a knife into it. Under this rationale for adversary theory, because of surrounding hostile forces it is only through self-protective efforts that the individual may secure or advance his own interests.

This pluralistic version of adversary theory has long been subject to attack, not only by communitarian and civic republican theorists but by certain liberal theorists as well.[16] To a certain extent, however, its skeptical elements have been used effectively by the most idealistic liberal forces in American society. For example, African Americans' political and legal efforts to bring about racial integration of privately owned public accommodations in the late 1950s and early 1960s were clearly grounded in the belief that individual dignity is inherently intertwined with the ability to challenge, through resort to adversary legal and political processes, powerful and long-established local communitarian traditions that reduce the advocate's personal welfare.

On the level of abstract political theory, the real-world example of the integration movement underscores the philosophical and pragmatic intersection between the skeptical pluralistic adversary theory on the one hand

and the considerably more positive and optimistic liberal democratic version often associated with the developmental theories of John Stuart Mill on the other.[17] According to a respected democratic theorist, the developmental theory associated with liberal democracy

> assumes that the individual will is the cause of all actions, individual and collective; it ascribes decisive epistemic and hence moral authority to the individual over his actions, on the grounds that he has privileged access to the contents of his own mind. For this reason individual consent becomes vital to the whole idea of political activity.[18]

The developmental model of democratic theory, so valued by liberal theorists, proceeds on the premise that

> Human dignity would be threatened by absolute power, for without an opportunity to participate in the regulation of affairs in which one has an interest, it is hard to discover one's own needs and wants, arrive at tried-and-tested judgments and develop mental excellence of an intellectual, practical and moral kind. Active involvement in determining the conditions of one's existence is the prime mechanism for the cultivation of human reason and moral development.[19]

The liberal individualist version of democratic theory posits that recognition of the individual's mental integrity and autonomy gives rise to corresponding recognition of the developmental value inherent in liberal democracy.[20] In the words of one commentator, "The most distinctive feature, and the principal orienting value, of classical democratic theory was its emphasis on individual participation in the development of public policy. . . . Above all else classical democratic theorists were concerned with *human development*, the opportunities which existed in political activity to realize the untapped potentials of men."[21]

Because the concern with human development may be described as instrumental, it possesses qualities reminiscent of traditional utilitarian theory. However, John Stuart Mill's version of utilitarianism differed substantially from those of his father, James Mill, and Jeremy Bentham. Where the theories of the elder Mill and Bentham sought to attain solely the greatest good for the greatest number regardless of the impact on any particular individual, the younger Mill sought to shape the instrumental goal more in terms of individual development and advancement. Additionally, the individual dignitary theories that underlie certain versions of liberal democratic theory have on occasion been grounded in Kantian moral abstractions, which posit individual liberty as a moral first principle.[22]

As the example of the 1960s civil rights sit-in movement in the American South demonstrates, both the pluralistic and liberal versions of adversary theory intersect on certain levels, even though developmental concerns appear to be of little immediate concern to those who adopt the pluralistic version. This is so because the pluralistic version of adversary democracy may effectively serve as a type of bodyguard for attainment of the developmental values inherent in the liberal democratic version. According to political scientist David Held, the Millian version of democratic theory posits that "the best safeguard against the disregarding of an individual's rights is when he or she is able to participate routinely in their articulation."[23]

While the two versions of adversary theory overlap to a certain extent, by no means are they identical. For example, pluralistic adversary theory, which is grounded in precepts of possessive individualism, is generally either agnostic or directly hostile to the developmental goals associated with liberal democratic adversary theory.[24] It is also true, however, that although liberal democratic theory sees individual development and growth as the ultimate goal, it recognizes the need for a healthy degree of concern about the potentially harmful impact that the behavior of others may have on an individual's ability to advance his own interests. For example, the skepticism of human behavior inherent in the separation-of-powers structure adopted in the U.S. Constitution[25] reflects a recognition of the need for such vigilance.[26] Thus, while liberal democratic theory extends far beyond the unduly truncated perspective of pluralistic theory, it nevertheless recognizes the need to employ the protections and skepticism inherent in the pluralistic version of democratic thought. The protections and skepticism serve as a means of shielding the individual's ability to develop her faculties by advancing her interests and ideals as she conceptualizes them against the hostile forces that exist in society.

ADVERSARY DEMOCRACY AND THE COMMON GOOD

The normative principle of adversary democracy recognizes that individuals' ability to further their own interests—by identifying them, by voting according to them, and by advocating that others vote in a similar manner—creates the possibility of a form of individual self-rule even within the context of collective decision making. In this sense, adversary democracy advances the core democratic notion of autonomy in a way that a purely cooperative democratic theory cannot: It values and protects individual autonomy. In this manner, adversary democracy reflects the Kantian notion that the individual is an integral unit worthy of respect, not a means to an end. Adversary theory thus contrasts sharply with exclusively participatory versions of democratic theory because those theories systematically marginalize pure exercises of individual autonomy, considering individual autonomy to be relevant to democracy only to the extent it facilitates collective autonomy.[27] And it contrasts starkly with those versions of democratic thought that completely ignore individual worth and integrity to the extent that they assume that democracy is simply a compact among citizens to govern for the common good.[28]

To understand how liberal democratic adversary theory interacts with the communitarian–individualist debate, one must first distinguish among concepts that are easy to confuse. Initially, it is necessary to distinguish between the concepts of "the common good," which communitarian and cooperative theorists proclaim as the only legitimate focus of citizen attention, and "altruism," which describes efforts to advance on protest interests other than one's own.[29] The confusion derives from the fact that both are often viewed as the antithesis of the narrow pursuit of self-interest. In a certain sense, of course, this is true; one who pursues only her own narrow self-interest is simultaneously not altruistic and not concerned with the good of society as a whole. Yet the two concepts are by no means identical.

The differences between altruism and pursuit of the common good can be grasped by attempting to determine the meaning of the phrase, "the common good." The concept is a surprisingly difficult one to define. Consider the following six options, each of which could plausibly be thought to grasp the essence of the phrase:

1. The interest of society as a whole, divorced from the interests of its individual members;
2. The attempt, where possible, to maximize the welfare of all individuals through the restriction or rejection of the shortsighted or information-lacking pursuit by each individual of his self-interest;
3. The sum total of each individual's private self-interests;
4. The determination of what policy choices would maximize the welfare of the collective as a whole, rather than the welfare of particular individuals, with the particular policy choices determined through an assessment of a consensus of the community, following a process of open deliberation;

5. If collective maximization of welfare is impossible because of inherent conflicts in individual interests and/or values, the choice of one set of those interests by those in power, combined with the simultaneous imposition of the label of "common good" on that set of interests; or

6. If collective maximization of welfare is impossible because of inherent conflicts in individual interests and/or values, the decision to abide by the free and fair choice of the democratic process, following free and open debate.

Closer examination of option (1) reveals its inherently nonsensical nature: There is no society that fails to include its individual members. Thus, a decision to pursue the common good must have as its goal the desire to benefit somebody. As Jon Elster has persuasively explained:

> We cannot coherently imagine a world in which everyone had exclusively altruistic motivations. The goal of the altruist is to provide others with an occasion for selfish pleasure. . . . If nobody had first-order, selfish pleasures, nobody could have higher-order, altruistic motives either. . . . The point is just a logical one. If some are to be altruistic, others must be selfish, at least some of the time.[30]

Recognition of the logical absurdity of option (1) as a definition of the concept of "the common good" thus underscores the inherent differences that necessarily exist between that phrase and the concept of altruism. The pursuit of the common good cannot be *purely* altruistic because such a process inevitably seeks to benefit at least some of those who are both making and being affected by the relevant decisions.[31]

Option (2) focuses on one version of the so-called prisoners' dilemma. In that hypothetical dilemma, each of two prisoners is asked to give evidence that will convict the other. If one remains silent but the other gives evidence, the prisoner who remains silent will receive a heavy jail term, and the prisoner who gives evidence will be released. If, however, each gives evidence against the other, they will both be convicted and sentenced to prison. If both remain silent, there would be insufficient evidence to convict either of them, and both would go free. However, they are not allowed to consult with each other, so neither knows what strategy the other plans to employ. Obviously, the welfare of both would be maximized if each remained silent. Yet if both testify, the interests of each will be negatively impacted. However, if one chooses to remain silent while the other chooses to testify, the latter would be considerably better off than the former. Clearly, the two could maximize each of their welfares by joining forces and working together, were that possible. The problem is that neither can know what choice the other will make. Under option (2), then, the common good is defined as the recognition that under certain circumstances, the welfare of every member of society may be maximized by resorting to collaborative efforts, rather than by the isolationistic pursuit of individual self-interest.

Such reasoning underlies the U.S. Constitution's Privileges and Immunities Clause.[32] Individual states are prohibited from pursuing narrow self-interest by discriminating against out-of-staters, despite the apparent creation of an immediate competitive advantage, because to do so would inevitably induce retaliatory behavior on the part of other states and thereby undermine all states' welfare.[33] As a result, the long-range interests of all the states are advanced. Under option (2), it should be noted, the concept of the common good still differs starkly from the concept of altruism: Efforts of individuals are joined, not to benefit others who are deserving of charity but rather solely to benefit the individual participants themselves.

Option (3) describes the version of the common good associated with pluralistic adversary theory.[34] In effect, under this option, there is no such thing as the common good: "From the interchange between self-interested voters and self-interested brokers emerge decisions that come as close as possible to a balanced aggregation of individual interests."[35] This is the version of adversary theory that has long been the subject of attack by modern civic republicans,[36] although in many ways it is little more than a caricature of adversary theory as it exists in prevailing liberal democratic thought.[37] As option (2) illustrates, even theories that begin with the premise of a need to further individual self-interest wisely acknowledge that under certain circumstances individual welfare may ultimately be maximized by eschewing the myopic pursuit of one's own narrow self-interest and recognizing how one's interests are intertwined with the interests of others. Such a version of the common good involves considerably more than a mechanistic summing of distinct individual interests. At most, a realistic version of this theory would recognize that at least in a variety of situations, individuals are likely to pursue nothing more than their own self-interests, divorced from any concern for either the interests of other individuals or society as a whole.

Option (4) roughly describes the concept of the common good as understood by modern civic republicans and communitarians. In important ways, this option is just as divorced from reality as is option (3). True, this option does not suffer from the logical fallacy that plagues option (1) because it does not purport to view the common good as a concept wholly distinct from the interests of society's individual members. Nevertheless, as already noted, on a purely practical level the idea that in a society as large and diverse as ours it is possible to derive a societal consensus that amounts to a monolithic community interest is pure folly.

This insight leads us inexorably to option (5), which basically amounts to a deconstructed version of option (4): Reliance on the language of the common good, consensus development, and deliberation is nothing more than a strategically motivated mode of argumentation that seeks to preempt expression of a diversity of views on moral, political, or economic issues by artificially placing the mantel of "the common good" on what is nothing more than one side of those various arguments.[38] This strategy adds an entirely new dimension to the process of democratic conflict and argumentation, for it enables its users to undermine their opponents' arguments, not merely by defeating the persuasiveness of those arguments in the minds of a majority of the electorate or its chosen representatives (two-dimensional argumentation) but also by effectively challenging the character and good faith of their opponents by accusing them of selfishness (three-dimensional argumentation). It is simply a more sophisticated version of the tactics employed by certain elements of the political right during the so-called McCarthy era of the 1940s and 1950s: efforts to defeat political arguments not only by responding on the merits but also by questioning the patriotism of those who take the opposite position.

Option (6), when combined with option (2), basically describes the concept of the common good as understood in liberal democratic adversary theory. It recognizes that an individual is simultaneously an integral whole and a member of broader, often overlapping communities. This option further recognizes that not only are pursuit of individual interest and pursuit of the common good not mutually exclusive; they are in fact, generally intertwined in a symbiotic intersection. Where individuals are viewed as nothing more than mindless spokes in a communitarian wheel, the entire community suffers because ultimately it must be acknowledged that the community is made up of its individual members. When they are viewed as part of a community, individuals are properly viewed not as isolated or atomistic entities but as socially interacting units. But to ignore the integral nature of the individual, even in this social context, threatens to disregard the essential premises of democratic theory.

Once it is recognized that individuals, even though members of a community, remain integral and mentally autonomous entities deserving of dignity and respect, it logically follows that individuals should be encouraged and expected to employ their personal resources to determine the choices and courses of action that will maximize the welfare of both them and their families. Where individuals prefer, they may base their choices on altruistic considerations, designed primarily to aid others in need of assistance. Where individuals so decide, they may also advocate a path that will benefit the greatest number within the community more than it benefits themselves. The point is, simply, that under the terms of liberal democratic theory, this choice is ceded—in the first instance, at least—to the individual members of society. It is not to be made for them by some external force.

When viewed as a means of implementing the fundamental values of liberal democratic theory, adversary theory plays a central and legitimate role in democratic thought. Once we conclude that, as part of the political process, individuals possess a fundamental right to advance their own interests as they assess them, the precepts of adversary theory flow inexorably. An individual or grouping of individuals may legitimately stake out a particular set of interests which they deem worthy of advancement because they believe advancement of those interests would maximize their own welfare, others' welfare, or the welfare of society as a whole. As a theory of political process, democracy must be formally agnostic among these choices. Liberal democratic theory simultaneously recognizes that individuals may properly differ as to the relevant interests to be fostered, and that on occasion it will be necessary to resolve those conflicts in a nonviolent but nevertheless contentious manner by resort to the democratic process.

Economic theory proffers the principle of externalities, which posits that where the impact of an action will not have an impact on one's own interests, the rational actor has no incentive to seek the effective and efficient performance of that action.[39] Thus, if an individual were required to entrust the protection or advancement of her own interests to another whom she has not selected of her own accord, she could not be assured that her interests would be effectively pursued because ceding such an authority would give rise to an externality.[40] Moreover, requiring the individual to entrust others with protection of her interests would undermine the developmental values that underlie liberal democratic theory.[41]

Adversary democratic theory, then, recognizes that: (1) Individuals and/or voluntary associations of individuals have both the moral right and the pragmatic need to resort to the political or judicial processes to protect or advance their own or other selected interests; (2) on many important issues, the interests or concerns of all relevant individuals and groups will not be identical—indeed they will, in fact, often be diametrically opposed to each other; (3) there exists no empirical or intuitive basis on which to believe that those in power who do not share an individual's or group's interest will have as their goal the protection or advancement of that interest; and (4) even in situations of identical or overlapping interest individuals or groups should not be required to trust in or defer to the competence, resources, or enthusiasm of others in the protection or advancement of their chosen interest.

Adversary democratic theory accepts that, in any but the most homogeneous society, there are likely to exist opposing interests and, therefore, a potential for conflict. Unlike the modern communitarian or civic republican philosophies, which purport to shun conflict—especially conflict that is grounded in disputes over competing self-interests—in favor of a search for consensus and universalism grounded in the use of deliberation and the vagaries of "practical reason,"[42] adversary theory embraces such conflict. Adversary theory views these conflicts as the reflection of the process-based values inherent in a democratic system. Those values acknowledge the virtual inevitability of individual diversity and differences of opinion on issues involving societal and individual needs, interests, and moral choices. The fundamental flaw in modern civic republican or communitarian philosophy is that by purporting to value consensus and moral universalism, these theories do not actually do away either with the stark reality of conflict or the existence of diverse and often competing interests of groups and individuals participating in the process. Indeed, in a society as large and diverse as ours, any hope of attaining such consensus through the voluntary use of deliberative processes is, at best, quixotic and, at worst, disingenuous.[43] It is likely, then, that what is going on in the modern civic republican revolution is reliance on these terms and concepts as little more than euphemisms for the imposition of the particular set of value choices favored by those urging attainment of some notion of normative consensus.

It logically follows from this discussion that under certain circumstances adversary theory as employed in liberal democratic society may apply even where an individual seeks to protect or advance an interest other than his own. Therefore the contentious nature of adversary democratic theory may operate comfortably within a framework of altruism or idealism. For example, right-to-life advocates, either in the political or legal processes, surely are operating in an adversary mode, yet the concerns they seek to promote would have to be called altruistic or ideological, rather than narrowly self-interested or purely for purposes of personal gain. Thus, adverseness, in either the political or legal contexts, is by no means synonymous with the exclusive and narrow promotion of personal self-interest. It is therefore important to understand that adverseness as it operates within liberal democratic theory does not necessarily equate with selfishness. Nor does adversary theory inherently imply a preference for antagonism and combat over reconciliation and cooperation. To the contrary, parties locked in an adversary competition may well choose to resolve their conflict by mutual agreement. By way of example, in the legal system, the overwhelming portion of formalistically antagonistic litigations is ultimately settled before any final judicial resolution has been made. This results not out of a desire to work cooperatively with others in an effort to seek out and advance the common good but rather because of the participants' recognition that under the circumstances mutually beneficial resolution will advance their interests more than would continued battle. Adversary theory, then, is necessarily characterized by neither a rigid, pluralistic, and isolationistic individualism nor an unremittingly antagonistic approach to issues of conflict resolution.

CONSTITUTIONAL ADVERSARY DEMOCRACY

Not only does adversary democracy provide the most normatively appealing and theoretically coherent explanation of American democracy, it is the only theory of democracy that is descriptively consistent with the political system we presently have and have always had since the nation's founding.[44] The democratic theory of the Constitution largely reflects an adversarial, rather than a cooperative, theory of democracy. It does so in both normative and descriptive senses. It does so normatively by embracing the liberal ideal of individualism and the notion that the government of many should not overpower the rights of the individual. It does so descriptively in that its separation-of-powers structure reflects an awareness that conflict and competing interests inevitably divide society and punctuate politics. Indeed, according to historian Gordon Wood, by the 1780s the Framers had discarded as "altogether fictitious" the conventional wisdom that a homogeneity of interests could exist in a sufficiently small republic such that the "the interest of the majority would be the interest of the minority also."[45] To the contrary, the Framers were acutely aware of the divisions that inevitably existed within society and the factions they produced.[46] In addition, the Constitution dispensed with the classical republican notion that collective self-government requires pursuit of the common good rather than self-interest. Writing in 1785, Noah Webster argued that "self-interest was all there ever was" but that "under a democracy . . . a self-interested man must court the people, thus tending to make self-love coincide with the people's interest."[47] And, according to Gordon Wood, Madison considered "the really great danger to liberty . . . in America . . . [to be] that each individual may become insignificant in his own eyes—hitherto the very foundation of republican government."[48]

To say that the Framers grounded the Constitution in an assumption of adversary democracy is not to deny their enormous concern for the pathological and tyrannical potential of the factions that are necessary by-products of that form of democracy. James Madison's *Federalist No. 10*, for instance, famously describes the danger of factions and describes "secur[ing] the public good, and private rights against the danger of [the] faction" as a "great desideratum" of government.[49] But, rather than deny the persistence of conflict and self-interest and propose a system of government that would purport to eradicate both, the Framers created a constitutional solution that actually encourages, and seeks to manage, ongoing conflict. Madison argued that their solution—representative government in a large republic—would control the danger of factions by "extend[ing] the sphere" to include even more interests.[50] By breaking society into "so many parts, interests, and classes of citizens . . . the rights of individuals or of the minority, will be in little danger from interested combinations of the majority."[51] As one political theorist writes:

> Large scale factiousness, together with a "multiplicity" of interests and sects, mitigate the deleterious effects of factions in two ways. First, "extending the sphere"—that is, releasing voracious self-interested behavior in the vast territorial frontier of the United States—might splinter existing groups rather than make them larger. Second, widespread factional behavior might encourage the formation of cross-cutting cleavages—that is, heterogeneous and overlapping memberships that tend to moderate the politics of large groups and prevent social stratification.[52]

In other words, Madison thought the solution was to fight fire with fire. The more that "each representative pursues the factious interests of his constituency," the more likely the "various factious interests in the nation [would] balance each other off in the government" and "be rendered harmless."[53] The solution Madison envisioned to the problems created by the pathological dark side of adversary democracy was *more* conflict and competition, not less.

According to political scientist Jane Mansbridge, "The framers of the American Constitution explicitly espoused a philosophy of adversary democracy built on self-interest."[54] This philosophy shaped the Constitution in several ways. First, by putting certain individual rights beyond the reach of majoritarian enactments, the Bill of Rights actually enshrines and protects conflict. The Establishment and Free Exercise Clauses of the First Amendment, for instance, protect religious diversity and the divergent ideas of the "good life" that result from different religious beliefs. The Free Speech Clause likewise protects the liberty of the individual to speak pursuant to her own will, even though her speech conflicts with the existing order and ideas of the "common good" that the majority accepts. The Constitution's countermajoritarian protections, in other words, reject the ideal of widespread societal consensus. To the contrary, out of respect for individual autonomy they constitutionalize individual interest and the conflict it will often produce.

The Constitution further manifests the theory of adversary democracy through its structural provisions for the federal government, most notably checks and balances and the separation of powers—the separation of the Congress into two houses, the presidential veto, and the institution of judicial review. Each of these constitutional structures reflects a fundamental assumption that disagreement between competing interests will punctuate American politics and an attempt to set out certain "rules of the game" to manage this conflict. In this sense, they represent the descriptive principle of adversary democracy: *Conflict is inevitable.* More important, these institutions also represent the normative principle of adversary democracy: They institutionalize opposing interests in the government itself on the premise that conflict advances, rather than impedes, democracy. By splitting the executive, legislative, and judicial powers into three separate branches of government, the Constitution gives each branch the "necessary constitutional means and personal motives to resist encroachments of the others"[55] in order to "utilize the inherent conflicts 'sown in the nature of man' as a means of preserving freedom."[56]

The Constitution also reflects adversary democracy in what it intentionally chose *not* to do: emulate the Athenian governmental form, the paradigm of cooperative democracy.[57] Athenian democracy was, quite literally, rule by the people. Citizens exercised the legislative power by participating in the Assembly, a body comprised of all Athenian citizens, who numbered as many as 40,000 to 50,000.[58] Consistent with the cooperative ideal of democracy, deliberation in the Athenian Assembly was to produce a consensus on the common good,[59] and citizens were to subordinate their private interests to that goal.[60]

The Framers so equated democracy with Athenian democracy that they considered the form of government they created quite distinct from democracy all together. For instance, in *Federalist No. 14* James Madison wrote that "in a democracy, the people meet and exercise the government in person; in a republic, they assemble and administer it by their representatives and agents."[61] Aristotle would have agreed. With its separate executive, courts, and representative legislative bodies, the U.S. government more closely resembled the "mixed government" of Sparta, which Aristotle considered an "oligarchy," rather than the democracy of Athens.[62] Notably, the Framers did not reject Athenian democracy solely because it was impractical. Rather, they considered "pure democracy"—"a society consisting of a small number of citizens, who assemble and administer the government in person,"[63] such as Athens—to be an inherently unstable form of government that invited "popular despotism."[64] In Madison's words:

> A pure democracy, by which I mean a society consisting of a small number of citizens, who assemble and administer the government in person, can admit of no cure for the mischiefs of faction. A common passion or interest will, in almost every case, be felt by a majority of the whole; a communication and concert results from the form of government itself; and there is nothing to check the inducements to sacrifice the weaker party or an obnoxious individual. Hence it is that such democracies have ever been spectacles of turbulence and contention; have ever been found incompatible with personal security or the rights of property; and have in general been as short in their lives as they have been violent in their deaths. Theoretic politicians, who have patronized this species of government, have erroneously supposed that by reducing mankind to a perfect equality in their political rights, they would, at the same time, be perfectly equalized and assimilated in their possessions, their opinions, and their passions.[65]

In this passage, Madison was suggesting that the cooperative ideal is an illusion—and a dangerous one at that. This was certainly an accurate assessment of Athens, as critical analysis suggests that the cooperative ideal of Athenian democracy is simply an historical myth. First, the principle of *isegoria* (the citizen's equal right to speak) ensured neither that every individual did speak nor that certain individuals would not emerge as more vocal and powerful elites within the Assembly.[66] Second, political elites in the Assembly[67] advanced their own interests by couching them in notions of the common good.[68] Likewise, citizens organized political clubs—based on existing familial relationships and friendships, not issues[69]—to further their own advantage in the discussion.[70] Third, consensus based on the force of the better argument, while the ideal, was rarely the reality;[71] when the Assembly could not reach consensus, it resolved disagreement by majority vote.[72]

Not only did Madison recognize the inevitability of conflict in collective self-government, he also recognized the threat of the cooperative ideal in a society without a singular interest: the danger that a majority united behind a "common passion or interest" will "sacrifice the weaker party or an obnoxious individual" to its will.[73] Indeed, even assuming only the wisest citizens participated in this direct form of democracy, Madison still believed the result would be the trampling of minority interests. "Had every Athenian citizen been a Socrates," he wrote, "every Athenian assembly would still have been a mob."[74] Athenian democracy was not only impractical, it risked the "democratic despotism" that the Founders feared.[75] Of course the irony, as Thomas Sowell notes, is that America during the Founding era itself demonstrated the tyrannical danger of a majority united behind a common interest: "The one area in which a united national majority was easily identified in colonial America was race, and it was here that the loss of freedom was carried to its extreme in slavery."[76] But this only further demonstrates adversary democracy's key principle that all individuals and groups must be free to represent their own self-interests lest they be marginalized by others.

Modern political theorists have further illuminated the core principles of adversary democracy that animated Madison's argument in *Federalist No. 10*.[77] They have argued that, by recognizing and institutionalizing competition among conflicting interests, a democracy paradoxically diminishes ideological conflict and the domination of majority interests over minority interests. For instance, Joseph Schumpeter developed the insight that competition between political parties for votes disciplines elected officials by forcing them to be more responsive to voters' preferences.[78] Ian Shapiro has similarly argued that "genuine competition by decision-makers for the votes of those who are actually affected by their decisions" provides the principal means for preventing "domination."[79] Likewise, Chantal Mouffe has suggested that unless democracy recognizes competition and creates "legitimate political channels for dissenting voices [to] exist," conflict will take "violent forms" that ultimately destroy democracy.[80]

The suggestion that the Framers rejected the cooperative ideal that democracy pursues the common good or forges a common will does not necessarily imply that they rejected the possibility or desirability of compromise. Nor does it mean that adversary democracy in its modern form does so. The point, rather, is that such compromise, to the extent it does in fact take place, is appropriately viewed not necessarily as a reflection of a generalized consensus but often as a pragmatic reconciliation of diverse and competing viewpoints, through mutual recognition of the political strength of the opposing position.

THE PRACTICAL BENEFITS OF ADVERSARY DEMOCRACY

Beyond the salutary theoretical implications of adversary democracy, the concept's practical impact is to promote a variety of values that in turn advance individual and collective self-government. First, competition among individual interests invariably leads to increased dissemination of information relevant to democratic decision making. An individual interest, be it economically, socially, or ideologically motivated, creates a positive incentive for the accumulation and dissemination of relevant information that supports the position of the speaker and thereby helps persuade the public. The more information the individual marshals to support his position, the more likely it is that others will accept his position and vote (or pressure their representatives to vote) accordingly. Thus, acting out of their own individual interests in enacting their private preferences, individuals have the incentive to spend the time and resources necessary to inform others of their positions and the factual predicates for them. And it will often be the case that other individuals will do the same for the opposing viewpoint. As in the economy, the effect of competition in the realm of public opinion is to create more and cheaper information for the individual decision maker.

The beneficial impact of this increased dissemination is not reduced by the existence of the speaker's personal or economic motivation. For example, a producer of wind energy who lobbies for a tax policy favoring renewable energy sources provides relevant information about the feasibility and desirability of renewable energy, despite—indeed, quite probably because of—her pecuniary interest in the matter. To the extent the information she provides is selective or slanted by her own self-interest, the competitive posture of adversary democracy alerts the listener to discount the information accordingly.[81] Indeed, one of the benefits of adversary democracy is that it strips away the rhetoric of impartiality and bares self-interest to the public in a way that permits the public to discount it.

This reasoning should sound familiar to any American lawyer. As one commentator has suggested, "A fundamental premise of the adversary system of jurisprudence is that a competitive rather than cooperative presentation and analysis of the facts underlying a dispute will produce a greater number of correct results."[82] Another commentator has suggested that placing control of the presentation of evidence in the hands of self-interested parties—rather than in the hands of the adjudicator, as an inquisitorial system would—"improve[s] the overall quality of the evidence upon which adjudication [is] based."[83] Indeed, the commitment to adverse interests between the parties is so profound that the federal courts' jurisdiction under Article III of the Constitution depends on the existence of a "case or controversy," meaning a real, live dispute with potentially concrete consequences, and the justiciability doctrines further ensure the existence of "concrete adverseness" between the parties.[84]

The standing doctrine is most conspicuous in this regard. Plaintiffs may sue in federal court only if they have "personally suffered some actual or threatened injury," which is traceable to, and redressable by, the defendant—in other words, only if the plaintiff has something to gain and the defendant something to lose.[85] "Such a personal stake in the outcome of the controversy," the Supreme Court has explained, "assures[s] that concrete adverseness which sharpens the presentation of issues upon which the court so largely depends on for illumination of difficult constitutional questions."[86] Indeed, to the extent that a personal economic injury is the prototypical form of injury-in-fact, standing doctrine suggests those with a personal, economic self-interest are most certain to "sharpen[] the presentation of issues" to the benefit of the decision maker.[87]

Of course, an analogy to the legal system is not seamless. First, the judge and the jury are at least presumed to be neutral and disinterested, while the public decision maker under the adversarial model is neither. This distinction, however, goes to the neutrality of the listener, not the incentives and motivations of the potential speakers to provide information. So long as the listener may conceivably be persuaded, the speaker has an incentive to provide information. Indeed, to the extent the listener is self-interested, the speaker has an even greater incentive to present the best possible support for her position.

Another critique of the analogy to the adversary system may be that in court the Rules of Evidence and the Rules of Professional Conduct moderate the adverse incentives of self-interest, which otherwise might entice a litigant to deceive or mislead the court, whereas there is little formally to constrain the adverse incentives of the self-interested speaker in public debate. The public decision maker, however, need not rely on the information presented to her by any single party the way a court must. She can affirmatively seek out additional information and verify the information provided by the self-interested speaker in a way that a court or jury cannot. In public, more speech can remedy the adverse incentives of self-interest in a way it cannot in court. In any event, the Rules of Evidence and of Professional Conduct are exceptions to the general principle that no one may deny the attorney the general latitude to shape arguments to influence the fact finder.

The second practical value that adversary democracy engenders is individual private deliberation. "Deliberation" is used here to refer to the process of internal self-examination and thought to resolve a conflict. This deliberation is quite different from the public deliberation that modern cooperative theories of democracy presume to be the essence of democratic self-government. Those democratic theories, which collectively are called "deliberative democracy," claim that democracy is defined by decision making on the basis of public deliberation: free, impartial, and rational public discussion among individuals who speak with the purpose both to persuade and to be persuaded and with the ultimate goal of reaching mutual agreement, or "rational consensus," on the meaning of the common good.[88] Because the ultimate goal of public deliberation is rational consensus about the common good, participants must refrain from arguments grounded in private self-interest.[89] Instead, public deliberation requires "reciprocity"—arguments based on "accessible" reasons (that is, those that all participants can equally understand), and on "moral" reasons (that is, those that "apply to everyone who is similarly situated in morally relevant respects").[90] Deliberation in deliberative democratic theories, then, is a collective and cooperative process aimed at agreement on shared interests, rather than an individual process aimed at determining and understanding one's own interests and how they are affected by competing interests. Private deliberation under adversary democracy is valuable in two respects. First, it is valuable in the Millian sense, because the process of deliberation helps individuals to develop their human faculties.[91] Adversary democracy promotes deliberation in the Millian sense because it requires the individual to know his individual interest to advance and protect it against competing interests.[92] Second, deliberation is valuable to adversary theory because the process of deliberation may cause the individual to consider and give due regard to opposing viewpoints.

Not only does adversary democracy prompt individuals to define their own self-interest, it also prompts individuals to consider opposing arguments and the interests they represent, if only to compete against adverse positions more effectively. This may sound similar to the "reciprocal justification" tenet of deliberative democracy,[93] but there is a fundamental distinction. Deliberative democracy assumes that all individuals share (or are capable of ultimately sharing) a common interest; adversary democracy does not make such an assumption (though neither does it deny the possibility of such sharing). Thus, when one makes a valid argument under deliberative democracy, one argues that a certain position promotes the common good; one does not argue that it promotes the speaker's own good. The premise of a concept of common good permits "the assumption that the other fellow wants what we want, or that he will want the same thing when his perception has developed to the level of our own."[94] As a result, it does not require thorough consideration of opposing interests. The adversarial premise, on the other hand, causes every individual to "understand as fully as he possibly can what the other party is like and what his wants are."[95] In a relationship where there is no assumption of a common good, we must know, if we are to obtain what we want, what the other fellow wants. It is true that, like Tom Sawyer when he got himself out of a fence-painting job, we may persuade the other fellow that he wants something that he really does not want, or like the modern advertiser we may elevate this persuasion to the level of a skillful manipulation of mass opinion. But even in this manipulation there is latent a certain regard for human dignity; we at least try to make the fellow over so that he will want what we have to give him. We do not merely thrust something on him and say, "Here it is."[96] Thus, while reciprocal justification masks (or at least blurs) difference, adversary democracy forces the individual to confront difference and, in doing so, to give due regard to the individual dignity of his opponent.

Ironically, adversary democracy's third practical value is its potential to encourage active democratic participation. The irony is that adversary democracy is posited here as a preferable alternative to the participatory theory of democracy—as a means of inducing individual participation in the democratic process. In many ways, the system of adversary democracy will encourage participation as much or more than theories that label themselves as participatory. Political scientists have long remarked on the low levels of participation in American democracy. Some, like Joseph Schumpeter, have suggested that ordinary citizens have little role to play in democracy, other than to periodically vote for their elected officials.[97] Others have argued that the lack of participation is not normatively problematic, to the extent it is merely a consequence of "rational ignorance" and abstention.[98] Still others have sought to find alternative means of gaining the developmental values of democratic participation through resort to areas of private decision making.[99] But assuming that some degree of participation and activity in democracy—through voting, campaigning, demonstrating, letter writing, or other activity—is to be considered normatively valuable, adversary democracy is the most likely democratic form to achieve it.

While self-interest does not explain all political participation, it certainly explains a good deal of it.[100] A 1993 study, for instance, found relatively low rates of political participation among the economically disadvantaged but also found that 71 percent of the time that the economically disadvantaged did communicate with public officials about the issue of basic human needs, they were addressing an issue that had "an immediate impact upon themselves or their families."[101] "Not only do [issues of basic human needs] weigh more heavily in their list of concerns," the authors conclude, "but when they communicate about these matters to public officials, they are more likely to be discussing issues that touch their own lives."[102] Likewise, a 2002 study found that participation among senior citizens with regard to Social Security is "an instance in which self-interest is highly influential: Those who are more dependent are more active."[103] A model of democracy that accepts the pursuit of self-interest as a legitimate goal of political participation at least permits that degree of participation directly motivated by that goal.

It is important to recall that adversary democracy is not confined to the pursuit of self-interest. Social action groups motivated by altruistic concerns are also likely to encourage participation in an effort to achieve their social and political goals. Under adversary democracy, individuals with similar interests and opinions are induced to organize together to compete with those who hold opposing interests and opinions.[104] And social and political organization established around common interests goes "hand in hand" with "high levels of [political] participation."[105] Indeed, after researching the effect of homogeneous and heterogeneous networks on political participation in a diverse society, one political scientist concluded that "homogeneous environments are ideal for purposes of encouraging political mobilization. Like-minded people can encourage one another in their viewpoints, promote recognition of common problems, and spur one another on to collective action."[106]

ADVERSARY DEMOCRACY AND THE FIRST AMENDMENT

Acceptance of the premises of adversary democracy has important implications for the scope of the theory of free expression. Free speech theorists are correct in positing a symbiotic intersection between democracy and free expression. Recognition of both the normative and empirical superiority of the adversary model of democracy, however, suggests that the First Amendment's domain extends significantly further than prior free speech theories would permit.

Adversary democracy, it should be recalled, posits that democracy invariably involves an adversarial competition among competing personal, social, or economic interests. Individuals are able to protect their own interests or to achieve their ideological goals by participating in the process of governing by exercise of the vote, and attempting, through exercise of their expressive powers, to persuade others to accept their positions. The First Amendment, therefore, must protect (1) all speech that facilitates the individual's democratic decision making; (2) all lawful advocacy;[107] (3) all speech that facilitates individuals' awareness of their self-interest; and (4) all speech that facilitates individuals' ability to maintain and develop their individuality in spite of their necessary participation in collective life. Notably, this does not mean that the government is absolutely barred from regulating speech that falls in these four categories. It simply means that it may do so only when the regulation survives strict scrutiny.

The following chapters explore the most important doctrinal and conceptual implications of this interaction between adversary democracy and free expression. In each inquiry, the analysis is guided by the premise that, in shaping the scope and reach of the First Amendment right of free expression, it is improper to exclude or reduce protection for speech solely because it is either designed to advance the self-interest of the speaker or appeal to the self-interest of the listener.

The adversary theory of free expression protects and even values the promotion of self-interest. It does so in part for the practical reason that self-interest creates an incentive for speech that facilitates democratic decision making. And it does so also on the basis of the recognition that the collective decision making process may ignore the individual's interest entirely unless the individual represents it himself. But, more fundamentally, it does so for the theoretical reason that autonomy requires that individuals have the freedom to decide how they want to govern themselves and how they want to engage in the process of collective decision making.

Cooperative Democracy and Public Discourse: The Flawed Free Speech Theories of Robert Post and Alexander Meiklejohn

Among the most prominent and widely accepted theories of the First Amendment are those that explain the Free Speech Clause as either a catalyst for or a protection of democracy itself.[1] Such "democratic" theories of the First Amendment posit that speech receives constitutional protection because it is essential to a functioning and legitimate democracy. Different democratic theories of the First Amendment suggest competing explanations of exactly how free speech advances or defends democracy. Some suggest that free speech facilitates the informed decision making that self-rule requires.[2] Others argue that free speech furthers democracy by allowing individuals to recognize themselves as self-governing.[3] Still others simply conclude, without elaboration, that democracy would be "meaningless" without the freedom to discuss government and its policies.[4] Every democratic theory of the First Amendment, though, in one way or another views free speech as a means to a democratic end.

The prior chapter described the political theory of adversary democracy and why it fits well with the American form of government and its commitment to the precepts of liberal democratic thought. It further explained the implications of adversary democracy for the theory of free expression. To date, none of the prominent democratic theories of free expression has either advocated or assumed the adversary form of democracy. This chapter critically examines the two leading democratic theories of free expression—those fashioned by noted free speech scholars Alexander Meiklejohn and Robert Post. Understanding the serious flaws in both theories will underscore the normative and descriptive superiority of the adversary form of democratic theory and the adversary version of free speech theory that grows out of it.

Before one can understand or critique the specific theories of Meiklejohn and Post, one must first understand certain definitional base lines of democratic thought. "Democracy" itself is an amorphous concept, both historically and theoretically.[5] Despite the concept's simple translation to "rule by the people," political theorists since Aristotle have advanced competing theories of democracy that are inconsistent, if not contradictory.[6] To say that the First Amendment advances "democracy" without more, then, is to say much less than First Amendment scholars often assume.[7] Still, "democracy" is not so empty a referent that it is impossible to evaluate whether so-called democratic theories of the First Amendment are indeed democratic. The central claim here is that the prominent democratic theories of the First Amendment propounded by Meiklejohn and Post are actually in tension with democracy, properly defined. Moreover, both theories conflict with democracy even as Meiklejohn and Post *themselves* define it. Most importantly, their theories are fundamentally flawed because they ignore or reject, either explicitly or implicitly, the premises underlying adversary democracy, which is properly deemed the preferable version of democratic theory.

As explained earlier in this book,[8] democratic theory encompasses two principles. First, the principle of self-rule is a foundational element of any democracy. Absent such a commitment, democracy necessarily degenerates into an authoritarian state. Thus, democracy must proceed on the premise that there is no "right" or "good" apart from what the people determine it to be (subject, of course, to whatever countermajoritarian limits are imposed constitutionally). Even when the electorate makes its initial moral or social choices, democratic theory demands that those choices remain open to the expression of criticism and dissent, so that the electorate may alter its initial choices at a later point. Commitment to this form of what I have called "epistemological humility"[9] constitutes a central element of democratic theory, for absent such a commitment the concept of rule by the people is rendered meaningless. Just as rulers may not place externally derived restrictions on the ultimate choices of the people, neither are they permitted to restrict the substance of speech or debate because of disagreement with the choices that that speech or debate advocates.

Second, democracy demands that the self-governing decisions of the people are respected by the government because in a democratic society elected officials must be made accountable to the electorate for their governing choices. Democratic theories may differ over how this process functions. But, at its foundation, democracy must assume that authority is controlled by public opinion, rather than the reverse.[10] If governing officials make choices with which the public ultimately disagrees, they will at some point be required to defend their choices to the public's satisfaction.

In important ways, the two principles overlap. Democratic theory necessarily restricts government's power to coerce or suppress public opinion because otherwise neither of the two foundational principles of democratic theory would be viable. Absent free recourse to information and opinion, the electorate cannot perform its central role in a democratic state. As Thomas Jefferson wrote, "If a nation expects to be [both] ignorant and free . . . it expects what never was and never will be."[11] Because Meiklejohn and Post disregard, or at least marginalize, different core aspects of these fundamental democratic principles, their theories of free expression necessarily fail as democratic theories of the First Amendment. They do so for varying reasons and to different degrees.

Alexander Meiklejohn's democratic theory of the First Amendment fails because, in some of its key elements, it contradicts the core democratic principle of epistemological humility. This flaw has long been largely overlooked by commentators, probably because other, more well-known elements of Meiklejohn's theory posit that the First Amendment absolutely forbids the suppression of any speech based on the viewpoint it conveys. Indeed, Meiklejohn famously insisted that democracy requires "an equality of status in the field of ideas" because "when men govern themselves, it is they—and no one else—who must pass judgment upon unwisdom and unfairness and danger."[12] At least on one level, then, Meiklejohn did appear to recognize that epistemological humility is a fundamental prerequisite for democratic self-government. Ultimately, however, Meiklejohn abandoned this superficial commitment to epistemological humility and consequently betrayed democracy itself. Despite insisting that democracy precludes any singular idea of what is "wise," "fair" or "American," and as a result, the regulation of speech based on the viewpoint it expresses,[13] Meiklejohn effectively screened speech according to his own viewpoint about how individuals should govern themselves in a democracy. Convinced that democracy entails a compact among citizens to pursue the common good, Meiklejohn summarily (albeit inconsistently) excluded from the First Amendment's protective reach speech in pursuit of private commercial self-interest.[14] He condemned such expression on the basis of his moral and political disdain for the pursuit of these narrowly focused personal interests and therefore for speech designed to further those interests. Thus, Meiklejohn allowed himself the very power he denied government: the authority to adjust the protection of speech on the basis of his particular opinion of what is "wise" and "American."[15]

The stark inconsistency between Meiklejohn's protective selectivity is in striking contrast to what is supposedly the essence of Meiklejohn's free speech theory. This is so not only because of its inescapable inconsistency with the foundational notion of epistemological humility but also because it undermines the central means by which Meiklejohn seeks to implement his democratic vision. Meiklejohn famously argued that democracy's objective is the "voting of wise decisions."[16] As a result, he suggested, the First Amendment protects speech solely to ensure the *listener's* access to information and opinion relevant to the processes of collective decision making. But Meiklejohn's disdain for private economically motivated speech effectively determines whether speech is entitled to First Amendment protection largely on the basis of the *speaker's purpose* for speaking, rather than exclusively on whether the speech conveyed information relevant to the people's wise voting decisions. He thus incoherently excluded speech from the First Amendment's scope despite the fact that it directly facilitates democracy as he himself defined it: It provides information and opinion to listeners, thereby making them more informed voters. Much as an underinclusive speech regulation suggests government's underlying motive to discriminate against a certain viewpoint, this mismatch between Meiklejohn's *theory* for protecting speech and his *criteria* for doing so further demonstrates Meiklejohn's willingness to censor certain types of speech he considered ideologically distasteful.

Robert Post's democratic theory of the First Amendment does not compromise the very notion of democracy in the blatant manner that Meiklejohn's theory does. Nevertheless, Post, too, proposes a democratic theory of the First Amendment that sets aside core democratic principles and that conflict with democracy as even he defines it. Post's participatory model fails as a democratic theory of the First Amendment because it fundamentally miscalculates both the nature and degree of autonomy that democracy presupposes and the necessary implications of that autonomy. Ironically, Post has faulted Meiklejohn for this very type of mistake, labeling the latter's approach a "collectivist" theory of the First Amendment that misunderstands the role of individual autonomy in democracy.[17] Post has argued that "the value of individual autonomy is inseparable from the . . . aspiration for self-government."[18] He has, moreover, insisted that "the ideal of autonomy is . . . foundational for the democratic process."[19] In reality, however, Post's commitment to autonomy—both individual and collective—is limited at best. Post's participatory theory of democracy grows out of the fundamental premise that "the value of collective self-determination does not inhere in the people's power to decide their own fate, but rather in their warranted conviction that they are engaged in the process of deciding their own fate."[20] As a result, Post concludes that the essence of democracy lies predominantly in the individual's ability to participate in public discourse, rather than in exercise of the vote, which he considers "merely a mechanism for decisionmaking,"[21] rather than the most basic exercise of democratic self-government,[22] because it is this participation that allows the individual to recognize herself as self-governing or to attain a sense of "democratic legitimacy."[23] Post's participatory theory, then, rests on the mistaken premise that legitimacy has a unique democratic value far more central than the value of the actuality of autonomy. In reality, the individual's subjective understanding of herself as self-governing is valuable if, and only to the extent that, self-government *itself* is valuable.

In fixating on participation as the one narrow aspect of democratic autonomy for its potential to create a subjective sense of democratic legitimacy, Post underestimates other aspects of autonomy that are at least as essential, both to the individual's subjective understanding of herself as self-governing and her actual status as such. As a result, he either grossly underestimates or mishandles the democratic value of information, understanding it as relevant only to the production of truth[24] or, alternatively, to what he deems the relatively less significant process of decision making.[25] He never recognizes, as Jefferson did, that information protects autonomy from the ignorance that can easily cripple it. If Meiklejohn's fundamental mistake was in allowing his personal ideological preferences to lead him astray from the logical implications of his listener-oriented theory, Post's fundamental mistake is in failing to appreciate the importance of the listener's role in democracy in the first place.

Because Post self-consciously anticipates this critique, his participatory theory is not quite the transparent affront to democracy that Meiklejohn's proves to be. Post acknowledges that the individual's ability to participate in public discourse cannot, in itself, constitute democracy.[26] Moreover, he often concedes that informed decision making is a necessary condition for democracy.[27] Yet on a number of occasions Post has insisted that informed decision making is of "lexically" inferior democratic value than participation in public discourse, without ever explaining how one necessary condition for democracy can be lexically inferior to another.[28] Ultimately, then, Post's concessions reveal that he at least has some basic awareness of core democratic principles, but such awareness does not stop him from failing to provide them sufficient recognition.

In any event, Post's participatory theory compromises democracy even in the unduly truncated manner in which he defines it. As already noted, Post defines democracy according to the value it furthers, which, he argues, is the individual's sense of "democratic legitimacy."[29] He therefore concludes that the First Amendment protects public discourse because it facilitates democratic legitimacy. Yet because he miscalculates the democratic value of information Post marginalizes the very speech that ensures that the individual's participation in public discourse truly reflects her own free will through its influence on the process of democratic selection of governing agents.[30] And, because he fails to acknowledge the true democratic value of the vote, he undervalues the very process that forces government to be responsive to public will. Post's participatory theory thus provides no protection to speech that ensures that public opinion controls governmental authority rather than vice versa and thus provides insufficient protection for the speech that guarantees the individual's actual *status* as self-governing.[31] Finally, because Post defines the category of expression falling within the "public discourse" in wholly manipulable terms and even on occasion incorporates majoritarian norms to determine its scope, his participatory theory actually *creates* the means for governmental authority to regulate public opinion. As a result, it compromises, rather than promotes, democracy as even Post defines it.[32]

Despite their differences, both Meiklejohn's and Post's theories share a failure to comprehend or implement core notions of democracy. Meiklejohn's theory does so by simultaneously disregarding the principle of epistemological humility and undermining his own listener-oriented perspective. Post's theory does so by effectively trivializing the inherent democratic value of voting and voter receipt of information and, consequently, the role listener autonomy must play both in democracy and free speech. His theory fails, moreover, because of his artificial distinction—even for speaker purposes—between public discourse and private speech, causing him to ignore the important role that private communication plays in fostering democratic values.[33]

Both Meiklejohn and Post, in varying degrees, understand democratic autonomy in its collective sense. Meiklejohn believed that democracy is simply a "compact" among individuals to govern for "the common good." Post likewise begins with the premise that "democracy is not about individual self-government, but about collective self-determination"[34] and ends with the conclusion that "democracy requires individual autonomy only to the extent that citizens seek to forge 'a common will, communicatively shaped and discursively clarified in the political public sphere.'"[35] As such, both ultimately understand democracy largely as a cooperative pursuit in which individuals collectively "plan[] for the general welfare"[36] or "forge a common will."[37] This chapter argues that because of their inherently cooperative and collectivist nature, the theories of both Post and Meiklejohn contravene fundamental precepts of democracy and free expression. Directly or indirectly, both theories contravene the principle of epistemological humility by imposing restrictions grounded in externally derived normative dictates.

THE DEMOCRATIC IRONY OF MEIKLEJOHN'S FIRST AMENDMENT

Meiklejohn's Theory of Free Expression

Alexander Meiklejohn proposed the earliest democratic theory of the First Amendment. Meiklejohn understood the First Amendment as "a deduction from the basic American agreement that public issues shall be decided by universal suffrage."[38] For that system of self-government to be a "reality rather than an illusion,"[39] he argued, the "voting of wise decisions" requires that citizens have access to all relevant information and opinion.[40] As a result, he argued, the First Amendment provides an absolute prohibition on the regulation of speech because of the offensiveness of the idea it expresses.[41] If (and only if) speech is relevant to the people's self-governing decisions, Meiklejohn concluded, the First Amendment guarantees it absolute protection against governmental regulation on the basis of disdain for or disagreement with the views expressed.

Meiklejohn's First Amendment thus assumed three fundamental principles. First, speech is constitutionally valued exclusively for its potential to facilitate democratic decision making. Second, speech facilitates democratic decision making by conveying relevant information and opinion to the *listener* so that the listener may make an informed decision when it comes time to vote. Thus, to the extent the First Amendment protects the right to speak, it does so only as incident to or facilitator of the listener's right to listen. Meiklejohn argued, for example, that the First Amendment's "ultimate interest is not the words of the speakers, but the minds of the hearers";[42] that the First Amendment "does not require that . . . every citizen shall take part in public debate" nor that "everyone . . . have the opportunity to do so";[43] that the "primary purpose of the First Amendment is . . . that all the citizens shall, so far as possible, understand the issues which bear upon our common life";[44] and that "it is th[e] mutilation of the thinking process of the community against which the First Amendment to the Constitution is directed."[45] Third, for the electorate to be sufficiently informed, Meiklejohn believed, the needs of democratic decision making require that citizens have access to *all* relevant information and opinion, not simply that information and opinion that the government favors:[46] "[U]nwise ideas must have a hearing as well as wise ones, unfair as well as fair, dangerous as well as safe, un-American as well as American."[47] As Meiklejohn wrote, "The reason for this equality of status in the field of ideas lies deep in the very foundations of the self-governing processes. When men govern themselves, it is they—and no else—who must pass judgment upon unwisdom and unfairness and danger."[48]

On the basis of these three principles, Meiklejohn concluded that, while the First Amendment prohibits regulation of speech for the ideas it conveys, it does not preclude the imposition of procedural regulations on the agenda or form of public discussion to ensure the quality of the public debate and to facilitate the voting of wise decisions. Thus, just as the "moderator" of the New England town meeting may rightly enforce certain rules of order to regulate "talking" and "get business done," so may the state regulate speech in a similar manner.[49] The moderator of the New England town meeting may suppress speech when she determines that "everything worth saying [has been] said" or when the question of the speech is not "before the house." Indeed, she may censor the "boor" or the "public nuisance," "by force if necessary," and may "deny the floor" or "throw[]out" of the meeting anyone who "threatens to defeat the purpose of the meeting."[50] Similarly, Meiklejohn suggested, the state may regulate speech in a democracy.[51] However, consistent with the third principle underlying Meiklejohn's theory of free expression, the moderator may not prohibit speech simply because he disagrees with the idea it conveys. Indeed, Meiklejohn insisted that "the First Amendment condemns with absolute disapproval" such viewpoint-based regulation.[52]

Meiklejohn's assertion that democracy requires an "equality of status in the field of ideas" has become the paradigmatic expression of the precept that democracy assumes that no absolute "right" or "wrong" exists and instead that democracy commits such substantive valuations to the people to decide through democratic procedures. Yet, as eloquently and emphatically as Meiklejohn defended this ideal (what can be described as the ideal of "epistemological humility")[53] more careful examination reveals that his theory of free expression ultimately severely undermines—indeed, arguably rejects—it.

The Democratic Difficulties Plaguing Meiklejohn's Theory

Meiklejohn's theory ultimately defies the very principle of epistemological humility with which he is so widely associated because it would deny speech First Amendment protection purely on the basis of Meiklejohn's personal moral or political views of what speech is "unwise," "unfair," and "un-American."[54] Put simply, because he considered "excessive individualism" to be toxic to democracy,[55] Meiklejohn concluded that speech that pursues an individual interest, rather than the common good, falls outside the scope of the First Amendment altogether.[56]

It cannot be emphasized enough that this critique of Meiklejohn's theory differs substantially from more traditional criticisms leveled by free speech scholars against Meiklejohn in the past. Previous critiques have questioned Meiklejohn's analogy to the New England town meeting as a metaphor for what speech regulations the First Amendment does *not* prohibit, suggested that Meiklejohn was blinded by a rather myopic understanding of the kinds of speech relevant to democratic decision making, and argued that the logic of Meiklejohn's theory requires that it apply equally to protect speech that facilitates an individual's decision making as it does to speech that facilitates collective decision making.[57] The claim made here is more basic and ultimately more damning. In contrast to prior criticisms, the point here is that Meiklejohn's approach to free expression fails as a democratic theory of the First Amendment simply because, in a number of its core elements previously ignored or overlooked by commentators, it abandons the principle of epistemological humility so central to the foundations of democracy.

This abandonment originates with Meiklejohn's division of freedom of speech into two different components: that freedom that is protected under the First Amendment and that freedom that is protected under the Due Process Clause of the Fifth (and by corollary, the Fourteenth) Amendment.[58] The former, which Meiklejohn describes as an "absolute" freedom, defends "public" discussion and "planning for the general welfare"; the latter guarantees only a limited freedom that, much like most other substantive interests protected by the Fifth Amendment's Due Process Clause, can be sacrificed for the interest of the common good without great difficulty, protects the individual's "private" speech in pursuit of his own interest or "advantage."[59] Meiklejohn justified this division of speech on the basis of an understanding of our dual roles as citizens. As self-governing citizens, Meiklejohn argued, we are both the "rulers" and the "ruled." As "rulers," "we think and speak and plan and act for the general good" and our speech is "public."[60] As the ruled, we "rightly pursu[e] [our] own advantage" and "seek[] [our] own welfare," and our speech is "private."[61] Only when we speak as "rulers"—that is, only when we are "planning for the general welfare"—is our speech protected under the First Amendment. Thus, despite insisting that the First Amendment's "ultimate interest is not the words of the speakers, but the minds of the hearers,"[62] Meiklejohn evaluated speech's claim to First Amendment protection based on the *speaker's* purpose for speaking. He argued that the First Amendment "offers defense to men who plan and advocate and incite toward corporate action for the common good"[63] but not to "men . . . engaged . . . in argument, or inquiry, or advocacy, or incitement which is directed toward [their] private interests, private privileges, private possessions."[64]

Meiklejohn's distinction between public and private speech, as well as his complete banishment of so-called private speech from the scope of the First Amendment, is immediately suspect because Meiklejohn's asserted criteria for drawing this distinction contradict his own theoretical premises. The problem is not merely that the distinction between private and public speech is ultimately illusory, though that is certainly the case.[65] Nor is it merely that the distinction incoherently excludes from the First Amendment's protective scope speech that facilitates self-government simply because it is an exercise of individual, rather than collective, self-government that is being facilitated.[66] Suspending disbelief as to those flaws and assuming that the line between public and private speech could somehow be drawn with perfect clarity and coherence under a plausible theory of free speech, the primary problem is that, in light of his very own democratic postulates, Meiklejohn's theory differentiates speech protection on the basis of wholly impermissible criteria.

Recall the three fundamental principles of Meiklejohn's theory: First, speech is constitutionally valued for its potential to facilitate democratic decision making; second, speech facilitates democratic decision making by conveying relevant information and opinion to the *listener* so that she may make an informed "governing" decision when it comes time to vote; and third, to perform their governing choices most effectively voters must have access to *all* relevant information and opinion, regardless of the government's judgment of its wisdom.[67] Given these theoretical principles, all of which proceed on the assumption that the constitutional value of free speech grows exclusively out of its impact on the listener, it is a non sequitur to differentiate "public" speech from "private" speech *based on the speaker's purpose for speaking* rather than exclusively on the speech's potential effect on the listener.

A democratic theory of free speech could conceivably distinguish public speech from private speech from two different perspectives, depending on one's choice of the underlying rationale for protecting speech in the first place. The first would evaluate speech from the perspective of the audience. From this perspective, speech would be "public" and deserving of First Amendment protection if and only if its content were relevant to the *listener's* self-governing decisions. Pursuant to this framework, the speaker's identity and motive for speaking would logically be immaterial: The sole determinative factor would be the content of the speech and its value to the listener as a facilitator of the performance of the self-governing function.[68] Evaluating the public/private speech distinction from this perspective logically follows from a theory of free speech, like Meiklejohn's, that assumes the democratic value of free speech to center exclusively on speech's role as facilitator of the audience's self-governing choices. If speech is constitutionally valuable solely because of its effect on its listeners, whether speech is "public" and deserving of First Amendment protection must logically turn solely on its significance for its listeners.

The second possible perspective from which to measure the democratic value of free speech would be that of the speaker. On this basis, whether speech is "public" would turn on whether it facilitates the *speaker's* self-government. The speech's effect on its audience, consequently, would be immaterial. This perspective logically flows from a theory that understands the democratic value of free speech to accrue to the speaker herself.[69] If speech is constitutionally valuable because of its effect on the speaker, whether speech is "public" and deserving of First Amendment protection must depend on its significance to its speaker.

Of course it is also possible to propose a standard that simultaneously incorporates both perspectives, either in the disjunctive or conjunctive. The disjunctive hybrid would define speech as "public" when it contributes to or facilitates *either* the audience's *or* the speaker's self-government. This standard would flow logically from a theory that understands free speech to be democratically valuable both to the speaker and the audience.[70] The conjunctive hybrid, on the other hand, would require speech to be relevant to the listener's *and* the speaker's self-government for it to be deemed "public" and therefore protected under the First Amendment.[71]

While Meiklejohn at certain points claims that his theory focuses exclusively on a listener perspective (a choice that could in any event be challenged as grossly underinclusive because it completely ignores speech's important benefit to the speaker), at other points he puzzlingly restricts the scope of expressive protection on grounds having absolutely nothing to do with that perspective. To the contrary, on a number of occasions he reduces protection purely on the basis of the speaker's motivation. For example, he argued that the radio is bereft of First Amendment protection because those who control it are motivated by considerations of profit rather than the pursuit of the common good.[72] He suggested that a paid lobbyist's speech may well be deemed "private" for the same reason.[73] Yet information valuable to the listener and private self-interest often coexist in the same speech. Indeed, the Supreme Court has recognized as much in routinely holding that speech does not lose its constitutional protection simply because it is in a form sold for profit.[74]

Meiklejohn's exclusion of commercially self-interested speech from the First Amendment is both a logical mistake (because it results from his adoption of criteria that are antithetical to his underlying theoretical rationale for protecting speech in the first place) and a pragmatic mistake (because it totally ignores commercially self-interested speech's potential to deliver information to the listener relevant to democratic decision making). To the extent that Meiklejohn's theory excludes protection for speech purely because of its speaker's self-seeking motivation, it illogically denies the people "acquaintance with information or opinion or doubt or disbelief or critics, which is relevant" to the process of self-government.[75] According to Meiklejohn's very own principles, then, his theory of free speech is decidedly *anti*democratic. By selectively altering speech protection on the basis of the personal motivation of the speaker, Meiklejohn is actually undermining attainment of his goal of facilitating listener self-government. The fact that the speaker is motivated by self-interest, of course, in no way necessarily implies that what the speaker has to say would be of no value to the listener. By selectively restricting expression that is potentially valuable to listener-based self-governing decisions, Meiklejohn has incoherently and counterproductively undermined his entire theoretical structure.

To understand how his public–private dichotomy undermines the goals Meiklejohn set for his theory, we need to apply it in a real-world context. Consider, for instance, a manufacturer of body and truck armor for American soldiers in Afghanistan. As part of its campaign to get the public to pressure the government to purchase its product, it begins an advertising campaign promoting recent technological advances in combat armor and the statistical decrease in combat-related casualties that such armor promises. The motivation for the manufacturer's expression is obviously grounded in the desire to make a profit. Does that fact make its speech any less relevant to its audience's self-governing decisions about whether government should reequip its military forces? Presumably not. Indeed, it is reasonable to presume that the manufacturer's personal interest gives it greater incentive to marshal supporting facts and to disseminate its message as widely as possible. It is true, of course, that the manufacturer's expression would likely be slanted by its self-interest. But in no sensible framework of free expression is advocacy excluded and the category of protected expression confined to impartial and objective speech. Yet there can be little doubt that, because of the manufacturer's underlying commercial motive, Meiklejohn would categorize the manufacturer's speech as "private" and therefore relegate it to the lesser protection of the Fifth Amendment.

As significant as Meiklejohn's mistake is, the ominous democratic irony of Meiklejohn's First Amendment runs much deeper. Meiklejohn's mistake concerning the definition of "public" speech under the terms of his own theory is not solely the result of confusion about the contours and logical implications of his approach. In effect, Meiklejohn's public/private distinction amounts to an indirect form of viewpoint regulation, which filters out the types of speech that Meiklejohn personally found ideologically distasteful and inappropriate in a democracy.

Of course, Meiklejohn recognized that different substantive visions of the common good exist, and he insisted that the First Amendment must protect expression of them all, regardless of how offensive those visions may seem to many of us. But by positing that speech cannot receive First Amendment protection if it is motivated by considerations of personal commercial gain, Meiklejohn's theory implicitly presupposes his own personal normative perspective on the process of democracy and free speech. To be sure, his viewpoint regulation is not equivalent to the direct censorship of speech for disdain of the substantive idea it expresses. But the form of viewpoint regulation Meiklejohn does employ is no less problematic as a matter of both constitutional and democratic theory. Instead of discriminating on the grounds of personal disagreement with the substantive message, Meiklejohn selectively excludes expression from the First Amendment's reach on the basis of his personal normative distaste for the self-interested motivation of the speaker (though, concededly, he is even inconsistent on that point). In Meiklejohn's normative world, a speaker who refuses to believe in the value of community and instead seeks solely to further his own personal interests through expression is to be constitutionally shunned.[76] But what is this, other than an ideological prerequisite that a speaker commit himself to a normative philosophy of communitarianism rather than to one of individualism and economic pluralism? Mystifyingly, Meiklejohn's entire free speech theory was created for the very purpose of constitutionally insulating communist speech of the 1940s from regulation grounded in ideological disdain.[77] Yet in fashioning his theory he proceeded to restrict expressive rights on the basis of the very type of ideological disdain and epistemological arrogance that his theory was explicitly designed to avoid in the first place.

Seriously complicating (and darkening) the epistemological arrogance inherent in Meiklejohn's focus on speaker motivation is his second level of motivational selectivity in his willingness to protect speakers. Reconsider the body and truck armor hypothetical, discussed earlier. Instead of the manufacturer, assume that the speaker is the mother of a marine serving in Afghanistan. It is reasonable to presume that her expression is "self-interested," in that her primary concern is most likely her son's well-being. Yet there is little question that Meiklejohn would extend full protection to this form of "self-interested" speech. The only difference between the two forms of self-interest is that the manufacturer's is commercial and the mother's is not. It was thus not purely personal interest that Meiklejohn disdained as speaker motivation. It was, rather, the presence of personal *commercial* motivation that led him to exclude a speaker from the First Amendment's scope. This fact renders his speaker selectivity even more ideologically suspect, for it suggests a form of anticapitalism that comes even closer to paradigmatic epistemological arrogance of a type wholly inconsistent with the foundational premises of democracy on which Meiklejohn purports to build.[78]

Adding a substantial element of total intellectual incoherence to Meiklejohn's First Amendment theory, which has already been shown to be plagued by intellectual and ideological inconsistency, is his addition of yet a third level of selectivity. When Meiklejohn asserts—again, without the slightest rational grounding in the logical dictates of his own asserted First Amendment goals—that speech motivated by economic gain is to be characterized as "private" expression unprotected by the First Amendment, it is easy to see that he could not possibly have intended to extrapolate that precept to its logical conclusion. To do so would surely have proven too much because it would have necessarily led to the characterization of all commercially produced books and newspapers as unprotected private speech—a conclusion Meiklejohn made clear that he in no way intended to reach.[79] But at no point did he ever attempt to distinguish the speech of radio broadcasters and lobbyists, which he excluded from the First Amendment's reach as private speech, from the sale of books and newspapers, to which he extended full First Amendment protection. Yet both forms of expression are sold; there exists no *ex ante* basis on which to assume that one is necessarily more motivated by profit concerns than the other.

This blatant internal inconsistency in his theory should clearly have served as a red flag to Meiklejohn, indicating that he needed to return to the theoretical drawing board. It should have signaled to him that if one focuses on the value of speech to the listener, the speaker's motivation logically becomes wholly irrelevant. In any event, he should have been aware that speech motivated by considerations of economic gain can be as valuable to maintenance of a vibrant democratic system as speech motivated by purely altruistic or communitarian concerns. He should also have realized that to exclude from First Amendment protection all economically motivated speech would cause serious harm to the health of a democratic system. In addition, he should have recognized that it is absurd to assume mutual exclusivity of expressive motivation: Just as a newspaper publisher or a book author may simultaneously intend to contribute to public discourse as well as to profit from their expression, so, too, may lobbyists or radio broadcasters have multiple goals and motivations for their expression. But Meiklejohn had none of these realizations, a fact that renders his free speech theory incomplete at best and totally incoherent at worst.

Essentially, Meiklejohn excluded self-interested speech from the First Amendment because he mistook his personal vision of democracy for democracy itself. Of course, on a purely normative level one might well agree with Meiklejohn that individuals engaged in democratic self-government *should* ignore private self-interest to pursue the common good, though even that point is itself the subject of reasonable debate. But that is merely one political opinion about what democracy should be, rather than a logical outgrowth of a commitment to a system of free expression.[80]

If epistemological humility means anything, it must mean that the state cannot regulate speech according to a particular viewpoint as to how democratic decision making should function—or, indeed, whether it should exist at all. It must mean that individuals possess autonomy over how and why to make substantive choices.[81] Without this citizen autonomy over the "how" or "why" of democratic decision making, government could control the outcome of democratic decisions simply by dictating the criteria for making them. Autonomy requires that the individual be as free to consider his own self-interest when he votes as Meiklejohn was free to ignore his.

Meiklejohn defied this core principle of epistemological humility by infecting his First Amendment theory with his own ideology as to how individuals should proceed when they engage in democratic decision making. He thus made himself far more than merely the moderator of debate at a nationwide version of a New England town meeting. Contrary to the limits he placed on the hypothetical moderator, Meiklejohn allowed himself full and unreviewable authority to assess what speech is "wise," "fair," and "American"[82] on the basis of his personal assessment of the speaker's motivation and, on the basis of that assessment, to determine whether the speech has any claim to First Amendment protection in the first place. As a result, his theory not only reveals an underlying inconsistency, it also fails as a democratic theory of the First Amendment.

POST'S "PARTICIPATORY" FIRST AMENDMENT

Participation, Self-Government, and Democratic Legitimacy

Robert Post developed his participatory theory as an alternative to Meiklejohn's democratic explanation of the First Amendment.[83] Although Post and Meiklejohn start with the identical premise that the First Amendment is designed to promote democratic self-government, they put forth alternative conceptions of democracy and, as a result, alternative theories of free expression.

Post adopts the basic premise that "democracy is not about individual self-government, but about collective self-determination."[84] He and

Meiklejohn agree on that much, at least. For Post, however, democracy is about values, not procedures.[85] Thus, while Meiklejohn found democracy to inhere in the collective "voting of wise decisions,"[86] Post considers the vote to be "merely a mechanism for decisionmaking."[87] What defines democracy is its ideal value—self-government—and the people's ability to recognize themselves as self-governing.[88] Thus, "the value of collective self-determination does not inhere in the people's power to decide their own fate, but rather in their warranted conviction that they are engaged in the process of deciding their own fate."[89] According to Post, democracy is not primarily about what individuals *do*, but rather about how they *feel*.[90] "Democratic legitimacy," according to Post, exists when and only when "citizens hav[e] the warranted belief that their government is responsive to their wishes,"[91] "experience their state as an example of authentic self-determination,"[92] and "identify [the] government as their own."[93]

How individuals identify themselves as self-determining is the "puzzle" at the heart of Post's participatory theory.[94] That puzzle, Post suggests, is how individuals are able to maintain a sense of self-determination though they will invariably disagree with some outcomes of collective decision making;[95] it is how they may feel "*included* within the process of collective self-determination"[96] and not "hopelessly *alienated*" from the collective decisions it produces.[97] This "reconciliation of individual and collective autonomy" is what Post calls the essential problem of democracy.[98] Thus, Post concludes, "Democracy requires individual autonomy only to the extent that citizens seek to forge 'a common will, communicatively shaped and discursively clarified in the political public sphere'"[99]—only, in other words, as an incident to participation in the collective process of public discourse.

Having concluded that the vote is assuredly not the exclusive solution to this puzzle,[100] Post reasons that individuals must derive their sense of democratic legitimacy from some process other than collective decision making itself. This process, Post suggests, is the individual's participation in the formation of democratic public opinion by engagement in public discourse. An individual may attain the sense of inclusion in the process of collective self-government, Post argues, if the individual is free to participate in the "communicative process relevant to the formation of democratic public opinion"—what he calls "public discourse"—and if the state is subordinated to the public opinion that emerges from this public discourse.[101] Thus, Post's "participatory" concept of democracy suggests that if individuals can participate in the formation of public opinion, and if the state is ultimately constrained by that public opinion, individuals can recognize their "potential[] . . . authorship" in collective decision making.[102] That recognition, in turn, creates the potential for individuals to recognize themselves as self-determining.[103]

To summarize, Post's participatory account of democracy makes four sequential points: first, that democracy is defined according to characteristic values rather than procedures; second, that the essential democratic value is self-government; third, that self-government inheres in the individual experiencing herself as included within the process of collective self-government (that is, in the individual's experiencing a sense of democratic legitimacy); and fourth, that in a heterogeneous culture individuals can attain a sense of democratic legitimacy only through participation in the formation of public opinion. From these four points, Post concludes that the purpose of the First Amendment is to "safeguard[] public discourse from regulations that are inconsistent with democratic legitimacy."[104] As this brief summary suggests, the starting point for Post's First Amendment theory rests entirely on the participatory theory of democracy. Because the faults within that theory are significant, and because they necessarily seep into Post's free speech theory, the next section will elaborate further on Post's participatory concept of democracy and its flaws, before the section after that explores Post's free speech theory itself.

The Participatory Theory of Democracy

Post's participatory theory fails as a viable theory of democracy for three reasons. First, and most fundamentally, Post's theory reflects a false and artificial dichotomy between autonomy and legitimacy. Post argues, for instance, that "the value of collective self-determination does not inhere in the people's power to decide their own fate, but rather in their warranted conviction that they are engaged in the process of deciding their own fate."[105] Democracy, in other words, is not valuable primarily for what it allows individuals to *do*, but rather for how it allows them to *feel*.[106] This distinction, however, is neither obvious nor even logical. If democracy is valuable for the feeling of autonomy that it produces, as Post suggests it is, autonomy itself must be valuable in a way that he fails to recognize.

Second, Post fails to see that, even accepting his assumption that self-government turns on the individual's sense of democratic legitimacy, potential participation in the public discourse is in no way a sufficient condition for its attainment. To the contrary, participation in the formation of public opinion is of little democratic consequence, standing alone. To be truly legitimating, participation in the public discourse must be free and informed. Moreover, if public discourse is to have meaningful effect, some mechanism must exist by which government may be required to internalize the public will that is an outgrowth of public discourse. Post's theory, then, is severely truncated to the extent he values the individual's ability to engage in public discourse over other democratic processes that ensure that such participation is democratically meaningful in real life. Absent the vote, participation is at best of limited value and at worst nothing more than a cynical and deceptive means of obtaining citizen compliance with an authoritarian regime. While Post does not completely devalue the vote, he never explains why it is of any less importance as a necessary condition to a viable democratic system than is participation and the feeling of legitimacy that supposedly accompany that participation. If, contrary to Post's understanding, the vote is to be deemed equal in democratic importance to participation, then it is mystifying why the voters' interest in receiving as much information and opinion as possible about issues relevant to performance of the self-governing function is not equally deserving of protection. It should be quite clear, then, that participation, as valuable as it is, is merely one equally necessary element in the democratic triumvirate: participation, voting, and voter access to opinion and information.

Finally, even assuming both Post's subjective definition of self-government *and* the diminished importance of other processes by which democratic legitimacy is achieved. Post provides no convincing explanation of exactly how participation in public discourse facilitates democratic legitimacy in a heterogeneous society. Nor does he explain how it does so in a way that voting does not. Indeed, his theory is confusingly contradictory on this point, especially because it fails to elucidate what are the precise conditions for democratic legitimacy in the first place.

The Subjective Concept of Democratic Self-government

Post effectively treats democracy as if it were a subjective phenomenon. The term *subjective* does not refer to the fact that democracy is an ambiguous concept, which may connote different things to different theorists. Instead, it refers to the fact that Post considers the essence of self-government to be found within each individual's psyche. That is, Post finds the primary value of democratic self-determination to lie not in the individual's ability to make autonomous self-governing decisions for herself, nor in the individual's power to participate equally in processes of collective decision making, but rather all but entirely in her mental recognition of herself as self-governing. It is a subjective concept of self-government, then, because it appears to be largely divorced from whether the individual is, in reality, self-determining. The troubling aspect of a subjective concept of democracy is plain: Equating self-government with the individual's ability to "imagine" herself as "included within the process of collective self-determination"[107] invites authoritarianism, so long as the individual is not the wiser for it.

To be sure, Post does recognize—at least to some extent—that democracy cannot be *exclusively* a product of the individual's imagination. Consider his description of democratic legitimacy as depending on individuals' "*warranted* conviction that they are engaged in the process of deciding their own fate."[108] That he requires that the conviction of self-determination be "warranted" suggests that Post does not mean to propose an entirely subjective definition of democratic legitimacy. Likewise, Post occasionally concedes that the opportunity to participate in public discourse—the process that directly facilitates the individual's subjective sense of democratic legitimacy—is not itself a sufficient condition for democracy.[109] My claim here is simply that Post's participatory theory grossly *undervalues* the objective component of democratic legitimacy, not that it denies it entirely. Thus, in one breath Post recognizes that actual exercises of self-government, such as voting, and actual conditions for self-government, such as the availability of information, have *some* democratic value. In the next breath, however, he suggests their value is "lexically" inferior to the value of public discourse.[110] He justifies this hierarchy by suggesting that voting does not allow individuals to feel "legitimated" in the way that participation in public discourse does.[111]

To explain his proposed structure, Post hypothesizes a society in which citizens vote on every mundane aspect of daily life—from what to eat to what color clothing to wear—but in which public discussion, political advocacy, and the press are banned.[112] Such a society would be "undemocratic," Post suggests, even though it ensures every individual equal power to vote and to decide the society's collective fate, because collective decision making is "oppressive" absent a connection between the "particular wills of individual citizens and the general will of the collectivity."[113] The "general will" to eat steak for dinner, for instance, will feel oppressive to the individual who prefers fish, and the equal power to affect that collective decision will apparently provide no solace. Thus, Post concludes that the vote fails to further the core value of democracy because it does not allow the individual to experience a sense of democratic legitimacy.[114] In reality, this hypothetical reveals only that Post's distinction between objective exercises of autonomy and subjective feelings of legitimacy rests on a false dichotomy. Because this hypothetical society is "undemocratic," Post concludes that democratic legitimacy must derive from processes other than voting. The problem with this analysis is that, to test this logic, Post never considers the exact opposite society, one in which there is an open public discourse and full freedom to participate in the formation of public opinion but absolutely no voting rights. Even if the state acts in good faith to determine the "general will" and to govern accordingly[115]—indeed, even if the state may perfectly determine what the general will is through some psychic process—we are left with a system assuredly closer to a benevolent dictatorship than a democracy. The reasonable and logical conclusion to draw from this scenario is not that open public discourse and democratic legitimacy are distinct but that an open public discourse, like majoritarianism, is necessary but insufficient, in and of itself, to ensure democratic legitimacy.[116] Yet it is this logically unsupported conclusion that Post seem at last to come close to adopting: that majoritarianism as determined by the vote is largely unrelated to democratic legitimacy while an open public discourse is its linchpin.[117]

In any event, resort to hypothetical societies is unnecessary to establish Post's mistake. Recall Post's statement that "the value of collective self-determination does not inhere in the people's power to decide their own fate, but rather in their warranted conviction that they are engaged in the process of deciding their own fate."[118] Post fails to recognize that a feeling is only valuable if its referent is itself normatively valuable. The subjective *feeling* of autonomy is valuable only if, and only to the extent that, the objective *reality* of autonomy is deemed valuable. Post, then, cannot have it both ways: If one values democracy for the feeling of autonomy that it produces, one must likewise deem autonomy itself equally valuable—and *valued*. Normally, it would go without saying that, in the words of the Supreme Court, "the right to vote freely . . . is the essence of a democratic society."[119] The vote is the most basic exercise of self-determination, the only guarantee that the people remain sovereign over their government, the principal distinction between democracy and autocracy, and the principal means (if not the only one) for individuals in an unequal society to have an objectively equal say in their collective government.[120] But whether or not one must accept this foundational precept of democratic theory, surely one cannot logically value the feeling of autonomy *over the autonomy itself.*

Because he divorces the feeling of self-government from the actual exercise of self-government, Post mistakes the individual's sense of democratic legitimacy, which should be seen as nothing more than an incidental, derivative effect flowing from the real-life commitment to democracy, for democracy itself. Because he does so, and because he undervalues aspects of self-government that are at least as essential as participation in public discourse, which he values almost to the exclusion of all else, Post proposes a theory of democracy that counterproductively undercuts the core democratic ideal of autonomy. In short, Post values the associated benefit more than he values the foundational activity. From a theoretical perspective, then, he places the cart before the horse. As a result, his theory fails as a democratic theory, however one defines democracy. But this by no means exhausts the flaws in Post's theory. The next section demonstrates that Post's theory fails as a democratic theory even if one assumes that the feeling of democratic legitimacy, in and of itself, serves as the predominant rationale for democracy.

The Underinclusive Conditions for "Democratic Legitimacy"

Post's entire participatory model is premised on the "precondition" that the state is responsive and accountable to public opinion. Inclusion of this condition makes perfect sense. If individuals are to sense that their contributions to public opinion affect the direction of the government, the state must be made to internalize public opinion in some fashion. Yet Post provides no explanation of how we assure ourselves that the state will internalize public opinion; he simply assumes it to be the case. Ironically, the very means by which the state is made to internalize public opinion is the same process that Post marginalizes for its purported inability, in his mind, to create democratic legitimacy: majority rule, implemented and assured through the vote.[121]

This criticism suggests that Post's participatory model rests on a defectively selective concept of democratic legitimacy. His model asks what structures create democratic legitimacy, and it privileges those structures as essential processes of democracy. However, it largely ignores the opposite side of the same coin: It fails to consider what structures are necessary because their *absence* would *destroy* democratic legitimacy.[122] This point becomes more clear when Post applies the participatory model to the First Amendment, and the next section will explore it in depth.[123] For now it is enough to note that a coherent concept of democratic legitimacy must embrace a condition if that condition either creates democratic legitimacy *or* its absence would destroy it.

The point is simple: The opportunity to participate in the public discourse (assuming, of course, that one is able to define that concept in the first place) may be a *necessary* condition for democratic legitimacy, but it certainly is not a *sufficient* condition. While Post acknowledges this point himself,[124] he nevertheless insists on a model of democracy that treats participation in the public discourse as the locus of democratic legitimation. If neither voting nor participation in the public discourse can independently ensure democratic legitimacy, elevating one over the other, as Post does, is illogical and unsupportable.

The Uncertain Connection Between Public Discourse and Democratic Legitimacy

Even forgiving these first two flaws, Post can appropriately be criticized because he never articulates a satisfying explanation as to how participation or potential participation in the public discourse actually ensures individuals' sense of democratic legitimacy. Part of the problem is that Post never clarifies the essential conditions for democratic legitimacy in the first place. He suggests vaguely that democratic legitimacy requires a "connection between the particular wills of individual citizens and the general will of the collectivity,"[125] or "reconciliation between individual and collective autonomy,"[126] but none of this says very much about the intersection between participation and legitimacy. It is arguable, for instance, that majoritarian voting itself provides such a "connection" or "reconciliation" to the extent it aggregates all individual decisions to determine the collective will. But, because Post made clear that he considers voting to be merely a *mechanism* of democracy rather than a process of democratic legitimation, we at least know that this is not the "connection" Post has in mind.

Post alternately suggests two competing explanations for this asserted connection. The first, which is the stronger of the two (in the sense that it expects public discourse to accomplish more, not in the sense that it is more persuasive) can appropriately be called the "substantive" explanation. The second, which is weaker in that it is designed to accomplish less, can be called the "procedural" explanation. Post seems to suggest both explanations at different points, but neither is satisfying. The substantive explanation, while theoretically plausible, is useless as a practical matter because it is so totally divorced from reality. And the procedural explanation, while practically plausible, is theoretically incoherent.

Post's substantive explanation reasons that public discourse facilitates democratic legitimacy because public discourse aspires to "agreement" or the discovery of a "common will."[127] This explanation is substantive because it values public discourse for its hypothetical result: "'agreement' (or the attainment of a 'common will')" by which "the individual will is . . . completely reconciled with the general will."[128] The reasoning is quite simple: If, through public discourse, individuals come to agree on a particular substantive outcome, each individual will be able to recognize the collective choice as her own. There will be no conflict between the will of the individual and the will of the majority; public discourse has made them identical. Thus, when public discourse creates consensus, it also creates democratic legitimacy as Post defines it: It allows individuals to recognize the government as their own.

If democratic legitimacy depends on achieving something approaching substantive consensus, and if consensus is the realistic outgrowth of public discourse, the participatory theory's emphasis on public discourse as opposed to voting would make perfect sense. Unlike public discourse, the vote provides no opportunity for consensus building. Standing alone, the vote is a private and individual act that registers individual preferences, not an act that permits discussion, compromise, and agreement. Indeed, absent the expectation of a unanimous outcome, the very act of voting reflects a recognition of the futility of any attempt to attain consensus. The vote presupposes that individuals disagree over the substantive choices that face them, that those differences are irreconcilable, and that the fairest way to resolve those differences is ascertainment of majority will. If democratic legitimacy does depend on individuals reaching agreement on the substantive outcomes of the democratic process, the vote would indeed be an ineffectual means for its attainment, as Post asserts.

The difficulty lies in Post's concession that public discourse is no better than voting at producing consensus. Consensus, he suggests, is merely the *aspirational* goal of public discourse rather than a probable or even reasonably possible result.[129] More likely, he concedes, division and disagreement will characterize the public discourse. In those circumstances, Post suggests:

> Even if a state were to subordinate lawmaking to public opinion, and even if all citizens were free to participate in the formation of public opinion, a particular group within the state that found itself perpetually outvoted, ignored, and alienated might well question whether the state were an appropriate vehicle for democratic self-governance. The group might even consider seceding from the state and founding its own democratic polity. . . . Persistent and

fundamental disagreement with other citizens may preclude the identification with the state that a system of open democratic participation is precisely established to promote.[130]

If Post is claiming that public discourse creates democratic legitimacy by creating substantive agreement among individuals, his concession of the likely "persistent and fundamental disagreement" among citizens—wisely made, given the realities of the situation—shatters that claim. It thus makes no sense to elevate public discourse as the locus of democratic legitimation on the grounds that it is more likely to bring about collective consensus.

Post's procedural explanation attempts to fashion an alternative rationale for how public discourse advances democratic legitimacy. It suggests that the outcome and even the goals of public discourse are far less significant to the individual's sense of democratic legitimacy than simply the ability to participate in the process of public debate.[131] For instance, Post suggests that as long as the state is subordinated to public opinion, the ability to participate in the formation of public opinion "authorizes citizens to imagine themselves as included within the process of collective self-determination."[132] Similarly, Post argues, "Although citizens may not agree with all legislative enactments, although there may be no determinate fusion of individual and collective will, citizens can nevertheless embrace the government as rightly 'their own' because of their engagement" in public discourse.[133]

This explanation is unsatisfying, in part because it is unsupported to the point of being conclusory. Post provides absolutely no empirical or psychological evidence that participation in public discourse actually does allow individuals to feel "reconciled" to their government, and even he recognizes that at times it may not.[134] But the explanation is unsatisfying also because its reasoning applies just as easily to voting. One could reasonably argue that individuals' ability to vote allows them to imagine themselves as included within the process of collective self-determination. In both cases, it could be argued, individuals feel "included" within the process of collective self-determination by the procedures that provide them a say in their government. Thus, the procedural explanation does little to support the unique status Post extends to public discourse among all democratic processes capable of promoting democratic legitimacy. To be sure, public discourse creates a unique opportunity that voting does not: It provides the individual the opportunity to advocate and to influence others so that the general will may more closely resemble her own. By the same token, however, voting provides a unique opportunity that public discourse does not. It provides an assurance, by law, that each individual has equal power to affect the direction of the government. In other words, *both* public discourse *and* voting provide unique opportunities for individuals to recognize government as their own.

The trouble with the procedural explanation, then, is that it provides no basis for the superior status that Post affords participation in public discourse over other democratic related processes. To the extent one recognizes that public discourse will never produce real consensus on substantive issues, it is no more essential than voting in creating substantive democratic legitimacy. And to the extent that public discourse and voting both create unique opportunities for the individual to have a say in her government, neither is better than the other in creating procedural democratic legitimacy. Post's entire participatory theory, then, depends on a premise that lacks any theoretical or empirical support. The point underscores the counterproductive impact of Post's puzzlingly artificial separation of the acts of participation in public discourse on the one hand and voting on the other.

The Selective Exclusions of Post's Participatory First Amendment

The prior discussion focused entirely on an effort to understand and critique Post's unique definition of democracy. With that understanding in place, including an understanding of that definition's foundational flaws, the analysis now turns to Post's First Amendment theory. That theory begins with the premise that the democratic purpose of the First Amendment is to "safeguard[] public discourse from regulations that are inconsistent with democratic legitimacy."[135] This follows directly from the participatory concept of democracy that Post adopts and its basic distinction between legitimation and decision making. Because Post's participatory model associates democracy with legitimation rather than democratic decision making and because it disassociates legitimation and decision making from one another, Post's participatory theory of the First Amendment enables legitimation far more than it enables or facilitates actual democratic decision making.[136]

Again, Post's First Amendment theory is automatically subject to question to the extent it incorporates the flaws of democratic theory described in the prior section. But its shaky foundation in democratic theory is not the only flaw in Post's First Amendment philosophy. Post's First Amendment theory is also flawed for its inexplicably underinclusive definition of "participation" in public discourse and thus its systematic marginalization of *listeners'* interests in free speech, its considerable inconsistencies and ambiguities in defining what speech comprises the "public discourse," and its resulting exclusion of at least some speech based on the completely incoherent considerations of speaker identity and presumptive speaker motivation; and, finally, its constitutionally illogical and dangerous incorporation of majoritarian norms to interpret the scope of the inherently countermajoritarian First Amendment. This section will describe Post's participatory theory of the First Amendment and each of these criticisms in turn.

As a threshold matter, though, it is first necessary to place Post's participatory theory within the broader context of First Amendment theory more generally. Post argues that his participatory theory is the most "powerful" free speech theory,[137] by which he means the theory that best explains the Court's existing First Amendment jurisprudence.[138] In an important sense, then, Post's First Amendment theory purports to be nothing more than a post hoc rationalization of existing Supreme Court doctrine. Post would likely object to this characterization, as he believes legal scholarship should glean from the doctrine insights about our "national commitments" and use those insights to formulate more coherent theoretical explanations for the doctrine—a kind of "First Amendment anthropology."[139] In reality, however, such an approach to legal scholarship mistakes judicial opinions for national commitments, precludes the meaningful formulation or discussion of normative first principles in constitutional theory, and ignores the role of the legal academy as the intellectual watchdog of the judiciary. One wonders, for instance, whether Post would have devised a theory to rationalize the highly unprotective Supreme Court free speech decisions of the early and mid-twentieth century concerning the rights of communists, rather than normatively attacking them for their gross underprotectiveness.[140] One can further wonder whether he would then have immediately altered his free speech theory to reflect the Court's subsequent shift to more protective standards.[141] If so, then while his "theory" could conceivably be valuable for narrow purposes of treatiselike doctrinal description and analysis, it would be valuable for little else.

Despite fashioning his own theory and tying it to existing Supreme Court doctrine, however, Post does not deny the legitimacy and applicability of other free speech theories.[142] Indeed, he understands his participatory theory only as a theory of inclusion, in that it describes a certain class of speech that deserves protection under the First Amendment, not necessarily a theory of complete exclusion.[143] Speech not deserving of protection under his participatory theory may nonetheless deserve protection under another free speech theory,[144] be it a different democratic theory of the First Amendment[145] or even a free speech theory that has nothing to do with democracy at all.[146]

That said, Post clearly does not regard all free speech theories as equals. Instead, he arranges them "according to a 'lexical priority.'" The participatory theory has top billing; other theories apply to protect speech only to the extent they are "not inconsistent with the requirements of participatory theory."[147] Post's treatment of commercial speech is the prime illustration of how this lexical approach functions. Post concludes that commercial speech (defined largely as commercial advertising), makes no contribution to "public discourse" and therefore is not protected under his participatory theory. Still, he concludes, it deserves *some* First Amendment protection for its "Meiklejohnian" value, meaning that it provides information to the listeners that can facilitate exercise of their self-governing choices.[148] Determining which theory protects certain speech, if any, is not purely an academic inquiry. That determination is intended to have significant implications for the nature and scope of protection the speech enjoys.[149] For example, the exact same regulation may be unconstitutional when applied to speech protected under the participatory theory and yet entirely constitutional when applied to speech purportedly protected solely under the less highly ranked Meiklejohnian theory valuing the conveyance of information to listeners.[150]

Under this logic, Post originally concluded that an overbroad regulation of commercial speech may be perfectly permissible even though an overbroad regulation of public discourse would not. The difference, Post reasoned, is that regulation of commercial speech threatens the loss of information—a form of communication that is fungible and can therefore be replaced from other sources—and not the loss of democratic legitimation. But this conclusion rests on a false dichotomy: The regulation of purely informational speech also undermines democratic legitimacy to the extent it endangers autonomous self-determination on the part of the communications' recipients.[151] More to the point, it also demonstrates that protection under a lexically inferior theory of free speech in Post's framework is a fairly puny consolation prize. According to Post, the state may enforce overbroad regulations of informational speech that is protected for its Meiklejohnian value on the wholly unsupported assumption that other speech will fill the informational void.[152] Not only does this represent a misapprehension of Meiklejohn's theory (Meiklejohn's moderator could silence speech on the basis of what had already been said, not on the basis of what potentially would be said),[153] it also demonstrates a shockingly cavalier attitude toward the value of informational speech generally.[154] The commercial speaker in many cases has unique access to certain information and a unique incentive to share it.[155] As a result, casual regard for her ability to speak represents a casual regard for the value of the information itself and its extremely important democratic benefit to its recipients. If the purposes of free speech protection have any significance at all, one cannot proceed on the empirically unsupported assumption that the information contained in the speech is easily replaceable. Indeed, the Court has squarely rejected the proposition that speech may be regulated simply because the information it contains is available from another source.[156]

Precisely because of the ominous implications Post's classification scheme has for the extent of speech's First Amendment protection, the following analysis criticizes Post's participatory theory of free speech for not protecting certain speech. To be clear, this criticism is not meant to suggest that Post himself leaves the speech entirely unprotected, only that his version of the participatory theory does. The criticism, then, is that the speech deserves protection *under the participatory theory itself*, properly understood. To the extent Post demotes the speech to a lexically inferior First Amendment position, he reveals just how theoretically truncated his version of the participatory theory is. In addition, his approach is subject to criticism for inexplicably devaluing certain forms and types of communication, wholly apart from their connection to his narrowly drawn theory. Also, because of the consequences of speech's classification as public discourse or not, it becomes all the more important to understand what speech the participatory theory protects, as well as what regulations of speech it prohibits. The analysis turns to those questions now.

Devaluing the Role of Listeners in the System of Democratic Discourse

Under Post's participatory theory, the First Amendment protects "public discourse" from "regulations that are inconsistent with democratic legitimacy."[157] Post asserts that regulations of the public discourse may undermine democratic legitimacy in two ways: First, they "cut off particular citizens from participation in the public discourse";[158] and second, they "regulate[] public discourse so as to reflect the values and priorities of some vision of collective identity."[159] But despite Post's clearly expressed concern for the need to avoid unduly truncating the scope of public discourse, Post himself improperly excludes, or at least devalues, wholesale categories of role players from their proper places within the system of democratic interchange.

Because Post explicitly equates participation in the public discourse with *speaking*, he overlooks the importance of individual *listener* autonomy not only to the practice of actual decision making but also to the process of democratic legitimation itself. In this sense, Post's mistake is the mirror image of Meiklejohn's: While Meiklejohn improperly truncated the scope of democratic discourse by excluding speakers, Post's truncation results from his dramatic undervaluation of the role of listeners. The common ground shared by their respective mistakes, however, is that both are counterproductively underinclusive in their characterization of the universe of democratic discourse.

The chapter has already explored Meiklejohn's numerous mistakes in this regard.[160] Here I explain why Post's mistakes are equally fatal to the viability of his democratic theory of free expression. To the extent that public opinion cannot be formed without the listener's evaluation and ultimate acceptance of certain ideas over others, the listener participates in the formation of public opinion as much as the speaker does.[161] Just as the speaker may benefit by contributing to public discourse, so, too, may listeners' moral and intellectual horizons be expanded by the receipt of information and opinion. Their ability to function as active participants in a democracy is improved as a result.[162] More importantly, government's decision to insulate citizens from information and opinion because of a paternalistic distrust of citizens' ability to make wise choices is as threatening to core democratic values as the suppression of any speaker.

The Confusing Role of Information in Post's First Amendment Lexicon

The fact that Post mystifyingly ignores the central role of the listener in fostering both public discourse and democratic legitimacy does not automatically imply his total rejection of the First Amendment value of information to the listeners who receive it. In two ways, however, Post's treatment of information under the First Amendment is confusing. First, as previously noted, Post posited, without any explanation or grounding in the theory of free expression, that the First Amendment value of information ranks substantially lower than that of public discourse.[163] This lexical ranking is flawed on several grounds. Initially, for reasons already explained, it is impossible to separate listener from speaker for purposes not only of the facilitation of democratic decision making but also of democratic discourse and legitimacy. Secondly, it is equally impossible to separate information from opinion because the use of information is often a central element in the persuasive nature of opinion.[164] Thirdly, even were one to assume that the listener-based value of information is somehow conceptually separable from the speaker-based value of public discourse, it is difficult to understand why it is nevertheless not considered at least the equal of public discourse in fostering attainment of First Amendment goals. Post appears simply to assume, rather than to explain, his chosen lexical ordering.

The clarity of Post's treatment of the First Amendment implications of information has been further undermined by his more recent, and possibly dramatic, shift in his proposed First Amendment treatment of information.[165] No longer, it seems, does Post classify information as necessarily of secondary First Amendment value (though at no point has he expressly rejected or modified his prior, well-established stance that the information value of speech to the listener is lexically inferior to its participatory value of speech to the speaker). Instead, he now seems to consider it to be simply of a *different* nature from public discourse and therefore to be deserving of a very different form of constitutional protection. Because the constitutional value of public discourse in no way turns on the factual or scientific accuracy of the speech, Post would let nothing turn on factual accuracy of expression in measuring the protection of speaker-based expression. However, because of Post's unduly narrow description of the protected speaker category (for example, excluding commercial advertising),[166] occasions arise where a listener could conceivably benefit from information conveyed by a speaker who is nevertheless unprotected. In these situations, because the *only* First Amendment value, in Post's mind, is the informational interest of the listener, he reasons that it would be illogical to protect false, as well as truthful information. After all, a listener gains no benefit from the receipt of false information; to the contrary, Post reasons, dissemination of such inaccurate information would actually undermine the values to be served by informational communication in the first place. This is what Post now describes as his "democratic competence" model.[167]

As superficially appealing as this reasoning may seem, closer analysis reveals serious logical and practical flaws. Most fundamentally, Post's information–discourse dichotomy ignores the practical manner in which the two are usually intertwined: Information is often conveyed, not as an end in itself, but rather as part and parcel of an effort to employ the system of public discourse to achieve certain normative and personal goals. Second, even if one were to ignore this serious difficulty, Post is far too willing to permit suppression or regulation of purely informational speech. The inadequate nature of his approach is underscored by his inaccurate reliance on Meiklejohn's theory as the source for his approach.[168] It is true, of course, that Meiklejohn recognized as the central value of the First Amendment the listener's receipt of information and opinion that would help the voters more effectively self-govern.[169] But he also was a strong believer in the Supreme Court's conclusion in *New York Times Co. v. Sullivan*[170] that, in the context of public figure defamation, we must tolerate much false speech (of no positive value in and of itself) in order not to chill true speech. Whether the economic incentive structure of commercial speech justifies an alteration in the assumption of an expressive chill is the subject of debate.[171] But Post's rejection of the protection of false expression is grounded primarily in the all too simplistic assumption that false information is harmful and therefore unprotected. This analysis misses the key lesson of the decision in *New York Times*: that the system often must protect even false speech to avoid chilling truthful speech. At the very least, Post has failed to satisfy his burden to prove that the same logic is for some reason inapplicable in the realm of commercial speech. To the contrary, Post fails even to acknowledge the issue's existence.

Even more problematic is Post's willingness to ignore the epistemological ambiguities inherent in the concept of falsity. Particularly in the case of scientific facts, reasonable disputes often exist as to what, exactly, is truth. Too often, seemingly well-established scientific assumptions have eventually been altered in light of stubborn insistence by minority voices challenging prevailing views.[172] Yet Post would all too readily defer to the supposedly expert judgments of those in power in his willingness to permit governmental suppression of commercial promotions that they deem false. This is so, despite the possibility of hidden political or economic agendas on the part of regulatory agencies possibly captured by private industries benefiting from the current scientific orthodoxy. As a result, listeners are deprived of information that might correctly cause them to question the judgments of those in authority. Yet by focusing primarily on "safeguarding the capacity of *speakers* to participate in the process of self-governance,"[173] Post systematically disregards the listener's role in the formation of public opinion[174] and in fulfilling the goals of democratic self-government.[175]

Of course, most of the time the participatory theory's omission of listener autonomy will have no effect on the listener's potential legitimation: The speaker's right to speak under the participatory theory, by proxy, indirectly protects the listener's right to listen. When the speaker has no right to speak under Post's grudgingly narrow participatory model, however, the omission of audience autonomy is fatal: The government is free to cut off listeners from information and opinion that would otherwise facilitate their own participation in public discourse as well as their own democratic decision making.

The Complexity of Speaker Motivation:
The Case of Commercial Speech

The chapter that follows explores in detail the implications of adversary theory for commercial speech. However, because it provides a concrete example of the situation in which the speaker has no right to speak under Post's participatory model, the subject of commercial speech is worthy of some attention at this point. Commercial speech provides the clearest, if not the only, example of Post's unduly truncated delineation of the category of protected contributors to public discourse. The commercial speaker, according to Post, neither seeks nor derives a legitimizing benefit from her speech.[176] As a result, Post believes that only information, rather than democratic legitimacy, is at stake when the state regulates commercial speech (ignoring the fact that information to the listener is as important to democracy as is discourse). Because democratic legitimacy is not at stake, Post reasons, the speech is not the kind of "public discourse" that the participatory theory protects. Regulation is therefore far more permissible than in the case of public discourse.

Rhetorically, at least, this provides a concise explanation as to why, in Post's mind, commercial speech deserves a lower quantum of First Amendment protection. According to Post's logic, because commercial advertisers are deemed not to be participants in public discourse, the only conceivable First Amendment benefit of commercial speech is its informational value to listeners, with all of the accompanying qualifications and limitations.[177] Post's failure here is his inability or unwillingness to recognize the potentially complex, multilayered motivations of most expression. Speakers do not always speak *solely* to contribute to public discourse or *solely* for purposes of narrow personal economic gain. A lobbyist on behalf of labor unions seeking to engender political support for higher tariffs or the repeal of NAFTA may on one level truly believe in the political wisdom and morality of his cause. Yet at the same time his expression is inescapably influenced by two levels of economic motivation: (1) his own, because he is being paid for his expressive efforts, and (2) his clients', because they obviously gain economically if their lobbyist's advocacy is successful. Is the lobbyist speaking to contribute to public discourse? The answer, of course, is yes—and no. Yet, in the case of the lobbyist, Post focuses exclusively on the effort to contribute to public discourse and thus provides the expression full protection.

What, then, about the commercial speaker? Here, Post summarily assumes that the expression is not made to contribute to public discourse but rather exclusively to sell a commercial product or service. Yet why we are to assume categorically that the desires to contribute to public discourse on the one hand and to gain economically on the other are mutually exclusive is far from clear. Moreover, how can Post be certain that even a commercial speaker motivated solely by considerations of economic gain who has been denied the opportunity to advance his interests through expression will not suffer the delegitimizing and alienating feelings due to his exclusion from public discourse? He cites no supporting empirical or psychological research to support so categorically sweeping a judgment about the human psyche, and his conclusion is far from intuitive.

In any event, Post's use of commercial advertising as an unbending surrogate for disqualifying economic motivation gives rise to the drawing of technical, formalistic distinctions that render his entire conceptual framework highly suspect. The problematic impact of Post's treatment of the commercial speaker can be demonstrated by use of a group of hypothetical permutations. Imagine that a beekeeper firmly believes that bee pollen possesses scientifically establishable health benefits. He wishes to publish an op-ed article in a daily newspaper asserting this position and mentioning his own product. Governmental authorities, believing that the beekeeper's assertion is scientifically inaccurate or at least unproven, seek to suppress the article's publication. It is reasonable to assume that in such a situation Post would characterize the expression as a contribution to public discourse and therefore fully protected, regardless of its accuracy. This is so, even though the beekeeper obviously possesses a strong economic motivation for expressing his viewpoint. Yet what if, instead of writing the op-ed article, the beekeeper seeks to take out an advertisement making the exact same argument and again promotes his own product? Now, the beekeeper's expression, in Post's view, has presumably been somehow magically transformed into far less protected commercial speech. And because he deems commercial speech not to be a contribution to public discourse, its only constitutional protection would derive from his "democratic competence" model[178] and remain unprotected if governmental authorities determine the claims to be scientifically inaccurate. Post would reach these opposite conclusions in the two hypothetical situations, even though the *identical speaker with the identical economic motivation is saying identical things to presumably a largely identical audience.* The only difference in the two situations, then, is that in the former case the expression is conveyed in an *article,* while in the latter it is conveyed in the form of an *advertisement.* This approach, then, amounts to the height of mindless formalism, leaving one at a complete loss to determine how Post would categorize an infomercial or a self-published promotional book.[179]

"Public Discourse" Defined and Gerrymandered

To this point the analysis here has demonstrated a number of grossly underinclusive aspects of Post's definition of the public discourse universe, which give rise to frustratingly formalistic distinctions. Even more troubling, however, is the malleability of his classifications. Post's participatory theory is confined to those communications that "regulate[] public discourse so as to reflect the values and priorities of some vision of collective identity."[180] Thus, Post criticizes Meiklejohn's free speech theory for subordinating public discourse to a "framework of managerial authority" that was based on a particular qualitative vision of what public debate should be.[181] In contemplating government regulation of the public discourse to prevent it from turning into a "Hyde Park" of "unregulated talkativeness,"[182] Post argues, Meiklejohn mistakenly imposed his *own* vision of what public discourse should be.[183] Traces of the very same mistake, however, appear in Post's theory as well.

Put simply, Post abdicates to the courts the authority to define what speech qualifies as public discourse. Whether through its political or its judicial branches, governmental definition of the scope of public discourse is itself a regulation of public discourse,[184] if not the most basic example of the agenda-setting regulations that Post rejects.[185] Of course, it makes perfect sense under the participatory theory that judicial review of speech regulation would give courts some role in determining the boundaries of the public discourse. But because Post's theory provides vague and contradictory guidance about the defining characteristics of public discourse and implicitly invites judges to pick the standard that allows them to reach the result they prefer, what is ultimately classified as public discourse is certain to reflect the "value and priorities" of the judge's own "vision of collective identity."[186]

Whether speech falls within the boundaries of public discourse is not only "uncertain" and subject to "case-by-case assessment," as Post openly concedes;[187] it also depends on a mercurial set of defining criteria. Two inconsistencies pervade Post's theory. First, Post vacillates on whether speech's inclusion within public discourse depends on the content of the speech or also (or instead) on the identity or motive of the speaker. Second, Post applies inconsistent units of analysis and levels of generality when considering different forms of speech and their inclusion within the boundaries of public discourse.

One would think, given the basic tenets of Post's participatory theory, that the scope of recognized contributions to public discourse should be relatively clear: If individuals attain democratic legitimacy by participating in the formation of public opinion, public discourse should encompass any speech relevant to the formation of public opinion. Indeed, Post appears to adopt this formulation, at least some of the time. At one point he defines "public discourse" as "encompassing the communicative processes necessary for the formation of public opinion."[188] He asserts that the relevant "public opinion" is not simply the overtly political but also all opinion relevant to the process of "collective self-definition."[189] And, perhaps most expansively, he argues that speech must be protected as a contribution to public discourse if it contributes to the "prior construction of a 'public'" because such a "public" is necessary for public discourse to exist.[190] Post applies this standard inconsistently, however. For example, though he applies this definition to bring wordless music and abstract art within the scope of public discourse, as already noted he fails to apply it to commercial speech. This is so, even though he acknowledges that commercial speech, like art, shapes a shared national identity and contributes to the construction of a "public."[191] Notably, this definition characterizes speech as public discourse according to its potential impact on its audience.

Despite the fact that this broad definition of public discourse is the most consistent with his participatory theory of democracy, Post often abandons it for a significantly more restrictive definition. That definition turns not on whether the speech contributes to the formation of public opinion or the construction of a "public" but on whether the speech reflects "a protected effort to shape public opinion"[192] or an "effort to engage public opinion."[193] Under this far more restrictive definition of public discourse, then, that the objective potential speech affect public opinion is a necessary but not sufficient condition to bring it within the public discourse. Not only must speech be relevant to the formation of public opinion, it must also reflect an *effort* to shape public opinion—a determination that turns, at least in some part, on the speaker's identity and what it reveals about the speaker's purpose in speaking.[194] Post's restrictive definition, then, plainly contradicts his broad definition: it will exclude certain speech despite its salutary impact on its potential audience. Most perniciously, Post applies this restrictive definition only in the context of explaining *commercial speech's* exclusion from the realm of public discourse. When asked about other speech in which the speaker has no conceivable participatory purpose, he mystifyingly reverts to the broader definition.[195]

Post's restrictive definition has two striking implications. First, by focusing on the "effort" motivating the speech, Post effectively shifts the constitutional analysis from the potential impact of the speech on its audience to the subjective motive of the speaker for speaking.[196] Second, as a result of the first implication, much speech that admittedly affects public opinion and "collective self-definition"—that is, speech not only at the heart of the broad definition of "public discourse" but speech that is absolutely necessary for *listeners'* capacity to "engage[] . . . in the public life of the nation"[197]—may not be protected at all under the restrictive definition.[198]

To be fair, Post would likely challenge the claim that his theory defines the boundaries of public discourse on the basis of speaker motive.[199] In the first place, he has recognized, at one point at least, that classifying speech according to speaker motive has the pernicious tendency to invite viewpoint discrimination and the suppression of unpopular speech.[200] In the second place, he contends that classifying speech based on the effort underlying it differentiates speech not on the speaker's motive but instead on the "social significance" of the speech.[201] For instance, he suggests that commercial speech's "social significance" is distinct from that of public discourse because "we most naturally understand persons who are advertising products for sale as seeking to advance their commercial interests rather than as participating in the public life of the nation."[202] Euphemistically labeling this an inquiry into the speech's "social significance," however, does not change the nature of the inquiry. In reality, this is not an inquiry into speech's *social* significance at all; it is an inquiry only into its *private* significance for its speaker. A principal evaluation of the social significance of speech would evaluate its impact in the public sphere.[203] Post's approach, instead, amounts to an evaluation of speaker motive and nothing more. Thus, Post concludes, commercial speech is not public discourse because commercial speech "should be understood as an effort . . . simply to sell a product" and not an effort "to engage public opinion."[204] As previously noted, in reaching this conclusion Post both disregards speech's potential to reflect multiple motives—in other words, he denies that a speaker may speak to sell a product *and* to affect public opinion—and logically implies that judges should engage in the futile and ultimately dangerous determination of the speaker's dominant motive (much as Meiklejohn had done).[205] The former would be absurd: The commercial speaker attempts to sell products *by* affecting public opinion and may even wish simultaneously to affect public opinion about *political* choices. For example, the pharmaceutical manufacturer may advertise its newly developed vaccine with the hope of influencing public opinion about whether the vaccine should be made mandatory.[206]

On the other hand, to the extent that an inquiry into a speaker's dominant motive necessarily lacks any objective evidentiary basis, the latter simply invites judges to punish speakers they dislike by concluding that the dominant motive underlying their speech is something other than an effort to "engage[] . . . in the public life of the nation."[207] Thus, Post suggests, the Supreme Court may rightly conclude that a Scientologist selling copies of *Dianetics* by L. Ron Hubbard door-to-door is not engaged in public discourse, even though it previously concluded that the speech of a Jehovah's Witness selling Bibles door-to-door is public discourse, because a Scientologist, unlike a Jehovah's Witness, is engaged in a commercial endeavor rather than an effort to shape public opinion.[208]

Moreover, regardless of whether Post's "social significance" inquiry amounts to an analysis of speaker motive, at the very least Post's restrictive definition classifies speech on the basis of its "significance" for the speaker to the total exclusion of its "significance" for the audience. Thus, commercial speech is not to be deemed public discourse under Post's framework because regulation of commercial speech "*merely* jeopardizes the circulation of information relevant to the 'voting of wise decisions'" and does not "endanger the process of democratic legitimation."[209] In drawing these distinctions as if informational speech and legitimating speech were mutually exclusive categories, Post either assumes that listeners derive no sense of democratic legitimacy from having access to informational speech or assumes that whatever legitimacy they derive is irrelevant to whether the speech should be defined as "public discourse."

Under this framework, judges evaluate speech in front of, rather than behind, the "veil of ignorance": Not only do they have the freedom to select the definition they prefer in a given case, they also have freedom to determine the "social significance" of speech according to their own subconscious, or even conscious biases. Under Post's definitional approach, then, judges are given the freedom to classify speech according to their "natural understanding" of the effort underlying it[210] and according to social norms of "when we instinctively perceive speech as 'public.'"[211] They are not required to decide speech's significance on the basis of evidence of participatory purpose or a lack of participatory purpose.

Even more troublesome is that under Post's approach courts are given the freedom to evaluate speech according to whichever analytical mode allows the result they favor. Post applies two contradictory approaches for determining whether speech reflects a participatory effort but does so without explanation or even any acknowledgment of his own distinction. Sometimes Post would have a court engage in case-by-case evaluation of speech and its speaker to determine whether the speech represents "an effort to engage public opinion,"[212] an "engagement [] in the public life of the nation,"[213] or an individual's "attempt to render the state responsive to [her] views."[214] A good deal of speech, not just commercial speech, would be excluded from public discourse if Post applied this approach consistently. For example, assume that Post and I had a private, heart-to-heart talk in which I explained to him exactly what I consider wrong with his theory of free expression. Assume further that, on hearing these concerns, Post then explained why he believes these concerns are unjustified. Under Post's "engagement[] in the public life of the nation" or "attempt to render the state responsive" definitions of public discourse, our private discussion about the foundation of free expression would presumably be unprotected by the constitutional guarantee of free expression—a truly preposterous result. Similarly, a wife's statement to her husband over the dinner table that the president and Congress are both incompetent would presumably be denied protection as well, because it is not an attempt to contribute to public discourse as Post defines it. Finally, if an individual wrote a stinging attack on the government in her diary, which was subsequently discovered by authorities, logically Post could not protect the diary, because it, too, does not represent an attempt to make the state more responsive to her views or to engage in the public life of the nation. It would be difficult to imagine that Post would deny full constitutional protection to the expression involved in these hypotheticals. But if he would in fact protect such communications, then there is little coherence left to his definition of public discourse.

On other occasions, however, Post has suggested that the reviewing court evaluate the speech generally to determine whether it represents the *"kind[] of communicative action* to which citizens must have unrestricted access" to sustain their warranted belief "that their government is responsive to their wishes."[215] Unlike the first approach Post describes, this approach does not focus on the specific speaker or the presumptive purpose that motivated her speech but instead assumes a hypothetical speaker with a participatory motive and asks whether *that particular* speaker would need to be able to engage in the speech to further her participatory goals. These inconsistencies in his definition of public discourse suggest that Post's theory would inevitably endow judges with significant authority to define—and thus to regulate—public discourse according to their particular "vision[s] of collective identity."[216]

Community Norms and the Majoritarian First Amendment

Post's participatory theory of the First Amendment reveals one additional and significant flaw, related to the question of how judges define the boundaries of public discourse. The prior section explained how Post expects judges to apply "contextual thinking" to determine the boundaries of public discourse. It also suggested that such a determination invites the implementation of bias against speech the judge disfavors. Even more problematically, on occasion Post suggests that the boundaries of "public discourse" should be drawn according to community norms. If so, the danger is not simply judicial bias against certain kinds of speech but also the judicial imposition of a kind of "heckler's veto" of speech that the community disfavors. If, as Post has argued, the "boundaries of public discourse . . . define the relative priorities of our national values" and if "in locating these boundaries we . . . exercise 'our capacity for human self-constituting,'"[217] then defining the concept of public discourse is exactly the kind of issue of national collective identity that Post believes must be determined and continually revised by the public.[218] Post attempts to resolve this tension by his suggestion that judges' determinations of the "social significance" of speech and the boundaries of the public discourse must depend in part on community social norms.[219] In suggesting that the court ascertain and apply community norms as part of its definition of public discourse, Post would have the court perform the function it is least structured to perform, namely, to determine and represent popular will.

The court's lack of institutional capacity to perform such a role enables judges to confuse their own social norms and values for those of the community. More importantly, even if the court were somehow able to perceive and represent popular will accurately, that the public instinctively devalues a certain kind of speech does not mean the First Amendment should do so as well. To have the reviewing court define the First Amendment's protective reach by reference to public will, as Post appears to advocate, would effectively force the court to abdicate its role as a countermajoritarian check on the popular will.[220]

By now it should be clear that Post's implementation of his participatory theory of free expression is plagued by both inconsistencies and dangers. First, as previously noted, at certain points Post suggests the line between commercial speech and public discourse should depend on the speaker's participatory purpose, yet at other points he suggests that the reviewing court evaluate the "social significance" of the speech, rather than the actual participatory purpose of the speaker. Second, when he does focus on social significance, Post would have the social significance of the speech turn not on judges' own principled understanding of the significance of the speech but rather on their necessarily imperfect understandings of community social norms. Post, then, would have judges decide the protection afforded a speaker not based on the speaker's subjective purpose for speaking, nor on a purely judicial evaluation of the participatory nature of the speech, but instead on the participatory nature of the speech as determined by reference to highly context-dependent community norms. The theoretical inconsistency in this result is notable: After consistently undervaluing and underprotecting speech by ignoring its possible value to the audience, Post gives the audience's perceived social norms a central role in justifying suppression of speech by allowing community norms to define the boundaries of the public discourse.

The danger of such an approach should be obvious: It invites the audience's bias against certain forms of speech and certain speakers into the judicial process, thus coloring the court's constitutional judgment with the majority's will, which is the last factor on which one should want First Amendment protection to turn. Furthermore, this approach contains an inherent regulatory bias. When government enacts a specific speech regulation it presumably reflects that popular will opposes the regulated speech. Thus, if the court accurately perceives the community norms it is likely to underprotect speech because the very same norms that motivated the regulation are those that the court will consider in setting the boundaries of the public discourse. On the other hand, if the court mistakenly perceives the community norms, the error will likely reflect the court's own preferred norms and values, resulting in regulation of the public discourse to reflect "some vision of collective identity" held by the judge.[221] Neither result constitutes an acceptable mode of First Amendment construction.

LINKING POST'S AND MEIKLEJOHN'S MISTAKES: THE FAILURE TO RECOGNIZE THE CENTRALITY OF ADVERSARY DEMOCRACY

In many respects Meiklejohn and Post propose almost polar visions of democracy and, as a result, of the First Amendment. To briefly review, Meiklejohn's theory equates democracy with the "voting of wise decisions." To him, therefore, the First Amendment protects the community's thinking process to prepare them to vote. As a result, Meiklejohn's version of the First Amendment focuses entirely on protecting the listener's ability to receive information and opinion. Post's participatory theory, in contrast, rejects the equation of democracy with voting. For Post, democracy consists primarily of those processes that allow individuals to recognize themselves as self-governing. As a result, Post's participatory theory of the First Amendment focuses, for the most part, on protecting the speaker's autonomy to participate in public discourse and not the listener's autonomy to receive information. Voting, to Post, takes a backseat to the value of participation and the legitimacy that supposedly flows from it.

Despite these differences, Post's and Meiklejohn's First Amendment theories share common ground. For example, through tortured definitions of "public speech" and "public discourse," respectively, both exclude from First Amendment protection certain classes of speech deemed to be motivated by private economic self-interest.[222] Similarly, both underestimate the extent and nature of the level of individual autonomy that is essential to democratic self-determination.[223] Indeed, running through both theories is the assumption that democracy is merely a process of *collective* self-government in which individuals cooperate to govern themselves as a society. Meiklejohn argued that democracy is simply a "compact" among individuals to govern for the common good.[224] Post likewise asserts that the premise that "democracy is not about individual self-government, but about collective self-determination"[225] and ends with the conclusion that "democracy requires individual autonomy *only to the extent that citizens seek to forge 'a common will,* communicatively shaped and discursively clarified in the political public sphere.'"[226] Thus, although Post recognizes the importance of individual autonomy in ways that Meiklejohn does not, he does so only to create the conditions for collective self-determination. Ultimately, both Meiklejohn and Post understand democracy as a cooperative pursuit in which individuals collectively "plan[] for the general welfare"[227] or "forge a common will."[228]

Both Meiklejohn and Post, then, adopt different forms of what can, in varying degrees, appropriately be labeled a "cooperative" theory of democracy. A cooperative theory of democracy does not necessarily presume that a universal common good exists (though the theory is not necessarily inconsistent with such a belief), nor does it deny the possibility of disagreement about what the common good is. It understands democracy as a shared collective endeavor to pursue a common good or to "forge a general will,"[229] however those concepts are defined. Neither theorist seems to have recognized, however, that in the rough-and-tumble of American political life, the supposedly ideal world of cooperative democracy and pursuit of the common good is far more the exception than the rule. It is simple political reality that speakers often pursue personal interests that are in direct social, moral, or economic conflict. As political scientist Jane Mansbridge made clear a number of years ago, the ideal of "cooperative" democracy is achievable primarily in a relatively small, homogeneous group with shared goals.[230] But it is surely not a realistic goal for the diverse and pluralistic American political society as a whole.

This does not mean, of course, that cooperation plays no role in American political society. In actuality, it performs two important functions. First, it is the process by which similarly interested groups and citizens join together to promote their position and attempt to defeat those advocating contrary positions. Second, cooperation provides both a floor and a ceiling to the adversary political battles that go on constantly in American society. It provides boundaries that the adversary political process cannot exceed: One side wins and one side loses, without bloodshed or civil war. A viable adversary democratic system can exist, then, only within a broader cooperative democratic framework. It surely does not follow, however, that adverseness and self-interest are foreign to American political society, or even the exception rather than the rule. For Post and Meiklejohn to focus their theories of free expression on an assumption of a predominantly cooperative and collectively deliberative mode of political decision making that excludes or reduces protection for much self-interested speech is to create a democratic theory that could function successfully only in fantasy-land. At least as important as the empirical deficiencies of both theories is their common failure to see the normative democratic value underlying the pervasiveness of the adversary political process. As a result, both theories grossly underestimate the nature and extent of individual autonomy that a viable democracy presupposes.

As a global alternative to the collectivist democratic visions of Post and Meiklejohn, this book has argued throughout that free speech theory must be shaped in accordance with the precepts of adversary democracy. The common linkage in their mistakes, then, is their failure to recognize the central role that adversary democracy both should and does play in the American political and constitutional structures. This theory, it should be recalled, posits that the purpose of democracy is to guarantee each individual the equal opportunity to affect the outcomes of collective decision making by lawful means, according to her own interests and values as she understands them.[231] The adversary theory of democracy, then, emphasizes individual autonomy as theoretically and practically interwoven into the processes of collective self-government.

Perhaps it is inevitable that cooperative theories of democracy, such as those of Post and Meiklejohn, would struggle to articulate a coherent theory of free speech, precisely because of their inherent rejection of the adversary premise and its centrality to core notions of democracy. Based on their theoretical premise that democracy is an exercise of collective self-determination in pursuit of shared objectives, cooperative theories of the First Amendment might always be faced with something of a difficult choice. They could remain true to their First Amendment premises for protecting speech—listener autonomy in Meiklejohn's model, for instance. But to the extent they do so, they might necessarily violate a theoretical premise of the underlying cooperative democratic theory, such as Meiklejohn's premise that self-government should pursue the common good rather than private self-interest. Another way of saying this is simply that cooperative theories of democracy are fundamentally inconsistent with the core principle of epistemological humility that the First Amendment embodies because, either implicitly or explicitly, they reflect predetermined conclusions about how autonomy should be exercised. In this manner, both theories suffer from the oxymoronic concept of externally determined autonomy.

Adversary democracy does not suffer from the same problem because it contains no underlying premise as to how or why autonomy should be exercised.[232] Instead, it commits these choices to the individual. Thus, if an individual wishes to vote and advocate to pursue the course of action she thinks is in the best interests of the community or the nation, adversary democracy authorizes her to do so.[233] On the other hand, if individuals wish to vote and advocate to pursue what they think is in their own private self-interest, adversary democracy says they may do that, as well. Because adversary democracy is consistent with these process-based autonomy decisions, one employing the adversary theory of the First Amendment is never tempted to exclude speech otherwise logically included within the amendment's scope simply because its speaker is not acting in accordance with some predetermined normative ideal of political behavior.

More importantly, the adversary theory of free expression is preferable to Meiklejohn's and Post's far more cooperative theories because it equally protects *all* aspects of democratic autonomy, rather than selectively privileging some aspects over others. Assuming that the purpose of a democratic theory of the First Amendment is to facilitate democracy, which in turn necessarily implies the notions of ideological humility and true voter autonomy, such comprehensive protection for all aspects and conditions of process-based autonomy is crucial to a theory's success. Unlike Meiklejohn's theory, which categorically excludes speaker autonomy and all forms of individual autonomy, and unlike Post's theory, which systematically underprotects listener autonomy and all forms of individual autonomy that do not facilitate the emergence of a common will, the adversary theory of free expression provides complete protection to democratic autonomy in all its manifestations.

It should be emphasized that the adversary theory of democracy confirms that Meiklejohn and Post are both correct to some extent. Individuals must have access to speech that helps them to make decisions as voters, and they also must be free to influence the opinions of others by participating in public discourse. In other words, the First Amendment must encompass *both* the listener autonomy that Meiklejohn would protect *and* the speaker autonomy that Post would protect. But the adversary theory of the First Amendment explains why neither Meiklejohn nor Post goes far enough in his protection of free speech. Given its descriptive principle—the recognition that different and often competing interests and ideologies will generally divide collective decision making—adversary democracy suggests first that it is necessary for every individual to possess the equal ability to influence the outcomes of collective decision making. This is why Meiklejohn is assuredly correct to focus on the vote as central to democracy and why

Post is assuredly mistaken to marginalize it. In such a setting, however, it is also necessary that every individual have a full opportunity to influence others around her. Otherwise, the majority becomes entrenched as the majority forever, and the promise of democratic self-determination benefits only those in that static majority. This is why Post is clearly correct to focus on the individual's right to advocate as a means of shaping public opinion and why Meiklejohn is clearly mistaken to deny it. Merely combining Meiklejohn and Post's theories, however, does not result in creation of a satisfactory free speech theory. Such a synthesis would still exclude the last two categories of speech that adversary democracy dictates must be protected: speech that facilitates individuals' awareness of their self-interest and speech that allows individuals to maintain their individuality in spite of the collectivizing pressures of modern life. Combining Post and Meiklejohn would still exclude (or, at the very least, reduce protection for) speech that is an exercise of individual autonomy—the very speech that the adversary theory dictates deserves protection.

Consider again Meiklejohn's stance concerning First Amendment protection for radio broadcasts. He suggested that because the radio is run by individuals who pursue profits rather than the common good of the nation, it should be denied First Amendment protection.[234] Now consider how Post's participatory theory would evaluate constitutional protection for radio broadcasts. Presumably, they are entitled to the presumption of qualifying as "public discourse" because radio is a form of media, and, according to Post, the media, purely as a matter of tradition, receive full First Amendment protection.[235] But consider the analysis in which a court would have to engage pursuant to Post's theory absent this unjustified presumption.[236] The judge would be forced to decide whether the most natural understanding of the radio is that it constitutes an "effort" to shape public opinion, or rather an effort to make money (as if the two were somehow mutually exclusive). Of course this is a misguided inquiry in the first place, but indulging it for the moment, it is difficult to imagine how rock-and-roll disc jockey Casey Kasem attempted to "engage in the public life of the nation" by broadcasting the Top 40 any more than General Electric does by advertising its "Ecomagination" philosophy. Purely as a logical matter, then, under Post's theory speakers' self-interest could potentially, if not inevitably, exclude their speech from First Amendment protection.

The adversary theory of free expression, on the other hand, protects and even values the promotion of self-interest. It does so in part for the practical reason that self-interest creates an incentive for speech that facilitates democratic decision making. And it does so also based on the recognition that the collective decision-making process may choose to ignore the interest entirely unless the individual represents it. But, more fundamentally, it does so for the theoretical reason that autonomy requires that individuals have the freedom to decide how they want to govern themselves and how they want to engage in the process of collective decision making, whether or not external observers approve.

CONCLUSION

The viability of any democratic theory of the First Amendment necessarily hinges on two considerations: (1) the validity of the vision of democracy that underlies it and (2) the consistency with which First Amendment theory is fashioned to best implement that vision. Alexander Meiklejohn's and Robert Post's democratic theories of the First Amendment fail on both counts. Neither grasps the true nature of autonomy that is central to any viable form of democracy. Moreover, even if one were to assume the correctness of their democratic visions, neither fashions a First Amendment theory that implements its vision in a logically consistent and coherent manner.

If one were forced to point to the single most fundamental flaw in both Post's and Meiklejohn's democratic theories of the First Amendment, it would be their failure to recognize the centrality of the adversary element in democracy or, at the very least, to understand its logical implications. In any functioning democratic society as large and diverse as ours, different personal or ideological interests will inevitably clash. On occasion, those advocating these competing interests will compromise. On other occasions, one side will defeat the other, politically. In all instances, however, the adversarial nature of the political battlefront is tempered by a cooperative ether—one that permits the peaceful resolution of disputes and a continuation of the commitment to the democratic process.

A purely or predominantly collectivist or communitarian vision of democracy ignores both the political realities of self-interested political combat and the normative foundational commitment of any democratic society to the ultimate integrity of its individual citizens. Any theory of free expression that ignores the insights of adversary democracy must therefore ultimately fail, much as do the theories of both Post and Meiklejohn.

CHAPTER FOUR

Commercial Speech and the Twilight Zone of Viewpoint Discrimination

Commercial speech is no longer the stepchild of the First Amendment. Long all but ignored and summarily excluded from the scope of the First Amendment's protective reach,[1] commercial speech took its first major step toward validation in the Supreme Court's 1976 decision in *Virginia State Board of Pharmacy v. Virginia Citizens Consumer Council, Inc.*[2] But as significant as *Virginia Board* was as a historical and doctrinal matter, it left much to be desired as a coherent statement of First Amendment theory. It was likely this failure that led to the stark second-class status and treatment the concept received in the Supreme Court for the better part of two decades.[3] Today, however, the situation in the judicial trenches appears to have changed dramatically. In every recent commercial speech case decided by the Supreme Court, the First Amendment argument has prevailed.[4] These results are in sharp contrast to the much more hit-or-miss record of the procommercial speech cause in earlier years. Although it would be incorrect to suggest that commercial speech is today deemed fungible with fully protected speech in all contexts,[5] it is at least true that the gap between the two is far narrower than it was in 1976.

Despite this significant alteration in judicial outcomes, certain aspects of the modern commercial speech debate, unfortunately, remain much the same as before. For one thing, the Court at least purports to be applying the "First Amendment Lite" type of protection that it first adopted in its famed four-part *Central Hudson* test in 1980. It does so despite the fact that the end results of what is supposedly the same diluted commercial speech-specific test are now far more protective than they once were. Moreover, a number of respected scholars have largely continued their vigorous opposition to commercial speech protection. Some object to the extension of any First Amendment protection at all.[6] Others have made clear their objection, not to the extension of *any* level of First Amendment protection but rather to the extension of *full* First Amendment protection. They reach these conclusions because they find unacceptable a First Amendment standard that would treat commercial advertising, for constitutional purposes, interchangeably with the works of Shakespeare, Martin Luther King Jr.'s "I have a dream" speech, or William Jennings Bryan's famed "cross of gold" speech.[7]

The nature of these scholarly attacks on commercial speech protection can be placed within three broad categories: (1) rationalist, (2) intuitionist, and (3) ideological. Arguments included in the first category put forward specific reasons to support the proposition that, as a matter of First Amendment theory and principle, commercial speech is undeserving of First Amendment protection, or at least the same level of protection given to more traditionally protected forms of expression. In contrast, arguments falling within the second category appeal to intuitive notions of what free expression is all about. They conclude, on the basis of those intuitions, that commercial speech is undeserving of full protection. Those objections falling into the third category differ from those in the first two categories in that they are openly based on the perceived evils of the economic system of which commercial speech is a part. In other words, arguments falling into the third category amount to nothing more than ideological opposition to the capitalist system from which advertising emerges.

The adversary First Amendment, grounded in the political theory of adversary democracy, has important implications for the current debate over commercial speech protection. Recall that the theory of adversary democracy acknowledges and accepts the possibility that the expression and actions of private citizens may well be motivated by considerations of economic or personal self-interest. It further recognizes, however, that those exercising regulatory power over private citizens' expression may also be motivated by personal or ideological agendas in deciding what expression is to be suppressed. Such strategically selective, politically driven suppression, of course, undermines the healthy functioning of the democratic process. The First Amendment must therefore put us on constant guard against such ideologically based interferences with free expression.

When one views the arguments against constitutional protection of commercial speech through the lens of the adversary First Amendment, one may reasonably reach two important conclusions: (1) The mere fact that commercial advertisers seek to profit by listener acceptance of their arguments cannot logically exclude their advertising from the scope of the First Amendment, or even lead to a reduction in the level of constitutional protection; and (2) one may reasonably invoke a healthy degree of skepticism about the underlying ideological agenda of those who argue against such protection. This chapter will demonstrate that, to all too great an extent, all three asserted bases for rejecting of commercial speech protection suffer from the same fundamental flaw: Each either constitutes or indirectly facilitates a constitutionally destructive form of viewpoint-based regulation. As such, each gives rise, ironically in the name of the First Amendment, to the most universally condemned threat to the foundations of free expression: suppression based on the regulators' subjective disagreement with or disdain for the views being expressed.[8]

To be sure, the three forms of constitutional attack on commercial speech protection differ significantly in how they ultimately reach their end result of viewpoint regulation. Criticisms that fall within the third category, for example, are refreshingly candid in their ideological cast, and it is therefore mercifully easy to expose their true nature. They are avowedly premised on acceptance of a particular political or ideological perspective that is hostile to capitalism and its logical outgrowths or implications. There is, of course, no reason in the world that, purely as a normative matter, scholars should not be able to vigorously attack what they see as the evils of capitalism and commercialism and argue that the logical result is that speech that fosters or furthers such an economic system should, purely as a political or ideological matter, be disdained. The problem, however, is that these arguments are made not merely on a purely normative or ideological level as part of a broader substantive political debate but rather as a supposedly principled basis on which to determine the reach of the First Amendment. Such a practice is a risky endeavor for those on both sides of any normative political issue. Any student of free expression should be able to explain that the level of constitutional protection extended to expression cannot be determined by the extent to which the regulator agrees or disagrees with the views expressed. Adoption of such an approach to determination of the First Amendment's scope would automatically transform First Amendment interpretation into a political state of nature. Whoever controls the official channels of constitutional interpretation would then be permitted to exclude from the First Amendment's scope any expression that *they* happen to deem deeply immoral or ideologically offensive. As is so often the case in constitutional law, then, we should warn those who wish to exclude commercial speech from the First Amendment's scope because they condemn the commercialism of which it is an outgrowth: Be careful what you wish for.

The other two categories are somewhat more complex and therefore more difficult to characterize as a form of invidious viewpoint regulation. Indeed, attacks in the first category appear, at least superficially, to represent the very opposite of an unprincipled, politically motivated approach to First Amendment interpretation. They appear, rather, to be grounded in a form of objective and principled constitutional analysis. However, closer analysis reveals that all such supposedly principled justifications are fatally and irrationally underinclusive. In each case, the justification asserted to support reduced protection for commercial speech applies with equal force to one or more categories of noncommercial expression that the scholar advocating reduced protection for commercial speech assumes to receive full First Amendment protection. Thus, what superficially appears to constitute a plausible and principled rationale for reducing protection for commercial speech in reality applies its basis for reduced protection in an irrational and unjustifiably selective manner to commercial speech but not to various forms of fully protected noncommercial expression. If the asserted criteria were employed properly as principled, legitimate, and neutrally applied grounds on which to reduce constitutional protection for speech, then logically they should also lead to the exclusion of or reduction in protection for the parallel noncommercial speech category, which is saddled with the identical flaw. On the other hand, if the asserted rationale is assumed not to justify reduced protection for various forms of noncommercial speech, then logically it should be considered equally insufficient to justify reduced protection for commercial speech. It is this very point that lies at the core of Herbert Wechsler's famed "neutral principles" analysis: Once a court interpreting and applying a constitutional provision has chosen a principled basis for decision, it may not selectively ignore that principle in subsequent cases when its use would lead to politically distasteful conclusions.[9] Rather, for judicial legitimacy to be maintained, the constitutional principle must be applied neutrally in all situations to which that principle applies.[10]

It does not automatically follow, of course, that opposition to commercial speech protection necessarily implies furtive politically based viewpoint regulation. Indeed, on occasion some of the strongest opponents of commercial speech protection have come from the political right—hardly the place from which one would normally fear anticapitalist viewpoint-based regulation.[11] However, these commentators' or jurists' views can largely be explained on the basis of their largely underprotective approach to free expression in general. The concern expressed here over indirect or furtive viewpoint-based discrimination, rather, focuses on scholars and jurists who are normally associated with a generally more protective approach toward free expression. It is their logically indefensible refusal to extend full protection to commercial speech that is appropriately seen as viewpoint driven.

Strategically selective application of rationalizing abstract principles is often associated with furtive or indirect forms of viewpoint-based regulation. For example, imagine an ordinance that makes it a crime to distribute antiwar literature on a city's main thoroughfare during rush hour. The asserted justification for the regulation is the viewpoint-neutral contention that distribution of literature at this particular time and place would be disruptive to important governmental interests, such as safety and traffic flow. Such a viewpoint-neutral rationale may or may not justify speech regulation. The answer to that question turns on a complex assessment of numerous criteria and is well beyond the scope of this inquiry. In the hypothetical ordinance, however, the validity of this asserted rationale is beside the point because the identical harm would result from distribution of prowar literature or, for that matter, *any* type of literature. The fatally underinclusive nature of the ordinance's limitation inexorably leads to the conclusion that the ordinance is effectively viewpoint based. A similar analysis is equally applicable to the fatally underinclusive justifications for reduced protection for commercial speech.

The remaining category of commercial speech opposition, which I have labeled "intuitionist," amounts to neither direct viewpoint-based discrimination nor furtive, indirect viewpoint discrimination. However, because of its inherently nonrational nature, intuitionist analysis may easily serve as either a catalyst or a cover for the implementation of such invidious discrimination. It is thus appropriately seen as an "enabler" of, or catalyst for, viewpoint discrimination. One can easily assert, in a conclusory manner, that one's own First Amendment intuition leads to the exclusion or reduction of constitutional protection for commercial speech. But because by definition an intuitionist justification need not be grounded in rational argument, such intuition may derive (consciously or subconsciously) from a background political or ideological prejudice against either the commercial speech itself or the capitalist economic system in which it functions. Equally troubling is the threat that this intellectual version of grunting causes to every aspect of First Amendment thought, right down to its core, for intuitionist justifications are, by definition, immune to any form of rational critique.

Even if one were to accept everything said to this point, there would nevertheless exist a significant analytical obstacle to characterizing any or all of these rationales as forms of viewpoint discrimination. Classical viewpoint discrimination selectively suppresses speech on the basis of regulatory hostility to a specific social, political, or moral position sought to be expressed by the speaker. This pathology, for the most part, is not technically true of commercial speech regulation, even when the reduced protection is openly grounded in hostility to commercial expression as a whole. By the Court's own definition, commercial speech is confined to expression that promotes sale of a product or service.[12] Such expression, therefore, does not directly express a political, social, or moral viewpoint. One may therefore challenge the characterization of scholarly or judicial hostility to commercial speech as a form of viewpoint-based discrimination. At most, it could be argued, commercial speech regulation constitutes a form of *subject matter* discrimination, a far less invidious—indeed, often readily accepted—type of constitutional classification. Although one can fully recognize this potential difficulty, it is nevertheless appropriate to conclude that any approach grounded in hostility to commercial speech is appropriately viewed not as subject matter categorization but rather as viewpoint-based discrimination. This conclusion is grounded in the argument that such hostility falls within a "twilight zone" category of viewpoint discrimination that, while not conceptually identical to traditional viewpoint-based regulation, gives rise to much the same invidious threat to the foundations of free expression.

This chapter contains three main sections. The initial section describes the three categories of argumentation usually relied on to justify a reduced level of protection for commercial speech.[13] The following section explores the nature of viewpoint discrimination and the reasons why, as a matter of constitutional and political theory, such discrimination must be categorically rejected as a basis for First Amendment analysis.[14] The final section integrates the first two sections by demonstrating that each of the categorical bases for reducing or rejecting First Amendment protection for commercial speech is, in one way or another, appropriately characterized as a form of invidious and therefore constitutionally impermissible viewpoint discrimination.[15]

THE ARGUMENTS FOR REDUCED COMMERCIAL SPEECH PROTECTION: A CATEGORICAL APPROACH

Defining Commercial Speech

Until relatively late in the twentieth century, neither court nor scholar invested virtually any effort in fashioning a defense of the summary exclusion of commercial speech protection from the scope of First Amendment protection.[16] It was generally assumed, without explanation or support, that commercial speech fell within the area of far less protected property rights, rather than constitutionally protected expression.[17] Since the Supreme Court's decision to extend at least some level of First Amendment protection to commercial speech, a scholarly cottage industry on the subject has mushroomed. Some of it has advocated full, or at least substantial, First Amendment protection.[18] Much of it—likely the overwhelming majority—has rejected full or, on occasion, any First Amendment protection for commercial speech.[19] Before the goal of categorizing and deconstructing the arguments against full First Amendment protection for commercial speech can be attained, however, it is necessary to define the concept. The term, it seems, is not self-defining, and how one chooses to define *commercial speech* can have an enormous impact on the validity of the attacks on its protection.[20]

Although the Supreme Court has cryptically offered a number of different—and not always consistent—definitions of commercial speech,[21] for all practical purposes the alternatives come down to two: (1) speech concerning commercial products or services[22] or (2) speech advocating the sale of commercial products or services (the definition on which the Court appears to have settled).[23] Under the first alternative, *all* expression concerning the quality, efficiency, or safety of products or services for sale, regardless of who the speaker is, would receive reduced or no protection. Thus, under this view both a manufacturer's speech advocating a product's sale and a consumer protection advocate's speech criticizing the product would be deemed less protected commercial speech.[24] Under the second alternative, in contrast, it is only speech motivated by the seller's goal of direct financial gain through sale that falls within the supposedly "second class" category of commercial expression.[25] Both alternatives represent linguistically plausible definitions of the phrase. But while the first alternative is at least theoretically conceivable, at no point has the Court ever chosen to employ it. It is probably reasonable to conclude at this point that the Court has unambiguously adopted the view that commercial speech is confined to expression advocating purchase.[26]

In categorizing, analyzing, and critiquing the various arguments relied on to reject full First Amendment protection for commercial speech,[27] it is essential to recognize that those scholars advocating this position have done so on the assumption that commercial speech is confined to expression promoting sale.[28] Indeed, in a number of instances the fact of sale promotion is central to the argument for reduced protection.[29] Thus, it should always be kept in mind that the very same scholars who urge reduced protection for commercial speech are at the same time proceeding on the assumption that expression criticizing or opposing the quality, safety, efficiency, or value of commercial products or services for reasons other than sale of the speaker's own product or service receives full constitutional protection.

Understanding the Nature of Principled Constitutional Analysis

Many years ago, Herbert Wechsler, in his famed article on "neutral principles," provided the modern basis for the argument that constitutional interpretation must ultimately rest on principle.[30] Though Wechsler's article clearly suffers from a number of flaws and has been the victim of often vigorous, and sometimes unfair, attack,[31] it properly remains the starting point for any argument that constitutional interpretation must ultimately be grounded in principled analysis. Anyone who seeks to defend the need for principled analysis in constitutional interpretation, of course, bears an obligation to explain the difference between principled and unprincipled interpretation—often not an easy task. Indeed, Professor Wechsler was largely agnostic on the question of how to choose an interpretation of a constitutional provision in the first place.[32] However, Wechsler's greatest—albeit today largely ignored—contribution was to point out what perhaps should have been obvious in any event: To satisfy the requirements of principle, a constitutional interpretation must be applied neutrally.[33] In other words, whatever rationale a court selects to justify its chosen interpretive doctrine must be applied consistently in all cases; it cannot be selectively altered in subsequent cases solely because the court finds the outcome dictated by use of that principle to be politically distasteful or offensive. Wechsler's insight, then, can play a valuable role in constitutional analysis, even if one remains uncertain of how to choose the applicable interpretive principle in the first place. His primary concern was not with the shaping of the principle but in maintaining the principle's consistent application once it has been adopted in the initial case.

In important ways, portions of the First Amendment's prohibition on viewpoint discrimination grow out of a Wechslerian concern for principle. When a regulation of expression is constitutionally justified on the ground that the regulated expression possesses harmful quality X or lacks the positive quality Y, the fact that the regulation fails to include within its prohibitory reach other expression that also both possesses quality X and lacks quality Y renders the regulation if not unconstitutional then at least constitutionally suspect. This is so even were one to assume that a regulation of *all* the expression characterized by X would satisfy the First Amendment. The constitutional flaw is that the regulation is irrationally underinclusive and therefore discriminatory.

It is important to understand that parallel underinclusiveness analysis applies to selective expressive *protection*, as well as to selective expressive *suppression*. Phrased in Wechslerian terms, when the guiding principle of First Amendment interpretation chosen by a reviewing court as a basis for excluding the regulated expression from the protective scope of the First Amendment simultaneously affects other types of speech that the court in subsequent cases chooses to protect, the court has failed to apply its interpretive principle in a neutral manner. Of course, nothing in Wechslerian jurisprudence would logically prevent a reviewing court from deciding to alter its underlying interpretive principle (putting issues of constitutional stare decisis to the side).[34] Thus, the court could now decide that it had been incorrect in its prior decision in believing that expression is disqualified from the First Amendment's scope because it is characterized by X. Such an alteration in underlying principle, however, would logically dictate a reversal of the decision not to extend protection to the regulated expression in the initial case; a failure to do so would lead to adoption of an analytical process equivalent to swimming halfway across a river, intellectually speaking. The court could, on the other hand, now decide that while X is no longer an appropriate basis on which to determine First Amendment protection, Z does provide such a basis, and the speech not protected in the initial case is characterized by Z although the speech the court chose to protect in the second case is not. If so, however, the court would obviously have to make its change in underlying decisional principle explicit. Absent such an explicit change in governing principle, exclusion of the expression in case one from the First Amendment's scope, combined with the protective inclusion of similarly characterized expression in case two, is inescapably unprincipled.

When a reviewing court engages in such inconsistent application of its chosen interpretive principle, two conceivable explanations exist: (1) The court simply fails to recognize or grasp the inconsistency or (2) the court is making a conscious (albeit concealed) choice to apply its guiding interpretive principle selectively because it dislikes the substance of the regulated speech in the initial case but is favorably disposed to the regulated speech in the second case. There appears to be no third alternative. The reviewing court could, perhaps, candidly acknowledge that it is refusing to protect the expression in case one, not because of any neutrally applied precept of First Amendment analysis but simply because it finds the substance of the speech politically or morally offensive. For example, the court could conceivably assert, quite openly, that its "principle" of First Amendment interpretation is that the speech of Socialists, or Fascists, or Communists, or (fill in name of hated group here) is so offensive or evil as to exclude itself from constitutional protection.[35] Applying this form of principled analysis, the court would be quite consistent in deciding not to protect the speech in case one but to protect the speech in case two because the speech in case one was by Socialists while the speech in case two was not. Such an approach to First Amendment interpretation, however, is unacceptable. It does not represent a good-faith attempt to reconcile and apply the competing historical, textual, and normative factors required by principled First Amendment analysis. It is, rather, nothing more than a thinly veiled attempt by those in power to use the First Amendment as a weapon to undermine the freedom of thought and expression underlying that very constitutional protection.

One may better understand this interpretive dichotomy by dissecting the reasoning that enters into the shaping of both levels of constitutional analysis. On the first level, the interpreter is seeking to glean an appropriate normative guide from the value or synthesis of values underlying the First Amendment. To be sure, reasonable people may differ over what the underlying value or values actually are or what is the correct translation from value to doctrine. Nevertheless, when engaging in truly principled analysis the interpreter is necessarily seeking to decipher the deep constitutional structure underlying the words of the First Amendment. When invoking unprincipled analysis, the interpreter cares not at all about the deep structural value or values underlying the protection of free expression but instead reflexively draws a superficial, unsupported, and manipulative equation between those values and the exclusion of what she deems politically offensive speech. But, in the final analysis, interpreters operating on this narrower political level are concerned not at all with what the First Amendment is all about. They are focused, rather, on how to find a way to suppress the speech they deem politically offensive and manipulatively interpret the First Amendment toward that end.

The Three Categories of Commercial Speech Opposition

With this structural background established, it is now appropriate to turn to explication of the three categories of justifications for the extension of reduced or no protection to commercial speech. Those three categories, it should be recalled, are here labeled (1) rationalist, (2) intuitionist, and (3) ideological. It should be emphasized that this categorization is solely my own. No one, to my knowledge, has ever even attempted to categorize the anticommercial speech arguments, much less chosen the specific categories selected here. Because none of the scholars who oppose full First Amendment protection for commercial speech has ever expressly categorized his or her own arguments in the manner I suggest, it is conceivable that particular scholars will object to my classification of their work. In each case, however, all of those opposing full commercial speech protection seem to fit with surprising ease into one of my three categories.

Rationalist Grounds

Rationalist grounds for opposition to First Amendment protection for commercial speech include those reasons that at least purport to be based on principled interpretation of the Amendment—in other words, efforts to construe and implement the values underlying the constitutional provision. To the extent these reasons justify exclusion of commercial speech, they do so not because of political opposition to commercial speech but rather simply because commercial speech is found not adequately to further First Amendment values. It is possible to discern six conceivable rationalist grounds on which one might seek to distinguish commercial speech from fully protected speech: (1) absence of relevance to the political process; (2) commercial speech's unique motivational hardiness; (3) characterization of commercial speech as conduct, rather than speech; (4) the corporate nature of the speaker; (5) the speaker self-interest that inherently accompanies commercial speech; and (6) the absence of improper regulatory motive for the suppression of commercial speech.[36] Closer analysis of each of these asserted rationalist grounds, however, readily exposes the grossly underinclusive nature of all of them.

Absence of Relevance to the Political Process. Although Professor Daniel Farber is undoubtedly incorrect when he asserts that "everyone seems to agree that political speech lies at the core of the First Amendment's protection,"[37] it is certainly true that a number of leading First Amendment scholars have advocated such a view.[38] If one were to define commercial speech as speech concerning commercial products or services, one starting from the premise that the First Amendment is primarily or exclusively designed to protect speech relevant to the political process might well conclude that commercial speech is deserving of little or no First Amendment protection. One may reasonably criticize the political speech theory as flawed because it fails to inquire into the normative reasons our system would choose democracy in the first place.[39] Such an inquiry would establish that speech concerning commercial products and services can facilitate private self-government in much the same way that political speech fosters collective self-government, and that both forms of self-government foster the values of democracy.[40] Both private and collective self-government are grounded in identical normative concerns about self-development and self-determination.[41] Therefore, it makes no sense to protect speech relevant to a situation where the individual has a minuscule fraction of a say in the outcome while simultaneously refusing to protect speech that will facilitate choices by the private individual that are solely her own.[42] The need for such an argument is rendered moot, however, once one chooses to define commercial speech not in terms of its subject matter but rather exclusively in terms of the motivation or goal of the speaker. If, as the Supreme Court currently maintains,[43] commercial speech refers only to speech that advocates purchase, there exists a great deal of expression concerning commercial goods and services—that is, speech about products and services by someone other than the seller—that is not classified as commercial speech and therefore not relegated to the second-class status given to commercial advertising. The magazine *Consumer Reports*, as well as consumer advocate groups, talk predominantly, if not exclusively, about the relative merits of commercial goods and services, much as commercial advertisers do, yet their speech is fully protected.

It might be argued that, unlike the expression of the commercial advertisers, speech of *Consumer Reports* and consumer advocate groups can be presumed to be objective, while commercial advertising will always be slanted strategically. But that fact, even if assumed to be accurate, surely has nothing to do with the characterization of the expression as political or nonpolitical because much political speech will be just as slanted as commercial advertising. Thus, it is at least arguable that a preference for political speech protection could logically lead to reduced protection, or even an absence of protection, for even purely objective speech about the merits of commercial products and services.[44] But it would amount to a total non sequitur to suggest that because we give primacy to political speech, we should therefore reduce protection for commercial advertising but not for nonpromotional comments about commercial products and services. Neither type of expression has any more to do with the political process than the other. Thus, reliance on a political speech preference as a principled basis for rejecting protection for commercial advertising breaks down. It is easily revealed to be an irrationally underinclusive, and therefore inherently unprincipled, ground for distinguishing commercial from noncommercial expression for purposes of First Amendment protection.

Motivational Hardiness. In choosing to extend substantial constitutional protection to commercial speech for the first time, the Supreme Court in *Virginia Board* noted that there existed "commonsense differences" between commercial speech and traditionally protected expression.[45] Chief among these differences is that "since advertising is the *sine qua non* of commercial profits, there is little likelihood of its being chilled by proper regulation."[46] The existence of the profit motive, in other words, provides a hardiness to commercial speech that makes it more resistant to chilling regulation. Putting the same point in the terms of public choice theory, Professor Farber has suggested that commercial speech is "at the periphery" of the First Amendment[47] because "commercial speech . . . [more] closely resembles a private good [than does political speech]. Most of the benefit of product advertising is captured by the producer itself in the form of increased sales. Consequently, we would not expect severe underproduction of commercial speech."[48]

It is conceivable that if accepted as a rationale for reduced protection of commercial speech, the argument grounded in motivational hardiness would, in fact, justify the drawing of a distinction between direct commercial promotion of sale, on the one hand, and a *Consumer Reports* discussion of products, on the other. As Professor Farber asserts, "Product information distributed by a third party produces benefits that are captured by persons other than the speaker. The speaker, therefore, has an inadequate motivation to produce this information."[49] One response to Farber's point is that *Consumer Reports does* have an economic incentive to produce and distribute its information, for the simple reason that it is able to sell its magazines because of that information. On the other hand, it is arguable that, unlike the manufacturer or dealer, *Consumer Reports* does not benefit economically—at least directly—by listener acceptance of, and action on, its expression. The problem with such a response is that if listeners or readers do not accept what *Consumer Reports* says, presumably they will not buy its publication and the publishers will lose money. The problems with this "motivational hardiness" rationale, however, are far more significant than this single concern.

In different ways, this rationale for refusing to protect speech manages to be simultaneously overinclusive and underinclusive. It is overinclusive in that it ignores vitally important differences among different forms of expressive regulation. When the governmental regulation is *partial*, it is at least conceivable that the motivational hardiness rationale is relevant. Thus, it might be argued that where government prohibits only false commercial speech—which itself is presumed to fall outside the First Amendment's protective scope—the spillover chilling effect on protected truthful commercial speech is diluted by the competing motivation of speaker self-interest. The speaker's desire to communicate truthful information would continue to exist despite the possible fear that what he deems truthful will subsequently be punished as false. But when the governmental regulation of expression is *total*, meaning that it has simply shut down all forms of that type of communication rather than prohibiting merely false or misleading speech, the motivational hardiness rationale makes no sense. Where government has chosen to suppress *all* of a particular form of expression, what possible difference can it make that the would-be speaker's motivation to speak remains strong due to self-interest? Under such circumstances, no matter how motivated the speaker may be, he is denied the right or opportunity to speak. In this context the motivational hardiness rationale has no relevance. The essence of that argument in this context would necessarily be the nonsensical logic that it does not matter that the speaker has been *completely prohibited from conveying truthful information* because he continues to have the motivation to disseminate truthful information. But of course, the conclusion in no way logically flows from the premise. To the contrary—to state the proposition is to underscore its incoherence. Nor is it the case that the overwhelming number of commercial speech regulations are aimed only at false or misleading commercial information.[50]

Thus, at the very least, those reflexively relying on the motivational hardiness rationale as a justification for reducing commercial speech protection need to be far more selective about the nature of the expressive regulation being justified.

It actually matters little how selective supporters of this rationale are in choosing among types of expressive regulation because the rationale's logic is fatally underinclusive in the scope of speakers penalized by its reach. It is true, as Professor Farber and others have suggested, that commercial advertisers have an enormous motivation, grounded in stark economic self-interest, to communicate with and persuade potential purchasers.[51] But it is surely not difficult to think of numerous other groups of speakers who fit the same description. Candidates for political office have an enormous motivation, grounded in self-interest, both to communicate and to persuade. In addition, it is often true that supporters of those candidates also have strong economic motivations for their expression because if elected their candidates will implement policies that will economically benefit those supporters. Perhaps one could respond that, while this is possible, it is also conceivable that the candidate and her supporters could be motivated by more public-oriented goals. Yet no one can know this *ex ante*, in the particular case. We nevertheless extend full protection to *all* candidate speech. Moreover, one can also assume that there are businesses motivated simultaneously by goals of personal economic gain and advancement of the public interest. In any event, one can hypothesize numerous categories of speakers who are obviously and unambiguously motivated by personal gain, yet whose speech unquestionably receives full First Amendment protection: Welfare mothers picketing for increased benefits, antitaxation groups, labor unions, and interest group lobbyists are illustrative.

The Speech–Action Dichotomy. It might be argued that the Court's focus on the proposal of a commercial transaction as the defining element of the less protected commercial speech category can be grounded in the well-established speech–action dichotomy. Both textually and theoretically, the First Amendment protects speech, not actions. To the extent that expression promoting commercial transactions is linked inextricably to the commercial transactions themselves, arguably the speech collapses into the nonexpressive commercial transaction. As a result, its status as protected speech is at least diluted, if not completely revoked.

At most, this reasoning could have relevance to promotion at the point of sale. It is only at the point of sale that commercial advocacy is, even arguably, so temporally and physically linked to the acts of purchase and sale that it can realistically be deemed an element of these acts. Moreover, to suggest that speech advocating action is automatically rendered the equivalent of action would defy both conceptual reality and at least seventy years of the Supreme Court's First Amendment jurisprudence on the question of unlawful advocacy.[52] The Court has long held that many forms of advocacy of conduct receive full First Amendment protection, even though the advocated conduct is itself unlawful.[53] For that reason, speech that advocates action is no less classifiable as "speech" for purposes of First Amendment protection. Indeed, speech advocating alteration in listener conduct in many ways lies at the core of the constitutional protection, which recognizes the inherent intersection between expression and political choice. Thus, the speech–action dichotomy fails to justify a categorical distinction between commercial and noncommercial expression.

The Corporate Nature of the Speaker. One could conceivably reject protection for commercial speech for no reason other than the nature of the speaker. The speaker proposing a commercial transaction is invariably a profit-making corporation, an artificial legal creation of the state whose sole reason for existence is profit maximization. Professor C. Edwin Baker, for example, argued that because free speech necessarily implicates the exercise of free will, the expression of corporations—which is nothing more than the reflexive, robotic attempt to increase profits—cannot qualify for protection.[54] For this reason, Professor Baker would deny protection not only to commercial speech but also to purely political speech uttered by corporations.[55]

Professor Baker's reasoning is subject to serious doubt. If one assumes that the values of free speech can be fostered by the receipt, as well as by the communication, of expression,[56] then it should logically make no difference whether the speaker itself deserves the benefits of the constitutional protection. But even if one were to accept Baker's reasoning, his argument remains grossly underinclusive as a justification for a surgical excision of commercial speech from the First Amendment's protective scope. The institutional media—from the *New York Times* to the *National Enquirer*—are as much profit-making corporations as is any commercial advertiser. Every publishing decision they make is therefore presumably as motivated by profit maximization as are those of nonmedia corporations.

There are several possible responses to the underinclusiveness attack on Baker's suggested distinction between the corporate press and speech by other corporations. First, Professor Baker has asserted a distinction grounded in the First Amendment's separate constitutional protection for freedom of the press.[57] Because the corporate media are appropriately classified as "press," he argued, they are to be treated differently, for protective purposes, from nonmedia corporate speakers.[58] Thus, the exclusion of robotic profit maximizers from the First Amendment is apparently to apply to "speakers," rather than to the "press."

There is much that is troubling in Baker's argument. First, historical support for Baker's grounding of his asserted distinction in the Framers' intent is weak for several reasons. Initially, one can appropriately question the interpretive legitimacy of any form of inquiry into original meaning or intent,[59] and it is only if one accepts the validity of an originalist inquiry as a form of constitutional interpretation that Baker's argument could even conceivably have relevance. Professor Baker himself appears wholly unconcerned with originalism when it comes to an understanding of the Free Speech Clause. More importantly, his argument fails because it amounts to an anachronism: At the time of the framing, there existed no corporate, profit-making institutional press in the sense that it exists today.[60] It therefore makes no sense to impute to the Framers the intent to exclude corporate *speakers*, but not the corporate *press*, from the scope of the First Amendment. Secondly, it would have been all but impossible at the time— and, indeed, today—to distinguish the institutional press from the "non-institutional" press, if one were even able to persuasively hypothesize such a distinction on a conceptual level in the first place. Finally, it is difficult to understand why, purely as a normative matter, one would choose to give greater protection to the institutional corporate press than to other forms of written expression. Inferring such a distinction from the First Amendment would effectively transform that provision into what today would amount to one big anticompetitive antitrust violation because it would use the amendment as a means of excluding expressive competitors to the institutional press—hardly a legitimate goal of the constitutional protection of expression.

Perhaps one could respond that it is necessary to provide the institutional press with greater protection, simply to assure the press's performance of its vital "checking function," by which it exposes—and thereby limits or deters—governmental excess and abuse.[61] But while checking governmental abuse is appropriately seen as a worthy aim of the First Amendment, it would make no sense to confine performance of that function to some sort of "in-group" of well-established institutional corporate media. One need point only to the *New York Times*'s dubious performance as a check on the Bush administration's long-since disproven charges of weapons of mass destruction in Iraq to see that the institutional press is often far more willing to jump into bed with government than it is to check it.[62] It makes sense, therefore, to view the scope of the press protection broadly to extend well beyond the institutional press. To do so would significantly expand the potential private check on governmental excess or abuse.

Most devastating to Baker's effort to rationalize his corporate press/ nonpress distinction is the simple fact that it is, at its foundation, wholly illogical. If the robotic goal of profit maximization is somehow assumed to justify exclusion from the First Amendment's scope when corporate speakers other than the institutional press are involved—a conclusion that, it should be recalled, is insupportable—then presumably it is exclusively the absence of speaker free will that justifies such exclusion. It is by no means evident that Baker's focus on speaker free will should logically matter only when the speech clause, rather than the press clause, is involved. If the institutional press is made up of profit-maximizing corporations, then presumably they, too, must be motivated solely by robotic profit maximization— the very fact Baker relies on to justify exclusion of corporate speakers in the first place. Reliance on the existence of a separate press clause, then, provides him no outlet. If the existence of a rigid goal of profit maximization is consistent with the notion of constitutional protection for communication in the press context, it logically follows that the values of the First Amendment can coexist with such profit-maximizing motivation. But if that is true, then one cannot rationally exclude constitutional protection for corporate speech solely on the grounds that it is robotically profit maximizing.

Yet one could possibly point to other asserted distinctions between commercial advertisers and the institutional press besides specious reliance on a press/nonpress distinction. It could also be argued, for example, that one does not necessarily know what positions will be taken in the institutional press on issues of public importance. In contrast, one knows for certain that a commercial advertiser will promote purchase. One could perhaps reason that it is this certainty that distinguishes commercial speech from the expression of the corporate press. But this argument amounts to nothing more than condemnation—and exclusion—of a speaker because she is speaking as an advocate. We know that a lawyer arguing on behalf of a client will take a position that, in one way or another, supports that client's interests, not necessarily because the lawyer agrees normatively with that position but because that is the lawyer's role within the adversary system.[63] But it does not logically follow that what the lawyer says is inherently unpersuasive or suspect. The same is true for countless noncommercial advocates whose views and positions are quite obviously predetermined by self-interest yet whose speech is universally assumed to be fully protected.[64] Again, neither Baker nor any other critic of commercial speech protection chooses for that reason to exclude the expression of those noncommercial speakers from the First Amendment's protection.

One might also point to the public interest that exists in the substance of what the institutional media report on, which is to be contrasted to the far narrower concerns of the commercial advertiser. But this argument, too, is fatally underinclusive, as long as one assumes that *Consumer Reports*, which deals with no issue beyond those of the merits of commercial products and services, is to receive full constitutional protection.

It could also be argued that the First Amendment right being asserted is not that of the corporate press but rather of the reporter or writer who works for the corporation. But what if, as common sense tells us is likely often the case, the reporter writes only what the corporation wants her to write?[65] At the very least, we can be reasonably assured that, in most cases, the reporter writes nothing that the corporation does not wish to be printed. No one has ever suggested that the press's First Amendment right in any way turns on the relationship between writer and corporate publisher in an individual case. Moreover, it cannot be forgotten that the corporate publisher was able to choose its reporters in the first place—and can fire them if it disapproves of what they have written. Thus, as long as it is the corporate publisher, rather than the writer himself, who is deemed the party injured by the abridgement of expressive rights, this factor cannot reasonably distinguish the profit motivation of the corporate institutional press from that of the commercial advertiser.

Finally, the ultimate refuge of one who has no other rational argument available is to fall back on a mindless adherence to tradition. According to the argument from tradition, the institutional press receives full protection, despite its inexorable drive to maximize profits, for no reason other than in American tradition it has been deemed to receive it, while commercial speech has not. But this form of "proof by adverse possession" makes little sense. Also part of our nation's "tradition," tragically, were slavery, Jim Crow laws, the near genocide of the Native American population, and the (shockingly recent) confinement of American citizens for no reason other than their national origin during World War II. Surely, not every part of our tradition is automatically deemed preserved by constitutional value. When in the past the Court discovered that our constitutional traditions were normatively or logically questionable, it abandoned them. There is no more reason to accept mindless tradition in the case of the First Amendment than in those situations. Thus, if one can defend the unprincipled distinction between First Amendment protection for the corporate press on the one hand and the commercial advertiser on the other solely on an appeal to tradition, one has effectively conceded the argument.

Speaker Self-Interest. In some ways, the argument grounded in speaker self-interest has already been referenced as part of the discussion of the possible distinctions between commercial advertising and the corporate media.[66] In a broader sense, however, the argument stands on a separate footing, as a distinct basis for excluding commercial speech from the First Amendment's protective reach. No commercial advertiser, it may be safely presumed, is likely to highlight the flaws or deficiencies in its product or the comparative advantages of a competitor's product. In this way, it might be argued that commercial speech is inherently misleading because of its strategic and selective incompleteness.[67]

This argument is transparently underinclusive in its reach. Whatever problems to which it may give rise, strategically selective advocacy is by no means confined to commercial advertising. To the contrary, casual experience and common sense tell us that preciously little fully protected expression could properly be labeled wholly objective. Countless speakers, whether in the political, academic, or social worlds, have an underlying agenda that they seek to further when they speak. This invariably leads them to selectively omit damaging arguments or information from the content of their argument. This is as true of political interest groups as it is of political candidates. For example, the National Rifle Association is no more likely to promote in its literature the number of people killed annually in gun accidents than gun control advocates are likely to highlight the number of crimes prevented due to gun ownership. Yet, somehow, this fact never leads the very same scholars who would reject protection of commercial speech to argue for reduced protection for the speech of interest groups or political candidates. Instead, we accept as a given that individuals and associations have a full constitutional right to promote their goals, which often involve personal economic gain,[68] through the use of expression as a means of persuading listeners, readers, and viewers to accept their positions. Yet, this is, of course, exactly what commercial advertisers are doing.[69]

Regulatory Motivation. The final conceivable rationale for the exclusion of commercial speech from the First Amendment is what is appropriately labeled "regulatory motivation." Simply put, the argument is that, when political speech is regulated, there exists an appropriate degree of mistrust of and skepticism about the motivation of the regulator. Such skepticism flows from the inherent incentive of those in power to suppress the expression of their out-of-power rivals. This fact gives rise to the need for a reviewing court to intervene more aggressively to counter the incentive to overregulate and to protect free speech interests.[70]

This reasoning resonates with the inherent skepticism that led the Framers to adopt systems of separation of powers, federalism, and checks and balances when they promulgated the Constitution—in many ways similar to the premises underlying adversary democratic theory.[71] Perhaps "if angels were to govern," the authors of the *Federalist Papers* believed, there would be no need for such protections.[72] The drafters of those documents were forced to recognize, however, that those who do govern are likely to be far from angelic and therefore need to be carefully monitored.[73] But whether this reasoning justifies reduced or excluded protection for commercial speech is a very different matter, for at least two reasons. First, the insights of public choice literature tell us that the legislative regulatory process is fraught with dangers of rent seeking or improper influence by special interests and private parties.[74] There is no reason to believe that these dangers are lessened when the subject of regulation is commercial, rather than political, behavior. Indeed, those with financial resources sufficient to influence political decision making are often commercial operators who are likely to be disposed toward suppression of their competition. Suppression of their competitors' advertising is often likely to be as effective, and far more furtive, than direct regulation of competitors' commercial behavior. To point to one of many conceivable examples, the drug industry might seek to influence the legislative process for the purpose of suppressing advertising of generic, compound, or homeopathic competitors, a strategic goal far more likely attainable than the total suppression of its competitors' business. There is, then, no *ex ante* basis on which to assume the good faith or neutrality of legislative regulators in the regulation of commercial speech.

The same skepticism might also affect administrative regulation. Scholars have often pointed to the danger of "captured agencies," in which regulators travel back and forth between governmental agencies and the industries they regulate.[75] This danger, under certain circumstances, could negatively affect competitors of those who have done the capturing. The problem for a reviewing court, of course, is that it is both difficult and unseemly to attempt to ferret out the presence of such pathological motivation in a particular case. It is therefore appropriate to generically presume the danger of regulatory abuse when commercial speech is the subject of regulation, much as we do when political speech is the subject of regulation. Moreover, exclusive focus on the danger of pathological regulatory motive unduly truncates both First Amendment interests and the threat posed to them by regulation, particularly of the administrative variety. Regulatory bodies exist for the very purpose of regulating.[76] It is all but inconceivable, then, that they can be presumed to provide protection for free speech interests when those interests stand as potential obstacles to what they deem an appropriate level of regulation. The danger here is not regulatory bad faith as much as it is the danger of regulatory overzealousness. It is not uncommon for regulators to focus their concern on a paternalistic desire to protect individuals by selectively suppressing promotion of sale of legal products.[77] This is so, even if we assume no ulterior or pathological regulatory motivation. It is simply a matter of the cognitive dissonance that inheres in holding the position of regulator in the first place. There is no basis on which to assume that this danger exists less when the subject of regulation is commercial speech than when it is noncommercial speech.

Finally, reliance on a focus on potentially pathological regulatory motivation as a justification for drawing a protective distinction between commercial and noncommercial expression is fatally underinclusive for yet another reason. Even were one to assume, for purposes of argument, that the danger of regulatory pathology exists for political speech regulation but not for commercial speech regulation, it would remain unclear why presumably objective commentators on products and services, such as *Consumer Reports*, would receive full First Amendment protection. Presumably, there is at least as small a danger of regulatory pathology when objective comments on commercial products and services are made as when commercial advocacy is regulated. Thus, as is the case for all of the conceivable "rationalist" defenses of reduced protection for commercial speech, the regulatory motivation argument is fatally underinclusive.[78]

"Intuitionist" Grounds

First Amendment scholarship is often characterized by what could appropriately be described as an "antirationalist" school of thought.[79] Though certain scholars somehow manage to fit themselves into both rationalist and antirationalist camps,[80] for the most part acceptance of this antirationalism allows its advocate to reach decisions about the scope of First Amendment protection without giving substantial attention to the internal logic of their analysis. Instead of worrying about how to deal with troubling logical inconsistencies in their conclusions, they choose to defend their decisions on grounds that are fundamentally right-brained and, therefore, presumably immune to rationalist attack. These intuitionist scholars are, in other words, focused exclusively on the intuitive appeal of the result of the extension or nonextension of First Amendment protection to a particular hypothetical situation.

Thus, Professors Farber and Frickey imply the preposterousness of suggesting a constitutional equivalence between political speech and an advertisement for soap, without enlightening us as to why, exactly, no equivalence can be drawn.[81] Professors Jackson and Jeffries conclusorily assert that whatever the First Amendment protects, it surely fails to protect "a seller hawking his wares."[82] Phrased in such a way, it does seem intuitively nonsensical to provide full constitutional protection to such fluff as that. But when one attempts to deconstruct their reasoning, one finds little more than hyperbolic pejorative in support of their sweeping exclusion of commercial speech from the First Amendment's scope.

Professor Emerson asserted many years ago that commercial speech implicates solely property rights, rather than those centered on expression.[83] But like Farber and Frickey and Jackson and Jeffries, Emerson fails to make even the slightest effort to explain *why* this is so or, for that matter, why the two are somehow assumed to be mutually exclusive in the first place. Each of them, in one way or another, employs (if only implicitly) a form of First Amendment intuitionism,[84] which, it appears, is simply another word for "conclusory." Whether the concept of "practical reason" demands more intellectual rigor than intuitionism appears to be the subject of debate. Farber and Frickey, for example, have suggested that it does. Yet their own suggested definition of practical reason certainly fails to instill confidence in their ability to translate the phrase's vague terms into something capable of providing meaningful guidance as to what expressive regulation is and is not appropriate.

Farber and Frickey suggest "an alternative view of the [F]irst [A]mendment's normative status. Rather than thinking of free speech as one level in a hierarchy of values, it may be better to think of it as part of a web of mutually reinforcing values."[85] The problem they see with more conceptually foundational, logically based theories is that such approaches often lead inexorably to "highly dubious applications, which the theorist presents as logically inescapable inferences from his premise."[86] They conclude that "when a concrete application of grand theory cannot be squared with our complex, situationally sensitive web of beliefs, it is the former that is likely to give way."[87] If all Farber and Frickey are saying is that pragmatic considerations must at some point be taken into account in shaping First Amendment jurisprudence, it would be difficult to disagree. But even pragmatic considerations can and should be developed first on a generalized basis as part and parcel of, or at least a gloss on, the general theory, and then applied to specific fact situations as a transparent potential qualifier or limitation on the remaining part of the theory. Thus, my own self-realization theory was expressly restrained by recognition of the need to take into account cases in which there exists a compelling need to prevent harm (narrowly defined), usually physical harm. But inclusion of this limited pragmatic gloss—itself appropriately disciplined by its own sets of internally principled restrictions[88]—is a far cry from the vague and malleable reference to a "complex, situationally sensitive web of beliefs" to which Farber and Frickey cryptically refer.[89]

Farber and Frickey assert that all forms of modern practical reason

> share some fundamental characteristics. Among them are a concern for history and context; a desire to avoid abstracting away the human component in judicial decisionmaking; an appreciation of the complexity of life; some faith in dialogue and deliberation; a tolerance for ambiguity, accommodation, and tentativeness, but a skepticism of rigid dichotomies; and an overall humility.[90]

Practical reason, they concede,

> is unruly. It specifies no certain starting point, follows no predestined path, may frolic as well as detour, and cannot rise above the abilities of its users. Indeed, the indeterminacy of practical reasoning might suggest that it cannot achieve the status of a theory at all. Like "prudence" and "wisdom" in everyday affairs, legal practical reasoning is explained better by example than by abstract methodological prescriptions . . . . The absence of a formula for practical reasoning is inherent in the enterprise.[91]

What seems to be missing from this discussion is any effort to explain how one actually goes about attempting to resolve a specific case on the basis of practical reason. In contrast to principled decision making, practical reason appears to rely on a far cruder resort to an often unstated preexisting set of widely shared prejudices and normative social instincts, untied to any effort to resolve individual cases by reliance on broader and deeper forms of constitutional value development, determined *before* examination of the specific situational context. Strongest evidence of this ominous absence of grounding in some consistently applied set of noncontextual values is Farber's and Frickey's total failure to explain exactly why "selling soap" is less deserving of First Amendment protection than other, more traditionally protected types of expression.[92] Yet they are more than willing to criticize the suggestion that no principled basis, grounded in accepted and transparent principles of First Amendment theory, justifies a gradation of protection between the two subjects of expression.[93] Instead of resorting to a theoretical and logical inquiry, Farber and Frickey appear to rely on a kind of intuitive situational judgment, largely inexplicable beyond the conclusory expression of a deep-seated feeling that somehow the two situations must be treated differently. This intuitive judgment, apparently, is to be derived from the observer's preexisting personal "web of values" and perceptions.[94]

How much the concept of practical reason extends beyond inherently antirationalist and logically inexplicable First Amendment intuitionism, like almost everything else about these frustratingly cryptic modes of First Amendment analysis, remains unclear. Although Professor Farber suggests that intuitionism, like practical reason, is part of "a movement away from grand theory,"[95] he ultimately rejects the notion that practical reason is identical to intuitionism.[96] But while Professor Farber extends a great deal of effort to tell us what practical reason is *not*,[97] he spends precious little time telling us what it *is*. Indeed, he attempts to define the concept primarily in terms of what it *rejects*. Practical reason means, he asserts, "a rejection of the view that rules and precedents in and of themselves dictate outcomes."[98] He adds that

> At the level of legal theory, practical reason means a rejection of foundationalism, the view that normative conclusions can be deduced from a single unifying value or principle. At the level of judicial practice, practical reason rejects legal formalism, the view that the proper decision in a case can be deduced from a pre-existing set of rules.[99]

The rejected techniques, Professor Farber explains, "rely heavily on deductive logic (i.e., the syllogism) as the primary method of analysis."[100]

While Professor Farber candidly concedes that practical reason "is easier to invoke than to define,"[101] perhaps his description of what the concept is *not* helps one understand that if practical reason is not identical to intuitionism, it is close enough to be considered a kissing cousin. Both seem to share a heavily antirationalist view, chafing at the restraints that syllogistic reasoning imposes on implementation of desired decision making. In this sense, the two can be treated fungibly for present purposes. Both modes of decision making free a reviewing court from the bonds of reason, consistency, and predictability that inherently characterize principled decision making. With what, exactly, do advocates of either approach fill the intellectual vacuum created by their rejection of the demands of principle and reason? One point seems clear: The antirationalism that they share suggests that under both approaches, decisions are made on the basis of some sort of unexplained—and, quite probably, inexplicable—value choices, external to the constitutional provision being interpreted. For if decisions did, in fact, derive from an analysis of the value or values gleaned from the provision's text or structure, they presumably could be explained transparently and supported rationally.

From where are these value choices, external to the interpreted constitutional provision, to be derived? One possibility is from the wholly subjective normative value structure of the particular judicial decision maker.[102] At the very least, it would be difficult to prevent such a result, even if it were not desired, were these nonrationalist decision-making models to be employed. The intellectual fog that flows from rejection of any demand of logic or principle would inevitably provide easy cover for implementation of the judge's personal moral or political value structure through the case-by-case process of constitutional interpretation. A second alternative, at least in theory, would be to fill the decision-making vacuum with a judicial implementation of what the court determines to be public sensibilities on the specific issue before the court.[103]

Neither of these alternatives provides a satisfactory solution. Indeed, both should frighten the stuffing out of any thoughtful observer of the constitutional decision-making process. An approach that condones as a guidepost for judicial application of the First Amendment right of free expression a judge's implementation of her own personal political, social, or moral value structure, disguised under some vague heading such as "intuitionism" or "practical reason," should be viewed as the worst form of judicial irresponsibility. Reliance on intuitionism or practical reason will let constitutional protection turn on the vagaries of subjective judicial preferences, and it will usually be impossible to determine what those preferences are, *ex ante.*

Even less appealing is the use of practical reason as a means of implementing some judicially perceived notion of widespread public sensibilities. Initially, it is difficult to imagine a branch of government less well suited to determine public sensibilities on a particular issue than the unaccountable, unrepresentative federal judiciary.[104] If one were to proceed on the assumption that assessment of public sensibilities should be deemed constitutionally significant, it would make far more sense to leave those choices to the representative and accountable branches of government. Moreover, the federal judiciary has no access to expensive and carefully performed empirical studies that could provide it with accurate information about public preferences.[105] Finally, and most importantly, to let First Amendment protection turn on some notion of public sensibilities on a subject effectively turns that countermajoritarian constitutional protection on its head. The idea of the First Amendment, at the very least, is to protect the individual's right to express unpopular ideas from suppression by the majority.[106] If the reach of the First Amendment is somehow to be coordinated with widespread public sensibilities on the subject of or views expressed in the challenged speech, then the First Amendment will have been effectively rendered a nullity.

It should be emphasized that rejection of both intuitionism and practical reason as the guidepost for First Amendment interpretation is not intended to put in their stead some sort of abstract Langdellian formalism. Cases will inevitably arise in which the outcome cannot be predicted simply on the basis of some formulaic statement of abstract law. The key, however, is that in such cases the issue will concern the nature of the *harm* to which the regulated speech gives rise and the extent to which, under the circumstances of the particular case, that harm can appropriately be thought to give rise to a compelling governmental interest justifying regulation of expression. But those who reject First Amendment protection for commercial speech cannot reasonably argue that commercial speech—at least truthful commercial speech—necessarily causes more harm than do all forms of fully protected political speech, such as advocacy of violent overthrow.[107] They are, instead, merely implementing some form of predetermined judgment about the nature or value of the expression itself.

The major distinction between use of practical reason and use of a harm standard as a qualifier of the implications of rational analysis is that the latter, unlike the former, requires resort to traditional legal reasoning: open, reasoned debate over the choice of a substantive standard of law and then application of that standard to individual cases. The decision as to whether to permit a showing of harm that will ever be sufficient to justify suppression of otherwise protected speech, and the nature and degree of the showing of harm to be required, are issues of general substantive law that are the proper subject of debate. They are to be made openly and consistently. When it is used as a justification for regulation of one type of expression, the harm factor cannot be mysteriously excluded as a measure of another type of expression, unless some other principled basis exists for distinguishing between the two types of expression. Decision makers employing First Amendment intuitionism or practical reason, in contrast, necessarily make contextual judgments that do not demand—indeed, apparently do not permit—attempted application of prior agreed-on general principles of decision to specific fact situations.

It is also important to make clear that neither practical reason nor intuitionism is the necessary outgrowth of a rejection of a single overarching value of free expression. One could conceivably conclude that free expression is appropriately deemed to foster a complex intersection of multiple values,[108] yet nevertheless view the creation of free speech doctrine as the application to specific cases of one or more permutations of those multiple intersecting values. This process would presumably be no more or less syllogistic than the shaping of doctrine through the application of an assumed single underlying value of free expression to specific cases. Intuitionism and practical reason, in contrast, eschew use of any such form of logical reasoning in favor of what is described—euphemistically—as a more "contextual" examination.

In the case of commercial speech, decision makers who choose to employ practical reason and intuitionism make their "rough judgment" that commercial speech is not worthy of protection before the issue of harm caused by the speech is even considered. The argument is not that commercial speech inherently gives rise to more harm than do more traditionally protected types and subjects of expression but rather that such speech is inherently less worthy of protection than more traditionally protected categories of expression. The initial question in every First Amendment case is whether government even needs to satisfy the compelling interest standard that is triggered when fully protected expression is sought to be regulated. Because the intuitionists and practical reason advocates conclude that, for whatever reason, commercial speech is not deserving of protection in the first place, they need never even reach the compelling interest question. In light of their initial conclusion, there is no First Amendment interest sufficient to trigger the demand for a compelling interest analysis. And their initial conclusion is never justified by resort to logic or reason that is applied consistently to all types of expression. No justification is provided to which reasoned response can be made. Instead, there is simply something "intuitive" that tells us that, as Jackson and Jeffries asserted, surely "a seller hawking his wares" deserves no constitutional protection for his speech.[109]

One could conceivably seek to defend resort to intuitionism or practical reason as an alternative to an effort to decide cases on the basis of logic and principle by challenging the feasibility of the rationalist enterprise. It is likely true that principled consistency will not function like clockwork in every case. Occasions arise, no doubt, where reasonable people differ as to how generally agreed-on principles apply to specific cases. But to resort to what ultimately amounts to a form of nonrational subjectivism and intellectual chaos as an alternative is most assuredly not a viable alternative.

Ideological Grounds

On relatively rare occasion, scholars have candidly evinced intellectual hostility toward commercial speech. These scholars have made clear that their opposition to the protection of commercial speech is grounded in their disdain for the expression's impact on the functioning of society—in short, their *ideological hostility* toward commercial speech.[110] This ideological rationale can take one of two forms. First, it may represent a generic ideological rejection of the very economic system out of which commercial advertising grows. Second, it may constitute a narrower form of policy preference that condemns the particular product or service being promoted by the commercial advertising in question. The thinking behind this narrower rationale is presumably that, as a practical matter, the only individuals who possess sufficient incentive to promote the product or activity to the public are those seeking to sell it. Thus, to stop the commercial advertising is tantamount to halting virtually all promotion of the use of the product or service. Under such a regulatory approach, it would make perfect sense to extend full protection to the speech of those attacking the product or service but to extend either no protection or only limited protection to speech promoting its purchase or use, simply because the former category of expression furthers the predetermined policy goal while the latter undermines it.

The problem with either of the conceivable forms of an ideological or policy-based rationale is that both of them are fundamentally inconsistent with the core premises of a system of meaningful free speech protection and the democratic structure of which free expression is a central element.

Surely, the Supreme Court today would not countenance a law restricting prosocialist expression on the grounds that those in power believe that socialism is unwise or immoral and fear that such expression might lead to society's adoption of socialist precepts. Nor would it uphold a law restricting antisocialist expression because those in power have deemed socialism to be the preferred social economic theory. Under such a blatantly viewpoint-based form of selective protection, the control of expression would be reduced to nothing more than a struggle for political power. Whichever side attains political power would presumably be able to constitutionally shut off all expression that it found to be offensive to the currently prevailing ideology.

Nevertheless, critics of commercial speech have on occasion openly acknowledged the relevance to their analysis of either ideologically oriented concerns or subjective social or political values. For example, Professor R. George Wright, a strong and articulate opponent of commercial speech protection, has argued: "Commercial getting and spending is, except in the case of the poor, at best weakly correlated with happiness or well-being."[111] He further expressed concern over "the ways in which commercialism and commercial values affect how we experience the otherwise noncommercial elements of our lives."[112] Wright thus overtly demonstrated his subjective ideological distaste for commercial speech as a predicate for his attack on its constitutional protection.

Reliance on ideological motivations effectively reduces free speech doctrine to a Hobbesian state of nature, in which a political war of all against all prevails.[113] In such circumstances, whichever ideological camp attains political power may, quite legitimately, suppress the speech of its opposition on no grounds other than naked distaste for or disagreement with the political viewpoints expressed in that speech. However, life in such a constitutional state of nature is, as Hobbes warned, likely to be nasty, brutish, and short. As a theoretical matter, then, preference for or opposition to a particular ideology should never play any part in justifying governmental restriction of expression.

OBJECTIONS TO COMMERCIAL SPEECH PROTECTION AND THE PARAMETERS OF NEUTRAL PRINCIPLES

For reasons already explained, each of the three categories of opposition to commercial speech protection—rationalist, intuitionist, and ideological—is seriously flawed in a variety of ways. The fundamental concern with the three categories, however, is not merely the manner in which each is logically or theoretically flawed but rather the way in which each threatens the core values underlying free speech protection. In attempting to construe the First Amendment, each of the three categories, in its own way, largely amounts to a form of impermissible viewpoint discrimination that undermines the very core of the First Amendment. It is thus reasonable to conclude that each of the three categories is ultimately grounded in distaste for what commercial speech represents, a rationale wholly unrelated to a value-neutral approach to First Amendment interpretation.

The reflexive response to this assertion, no doubt, is that one cannot demand value neutrality in First Amendment interpretation. To the contrary, the argument would proceed, First Amendment construction necessarily involves a choice among competing values that free speech protection could conceivably be designed to foster. This is no doubt true. However, the value neutrality that is necessarily implicated in First Amendment analysis differs fundamentally from the form of value invocation triggered by the three categories of objections to commercial speech protection. As already demonstrated, those objections are not premised on a plausible selection of one conceivable free speech value over another. If they were, the objections would logically also be applied consistently to the other types of expression that opponents of commercial speech protection would readily protect.[114] Rather, they are grounded in the decision maker's preference for particular political or ideological value choices that would, in the decision maker's view, be threatened or undermined by the extension of constitutional protection to commercial speech. Recognition of these alternative levels of value analysis is essential to an understanding of the judiciary's appropriate—and limited—role in enforcing First Amendment protections.

The essence of this distinction in levels of value analysis is embodied in and policed by the doctrinally well-established prohibition on viewpoint-based discrimination. Therefore, I now turn to a description and analysis of this core First Amendment doctrine.

Viewpoint Discrimination and the Foundations of Free Expression

The Uniquely Invidious Nature of Viewpoint Discrimination

How absolute in its protection the First Amendment should be has long been the subject of scholarly and judicial debate.[115] What should not be—and, for the most part, has not been—the subject of serious dispute, however, is that regulation of expression grounded in nothing more than governmental hostility to the normative viewpoint expressed is necessarily unconstitutional. There can be no exceptions to the constitutional bar of viewpoint-based regulations because to permit one exception is effectively to permit all viewpoint-based regulations;[116] whoever is in power will choose as an "exception" any viewpoint to which they are hostile.[117]

Viewpoint-based regulations are, by definition, grounded not in a principled effort to interpret and apply the structural values underlying the free speech protection but rather in a subjective assessment of moral and/or sociopolitical considerations that are external to the First Amendment. These considerations necessarily grow out of normative concerns that exist wholly external to the First Amendment. The First Amendment's focus is on allowing the private individual or entity, not the government, to decide what ideas are normatively appropriate. The viewpoint neutrality of the First Amendment's free-expression guarantee is the logical outgrowth of the nation's original commitment to democratically based rule. Commitment to a democratic form of government necessarily means that the electorate possesses the fundamental freedom to choose those who will make day-to-day policy choices.[118] It will presumably choose those whose policies are closest to its own. Moreover, the electorate is even permitted to alter the countermajoritarian limits imposed by the Constitution by resort to the supermajoritarian amendment process.[119]

Free expression, as Alexander Meiklejohn correctly argued, facilitates performance of the democratic function by providing the electorate with information and opinion concerning policy making choices that will be faced by those chosen to serve.[120] Because the electorate possesses the ultimate authority to put into office candidates who take any political position, no matter how offensive to either those in power or the majority of the electorate, it logically follows that those in power cannot be permitted to manipulate political debate in a manner designed strategically to control the available scope of governmental choices. Any other result would undermine the individual citizen's integrity as a free-thinking human being worthy of respect. It would also effectively gut the operation of the democratic process of which the First Amendment is a logical outgrowth.

The absoluteness of the constitutional prohibition on viewpoint discrimination flows from recognition of the unique harm that such regulations necessarily cause to the foundations of free expression. It is impossible, *ex ante*, to authorize exceptions to this prohibition because the content of those exceptions would necessarily be determined by those in power; it is those in power who would determine which viewpoints are to be deemed sufficiently offensive as to justify suppression of their expression. Presumably, governing officials would choose to exempt from First Amendment protection regulations of those particular viewpoints that, as a subjective matter, they found to be the most offensive. If power were to be subsequently transferred to a competing ideological group, the exemptions to the constitutional prohibition on viewpoint discrimination would be changed to comport with the subjective preferences of that group. For example, if conservatives were in power, they might well deem sufficiently offensive as to justify exemption from the bar against viewpoint discrimination the expression of viewpoints such as that a woman should have a right to choose to obtain an abortion, or that the United States is an imperialist nation, or even that we should withdraw from Afghanistan. If the political left were to replace the conservatives in power, viewpoints exempted from the bar against discrimination might well be changed to include expression of the view that abortion is murder or that affirmative action is evil.[121]

The most fascinating aspect of the constitutional prohibition of viewpoint discrimination is that it is simultaneously so obvious as a core element of First Amendment theory and so counterintuitive to those functioning in the real world, away from the lofty heights of constitutional theory.[122] The classic illustration is the Skokie case of the late 1970s, where a ragged—but, to most, highly offensive—band of self-styled Nazis sought to march in a Chicago suburb with a large Jewish population (including, at the time, many concentration camp survivors).[123] The courts that dealt with challenges to Skokie ordinances designed to prevent the march were quite clear that those ordinances were unconstitutional, regardless of the distaste that prevailed in the community for the political message of the march.[124] This conclusion was constitutionally required because any other result would have led to normative censorship by those in power—a result wholly inconsistent with the foundations and premises of a democratic society. That the bar to viewpoint-based discrimination must be deemed absolute, however, is of little help in recognizing when a regulation of expression is viewpoint based and when it is not. It is to this question that my analysis now turns.

Defining and Recognizing Viewpoint Discrimination

The Essential Characteristic of Viewpoint Discrimination

On a purely conceptual level, viewpoint discrimination is not difficult to distinguish from more principled forms of First Amendment selectivity, even those forms with which one ultimately disagrees as a matter of free speech theory. Principled disputes over the scope of First Amendment protection concern factors that can be considered "internal" to the First Amendment. The debate over which principled means of construing the First Amendment should prevail concerns one of two issues: (1) the extent to which the expression in question is deemed to foster the value or values that underlie the guarantee of free expression or (2) the extent to which the unlawful harm to which the expression would likely give rise justifies restriction. Viewpoint discrimination, in contrast, is grounded in considerations that are "external" to the First Amendment. This means that the driving normative force underlying the selective regulation has nothing to do with a good-faith effort to determine the process or structural values of free expression. Rather, it flows from normative premises determined by factors of political, social, economic, moral, or religious beliefs or concerns wholly external to the First Amendment. They grow not out of a principled analysis that seeks to create the most viable or appropriate constitutional system but rather from the personal ideologies of those imposing the restriction. To those seeking to impose viewpoint discrimination, the First Amendment is not something to be deciphered and structured but rather a potential obstacle to attainment of their political or ideological values and goals that needs to be circumvented.

Although this dichotomy seems relatively easy to recognize as an abstract matter, it is not always a simple task to separate legitimate, principled (if controversial) constitutional analysis, on the one hand, from invidious viewpoint discrimination that grows out of normative premises wholly unrelated to constitutional analysis, on the other. As the following sections demonstrate, however, certain guideposts may be recognized to help draw this vitally important distinction in the First Amendment trenches of real-world adjudication.

Viewpoint Discrimination and the Avoidance of "Harm"

In its starkest form, viewpoint discrimination is relatively easy to recognize. Classic illustrations are not difficult to hypothesize: a law prohibiting speech that argues against (or in favor of) the government's economic policy; a law prohibiting expression advocating (or opposing) abortion rights; or a law prohibiting anticapitalist advocacy. When such cases have arisen, the Supreme Court has generally been quick to strike them down.[125] A problem quickly arises, however, when supporters of the selectively based restriction reflexively invoke the fear of "harm" that might result from allowing the regulated expression. After all, if expression is being suppressed or punished to prevent "harm," then it is being regulated for reasons other than the desire to quiet expression of an offensive viewpoint. For example, a constitutional prohibition on viewpoint regulation would not prevent the government from punishing advocacy of violent criminal behavior. Sloppy or conclusory invocation of the threat of harm as a justification for suppression, then, could easily consume the beneficial impact of the constitutional prohibition on viewpoint regulation because virtually all viewpoint-based regulations could then be rationalized as the avoidance of harm.

There exist three ways in which this risk can be averted. First, at the outset it is important to distinguish between "harms" that flow from illegal or extralegal behavior, on the one hand, and harms that flow from either lawful behavior or from efforts to bring about alteration of existing law through lawful means, on the other. Individuals have a First Amendment right to urge a governmental body—judicial, legislative, or executive—to alter existing legal standards, even if those currently in power would find that such legal changes lead to normatively unacceptable results. For example, if the First Amendment means anything at all, it must protect an individual's right to urge that the Supreme Court's decision in *Brown v. Board of Education*,[126] finding unconstitutional so-called separate-but-equal laws, should be overruled, even though most of us today would no doubt be morally outraged by such a reversal. An individual must also possess a First Amendment right to urge Congress to repeal Title VII of the 1964 Civil Rights Act,[127] which prohibits racial, religious, or gender-based discrimination in private hiring, though, once again, most of us today would find such a change in the law morally repugnant. On a political level, one could easily oppose such proposals on the ground that their acceptance would cause significant "harm" to racial minorities or women. But for the First Amendment to function successfully, the "harm" that is considered sufficiently severe to justify suppression of expression cannot be defined to include bringing about a distasteful, albeit lawful, political result.

In addition, the courts must be wary of laws that seek to avoid harm by resorting to a suspiciously underinclusive invocation of the danger of harm. To point to an earlier example, an ordinance prohibiting distribution of antiwar literature during rush hour because of the danger of harm cannot be permitted to stand unless *all* forms and subjects of expression at the same time and place are also banned. The same would be true of an attempt to justify a law making criminal the burning of the American flag on grounds that such action would give rise to a serious fire hazard. Finally, we should demand that any claim of even potential unlawful harm be established not as some vague, undefined possible injury at some point in the unspecified future but rather as a more definite and proximate threat.[128] This is the goal of the "clear and present danger" test, currently embodied, in its most protective form, in controlling Supreme Court doctrine.[129]

Recognizing the Different Forms of Viewpoint Discrimination

Unconstitutional viewpoint discrimination is not always as direct or obvious as many of the examples described in the prior discussion. Those are situations in which the government sought to regulate expression of a specific viewpoint, regardless of who was expressing it. The perceived offensiveness of the words themselves, standing alone, was what triggered suppression. Other, less obvious or direct situations of viewpoint regulation, however, will arise, and it is important to see them as equally invidious forms of speech regulation.

One example of such indirect viewpoint regulation could be described as a type of "heckler's veto." In these situations, government will prohibit expression of derogatory comments about a particular ethnic, racial, or religious group, even where the speech in question is not spoken directly to a member of one of those groups and lacks any immediately coercive quality,[130] for no reason other than that the speech is thought to be demoralizing or hurtful to the affected group. Here the governmental regulator is effectively operating as the agent of the affected group. Even more clear are classic "heckler's veto" situations, where government suppresses speech because of fear that others who hear it will be so offended that they are likely to harm the speaker. Here, too, the regulator is operating as a type of agent for those who are likely to find the speaker's views offensive. A viable system of free expression could not possibly function under such a framework. At most, reliance on these concerns to justify suppression could be accepted only in the most compelling of immediate, narrowly defined circumstances, where authorities reasonably conclude that they would be unable to prevent serious violence.

A second form of indirect viewpoint discrimination occurs where government suppresses speech not because of the words of the speech but because of who the speaker is. For example, a law prohibiting Democrats from speaking should still be deemed invidious viewpoint discrimination, even though it does not directly focus on the expression of a particular viewpoint. In this example, the restriction of expression turns not at all on the specific words that the Democrat would utter. But focus on the nature of the speaker here serves as a relatively simple surrogate for viewpoint discrimination. The speaker is prohibited from speaking on the basis of his or her preexisting ideological association.

Because these regulations are aimed at the speaker and not the speech, it might be suggested that their unconstitutionality is more appropriately grounded in the Equal Protection Clause[131] rather than in the First Amendment right of free expression.[132] Either way, the end result would appear to be the same. However, that the First Amendment, standing on its own, is appropriately construed to invalidate such a law as invidious viewpoint discrimination. The fact that the viewpoint regulation is one step removed from the expression itself should make no difference because the right of the speaker to speak is being "abridged" as a result of his preexisting ideological and political expressive associations—the core concern of the ban on viewpoint regulations.

Judicially Imposed Viewpoint Regulation

The judiciary, like the other branches of government, is constrained by the First Amendment.[133] It is therefore at least conceivable that the actions of the judicial branch, as easily as the executive or legislative branches of government, could contravene the First Amendment's absolute prohibition on viewpoint discrimination.

Judicial action can interact with viewpoint discrimination potentially in one of two ways: (1) by condoning or facilitating implementation of viewpoint discrimination initiated by one or both of the majoritarian branches of government, or (2) by shaping or applying First Amendment doctrine selectively, where no basis for such a disparity in First Amendment treatment—apart from the differences in viewpoint—exists to justify such distinctions. It is important to recognize, then, that the judiciary may well be the culprit, rather than merely the enabler. The difference in judicial culpability can be best understood by use of hypothetical examples. First, imagine an action taken by one or both of the political branches selectively discriminating against expression of one viewpoint. If the judiciary upholds this discrimination against First Amendment attack, it will have acted as an enabler. Now imagine a law that indiscriminately restricts expressive activity by all. Were the courts to uphold that law against constitutional attack when it is used against speech expressing one viewpoint but invalidate it as to the expression of a different viewpoint, the judiciary itself would be imposing the viewpoint discrimination.

Recognizing the "Twilight Zone" of Viewpoint Discrimination

To this point, the descriptions, explanation, and analysis of the concept of viewpoint discrimination, while hopefully illuminating, should hardly be considered controversial to First Amendment theorists. Few knowledgeable observers would dispute the inherently invidious nature of viewpoint-based discrimination in light of the manner in which it inevitably undermines the values served by democracy and the system of free expression of which it is a part. However, there exists a form of viewpoint discrimination that may not be as readily recognized as either the direct, indirect, or judicial forms of the First Amendment pathology described to this point. This category is appropriately described as "twilight zone" viewpoint discrimination because the resulting invidious harms to free speech interests are just as great as the more classic forms of the category, even though they are, superficially at least, one or two steps removed.

What distinguishes twilight zone viewpoint discrimination from the more classic variety is that it focuses on neither the normative positions taken in the substance of the regulated speech (direct viewpoint discrimination) nor the ideological or political affiliations of the speaker (indirect viewpoint discrimination). It is, rather, grounded in hostility toward what might be called the "ideological ether" of which both the speech and the speaker are a part. In these situations, the speaker herself may have no *ex ante* offensive sociopolitical affiliations, and what she says, in and of itself, asserts nothing to which the regulator is normatively hostile. However, both the speaker and the speech are themselves outgrowths of, and participants in, a broader process or practice that the regulator finds offensive on ideological grounds. Of course, if the speaker and the speech are part of a broader nonexpressive, conduct-based activity deemed harmful by those in authority, the government may prohibit the relevant conduct, consistent with constitutional protections other than the First Amendment. In so doing, the government may sweep within its reach any communicative activity that forms an essential element of that conduct, subject to whatever limited First Amendment protection is extended to advocacy of unlawful conduct. But where the primary or intended impact of a regulation is on expression or communication, the fact that regulatory hostility focuses not on the specific speech or speaker, but rather on the ideological foundations of the system of which the speech and speaker are an inherent part, does not alter the invidious viewpoint-discriminatory character of the expressive regulation. As in the case of classic viewpoint discrimination, government is regulating expression on the basis of ideological hostility, and for that reason it is seeking to prevent communications among free-willed private individuals or entities. As in the case of classic viewpoint discrimination, under these circumstances the penalization of expression is premised on grounds wholly external to the First Amendment, and government is selectively restricting expression in an attempt to foster one ideology and hinder another.

It is likely that relatively few categories of twilight zone viewpoint regulation actually exist. But this fact makes them no less problematic when they do occur. One example of this category is obscenity. When government suppresses or punishes obscene publications, it is probable that neither the regulated expression nor the speaker has directly assumed an ideological position found to be offensive by the regulators.[134] For example, regulated obscenity usually does not, on its face, urge creation of a society characterized by free love. Were government to prohibit expression of the view that society should adopt a free-love system, a court would presumably strike the prohibition down as unconstitutional viewpoint discrimination. However, in the case of obscenity both the speaker and the expression grow out of a system whose essential (if implicit) premise is a belief in a significant loosening of societal mores about sex. Suppression of obscene expression, then, grows out of regulatory hostility toward the moral and sociopolitical premises implicitly advocated by the obscene communication. Thus, the regulatory hostility is effectively directed at the "ideological ether" surrounding the obscenity. If government may not punish expression that voices a particular ideological position, the same logic should prevent it from punishing such "satellite" expression because of hostility to that ideological position. In both situations, government seeks to prevent speakers from directly or indirectly communicating ideas that those in power deem objectionable.

The one conceivable distinction between direct regulation of expression of the ideological position itself and regulation of such satellite expression is the possibility that the satellite expression gives rise to regulable harm to which direct ideological advocacy does not. Advocacy of violent overthrow, for example, is surely not the same thing as an actual attempt to overthrow. But as long as we are speaking solely of satellite *expression* rather than *conduct*, the harms that allegedly flow from both ideology and satellite expression are basically communicative in nature, and no coercion of unwilling listeners is involved, this distinction should be considered irrelevant. In the case of obscenity, for example, government seeks to control obscene narratives for much the same reason that it seeks to prohibit advocacy of free love. In both situations, government regulates because it does not wish to allow private individuals to decide for themselves whether to alter their mores in ways found offensive by those in power.[135]

COMMERCIAL SPEECH AND THE TWILIGHT ZONE OF VIEWPOINT DISCRIMINATION

As in the case of obscenity, exclusion of commercial speech from the protective scope of the First Amendment may be characterized as a form of twilight zone viewpoint discrimination. If we assume, for purposes of argument, that exclusion of commercial speech from the First Amendment's protective scope is based on something other than principled constitutional analysis, the only alternative is to assume that it grows out of some form of hostility to or disdain for the capitalist system of which commercial speech is a part. While exceptions may exist, political hostility to commercial speech will usually not be grounded in either the ideological affiliations of the speaker or in any ideological viewpoint expressed in the substance of the regulated speech. But if the basis for the exclusion of commercial speech grows not out of a principled "internal" analysis of First Amendment value but rather from political or socioeconomic hostility to the capitalist system of which commercial speech is a part, then the discriminatory treatment given commercial speech is appropriately characterized as an invidious form of viewpoint discrimination.

Does this analysis necessarily imply that any jurist or scholar who opposes full First Amendment protection for commercial speech is necessarily engaged in the surreptitious and manipulative process of stratifying First Amendment protection to furtively undermine capitalism? As a practical matter, it would be difficult to maintain this position, in light of the fact that several jurists associated with the political right—an ideology hardly considered hostile to capitalism—have consistently opposed full First Amendment protection for commercial speech.[136] There are, to be sure, scholars and jurists who have no moral, economic, or political problem with the capitalist system but who strongly believe in generally limiting countermajoritarian judicial interference in decisions of the democratic process.[137] These jurists or scholars—Judge Robert Bork, for example—may consistently seek to confine First Amendment protection narrowly to speech directly affecting the political process.[138] One may reasonably conclude that such skimpy protection of free expression is grossly underprotective,[139] but it would be difficult to characterize their rejection of commercial speech protection as a form of furtive ideological manipulation.

Scholars or jurists who reject full First Amendment protection for commercial speech, but who are simultaneously willing to extend such protection to other forms of nonpolitical economically motivated expression, must fall into one of two categories. On the one hand, they may simply fail to recognize the inescapable intellectual inconsistency in their positions. On the other hand, they may be employing a form of indirect, twilight zone viewpoint discrimination. There is no third alternative for speech-protective scholars or jurists who purport to employ a rationalist approach to First Amendment interpretation. To the extent these jurists reject commercial speech protection, at least to the extent that they would simultaneously protect other forms of equally nonpolitical or economically motivated expression, they have drawn logically indefensible distinctions in their efforts to avoid judicial disruption of democratically ordained choices.

To the extent that scholarly observers choose to exclude commercial speech from First Amendment protection by resorting to some form of intuitive nonrationalist process, it is conceivable that they do not themselves recognize that they are actually implementing a form of implicit viewpoint discrimination. Ultimately, the argument fashioned here comes down to the following points: Unless observers who choose to reduce protection for commercial advertising (1) simultaneously reduce protection for *Consumer Reports* and the expression of consumer advocate groups, (2) reject or reduce protection for political speech motivated by goals of personal gain on behalf of the speaker, or (3) put forth a consistent, coherent, non–viewpoint-based justification for drawing such a First Amendment distinction (the potential content of which escapes me), their refusal to protect commercial speech at the very least must be considered presumptively either an illustration of indirect viewpoint-based discrimination or a failure to understand the inescapable logical implications of their own analysis.

The viewpoint discrimination that appears to plague the arguments for reduced protection of commercial speech is made up of a synthesis of two categories of discrimination: twilight zone discrimination and judicially imposed discrimination.[140] It belongs in the twilight zone category for the reasons just described.[141] It also belongs in the judicially imposed category, however, because those urging the reduction or exclusion are doing so not in the form of legislatively or imposed discrimination but rather through the judicial exclusion of commercial speech from the First Amendment's protective scope. While this exclusion will of course facilitate legislative or executive discriminations, even standing alone it represents an impermissible, judicially imposed expressive discrimination. It is as if the Court invalidated a ban on picketing by prochoice demonstrators but refused to invalidate an identical ban on picketing by prolife demonstrators.

Ironically, in *Sorrell v. IMS Health, Inc.*[142] the Supreme Court recently subjected a governmental regulation of commercial expression to strict scrutiny because the laws discriminated among speakers, favoring non-manufacturer expression over speech by manufacturers.[143] But is that not exactly what the Court's own commercial speech doctrine does? The reduced protection for commercial speech is determined not on the basis of either the subject or content of the speech but rather by the economic motivation of the speaker. Yet as the Court in *Sorrell* acknowledged, a great deal of vital and fully protected expression results from an economic motive.[144] While the *Sorrell* Court attempted to rationalize the reduced protection for commercial expression on the basis of government's legitimate interest in protecting consumers from commercial harms,[145] such a rationale ignores the fact that the same expression by nonseller speakers may cause even more harm than harmful expression on the part of sellers because listeners are less likely to be skeptical of recommendations made by objective observers. Thus, the court itself is guilty of the very speaker-based discrimination it found so troublesome in *Sorrell*.

The viewpoint-based nature of the constitutional segregation of commercial speech is especially underscored in situations in which a commercial enterprise is enmeshed in a dispute about its product or service with consumer advocates or members of the media. For example, consider Ralph Nader's attack on the safety of the Chevrolet Corvair.[146] No one, it is fair to suppose, would suggest that Nader possessed anything short of full First Amendment protection for his critical comments. However, were General Motors to attempt to spend its financial resources to defend its product's safety in response to Nader's attacks, presumably its comments will be automatically transformed into lesser protected—or, in the view of some, completely unprotected[147]—commercial speech. The same is true of the more recent dispute between the media and Nike. When *New York Times* columnist Bob Herbert criticized Nike for using near slave labor in Third World countries to manufacture its sneakers,[148] no one could question the extension of full First Amendment protection to his statements. But when Nike sought to respond through use of advertising, because it was effectively promoting sales of its product a majority of the California Supreme Court found that Nike's expression received only the reduced protection afforded commercial speech.[149] In these situations, as Justice Scalia accurately suggested in a different context, one side is forced to fight according to the Marquis of Queensbury Rules while the other side is allowed to hit below the belt.[150] Most importantly, the viewpoint always afforded the lesser level of protection is the probusiness side of the debate. It would be difficult to hypothesize a starker illustration of intentional and invidious viewpoint discrimination—discrimination that takes place only because of the reduced protection given to commercial speech. That the viewpoint discrimination is imposed by the judiciary, rather than the legislature or the executive, makes it no less constitutionally unacceptable.

Whether the urged exclusion or reduction of commercial speech protection *necessarily* derives from "external" ideological hostility is another matter. It should be recalled that a number of purportedly principled arguments have been made to support a logically grounded basis for a reduction in commercial speech protection. But as already demonstrated, even if they are assumed to provide valid bases for reduced protection in the abstract, these asserted distinctions are inevitably applied in an irrationally underinclusive manner: In most cases, noncommercial speech is never measured by the same criteria sought to be relied on to reduce protection for commercial speech. For example, one cannot rationally base the reduced protection for commercial speech on the ground that commercial speech involves matters not worthy of First Amendment concern because it is universally accepted that *Consumer Reports*, which focuses on identical issues, receives full protection. Nor can one rely on the ground that commercial speech is motivated by base concerns of personal economic gain because much fully protected expression is also motivated, largely or exclusively, by considerations of personal economic gain. The exclusion cannot be premised on the ground that in commercial speech cases the speaker is a profit-making corporation because much expression by profit-making corporations is fully protected in other contexts. Finally, an equally insufficient basis for exclusion is that commercial speech, because of its inherently self-interested nature, will always be misleading due to its strategically motivated selectiveness and slant. The exact same thing can be said of any form of advocacy that is fully protected by the First Amendment, when the speaker is motivated by self-interest.[151]

When every conceivably principled (or what here has been called "internal") basis for discrimination against commercial speech is shown to be irrationally underinclusive, it is possible to draw only one of two conceivable inferences: (1) the asserted bases of distinction do not represent the true grounds for exclusion of commercial speech from the category of fully protected expression or (2) the First Amendment interpreter has mistakenly failed to recognize the illogical underinclusiveness of the asserted basis of distinction. It should be recalled, however, that discovering irrational underinclusiveness is a classic method of unearthing furtive viewpoint-based discrimination. Otherwise, the prohibition on viewpoint discrimination could be easily circumvented simply by invoking a form of legalized sophistry.

Reliance on First Amendment "intuitionism" (or "practical reason") as a basis for exclusion of commercial speech from the scope of the First Amendment gives rise to a more complex issue. However, careful and critical analysis of the essential nature of intuitionist constitutional thinking leads to one of two conclusions: (1) The intuitionist label disguises what is at its foundation a form of unprincipled constitutional analysis that in reality represents a form of viewpoint discrimination or (2) at the very least the intuitionist approach functions as an unwitting enabler, implementing preexisting societal hostility to or disdain for particular types of expression.

Both intuitionism and practical reason, it should be recalled, call for an analysis that turns on a nonsyllogistic, emotive form of contextual reaction to a given set of circumstances. Although it is not entirely clear exactly what either approach actually entails, it is clear what they do *not* entail: neutral, consistent application of preexisting generalized principles to specific fact situations.[152] Absent this intellectually disciplined form of inquiry, what remains amounts to nothing more than some vague synthesis of personal impressions and instincts, untied to any effort to discern enduring, generalized and consistently applied constitutional principles from the document's text, structure, or history. As a definitional matter, then, use of intuitionism inevitably relies on the decision maker's preexisting prejudices, instincts, and predilections. It is only a small step from personal prejudices, instincts, and predilections, untied to a careful and reasoned analysis of abstract constitutional principles, to a decision grounded in nothing more than the decision maker's normative viewpoint.

To the extent that practical reason seeks to implement not the deci-sion maker's personal preferences but rather those of society at large,[153] it simply transforms the source of the external viewpoint that is to be imple-mented. In so doing, practical reason effectively turns the entire basis of the First Amendment on its head. The assertion that the First Amend-ment is designed to *protect* the expression of *unpopular* views, positions, perspectives and ideologies from *suppression by the majority* should hardly be a controversial proposition. It therefore makes no sense to let the scope of First Amendment protection turn on an assessment of the normative instincts of society as a whole. And this is so, even if we ignore the flawed assumption implicit in this approach that somehow the unrepresentative, unaccountable judiciary possesses an empirical pipeline to popular prefer-ences.[154] For example, it is hardly consistent with the foundations of the First Amendment to suggest that during the "pathological" periods of World War I, the post–World War I "red scare" period, or the McCarthy era of the 1950s it was appropriate for the judiciary to implement, through a judicial assessment of public "sensibilities," the strongly held ideological prejudices of the majority to justify suppression of contrary views.[155]

Reliance on intuitionism or practical reason to justify the exclusion of commercial speech from the First Amendment, then, constitutes no more principled a form of constitutional analysis than is reliance on superfi-cially principled but irrationally underinclusive bases of distinction. The fact that the decision maker's reflexive personal instincts or the decision maker's rump assessment of societal predilections and preferences suggest that commercial speech is somehow not worthy of First Amendment pro-tection in no way removes such analysis from characterization as invidious viewpoint discrimination.

The most obvious form of viewpoint discrimination relied on to justify reduced protection for commercial speech is open and candid reliance on ideological disdain for commercialism.[156] When this transparent ideologi-cal disdain is employed, we are left with a justification for the exclusion of commercial speech from the First Amendment's scope that is the paradig-matic example of twilight zone viewpoint discrimination. It is true that, in this situation, normative preferences untied to any good faith effort to decipher and apply the First Amendment's underlying values do not lead to classic forms of viewpoint discrimination. The fact remains, however, that in such a situation the decision to discriminate against commercial speech in the reach of constitutional protection is made on the grounds of the decision maker's personal ideological predisposition. It is difficult to imagine a more pathological undermining of fundamental First Amendment values.

CONCLUSION

The preceding analysis was designed to provide two important insights about the judicial and scholarly treatment of commercial speech. First, it underscores the importance of separating personal political and ideological preferences from an understanding of the ideological humility central to a commitment to a viable system of free expression. No viable system of free expression can survive where the guardian of the First Amendment determines protection on the basis of the speech's consistency with her own ideological predilections. Second, it demonstrates the close—and often unrecognized—link between commercial speech and political ideology. Commercial speech, as defined by both the Supreme Court and hostile commentators, does not include *all* speech concerning commercial products and services. As previously noted,[157] none of the scholarly opponents of commercial speech protection would suggest that Ralph Nader's criticisms of the Chevrolet Corvair's safety, *New York Times* columnist Bob Herbert's criticisms of Nike's foreign production process, or an article in *Consumer Reports* falls into the category of less protected commercial speech.

The goal of this chapter has been to connect the constitutional and political dots. Many scholars have incorrectly assumed that the arguments for excluding commercial speech from the scope of the First Amendment represent plausible contributions to the debate over the shaping and application of principled constitutional analysis. It has also been widely—but incorrectly—assumed that commercial speech may appropriately be excluded from the First Amendment's scope without undermining any fundamental constitutional values because commercial speech is, at best, only peripheral to those values. Ironically, the inaccuracy of both of these assumptions is best underscored by understanding the link between these two flawed assumptions about commercial speech: The very fact that many wish to exclude commercial speech from protection on grounds completely ignored when relevant to other types or subjects of speech actually suggests the invidious political and ideological presumptions that often implicitly underlie the attacks on commercial speech.

When, in the 1940s and 50s, constitutional scholars opposed First Amendment protection for the speech of Communists, they often did so on the basis of a world view that found such expression ideologically offensive.[158] One can only hope that, if an identical political situation were to arise today, cooler heads in the world of free speech scholarship would prevail, allowing them to recognize that ideological hostility to the views of Communists cannot properly be used as a basis to exclude their speech from the First Amendment's scope. And this is true, whether we seek to achieve that end by irrationally (or strategically) selective use of more principled grounds, vague notions of intuitionism or practical reason, or open reliance on political ideology.

It is true that hostility to commercial speech is probably one step removed from hostility to Communist expression because in the case of commercial speech the suppressed expression is usually not, standing alone, what is deemed offensive by the regulators. However, as this chapter has demonstrated, where the speech is suppressed because of the regulators' hostility to the "ideological ether" that pervades the regulated speech and speaker, the harms to First Amendment values are just as great. It is time to recognize opposition to commercial speech protection for what it all too often is: a form of ideological hostility to the premises of capitalism and commercialism. As was true of those who sought to protect the free speech rights of Communists in the mid-twentieth century, one surely need not agree with the ideological premises underlying either capitalism in general or the commercial speech sought to be regulated in particular to find such suppression ominous.

CHAPTER FIVE

The Anticorruption Principle, Free Expression, and the Democratic Process

> There are again two methods of removing the causes of faction: the one, by destroying the liberty which is essential to its existence; the other, by giving to every citizen the same opinions, the same passions, and the same interests. It could never be more truly said than of the first remedy, that it was worse than the disease.
>
> James Madison, *The Federalist No. 10*

A number of scholars and jurists have long deplored what they see as the corruption of the American political process.[1] In their view, too much money is having too large and unsavory an impact on American politics, simultaneously distorting political power toward the wealthy and seductively drawing politicians away from pursuit of the public interest.[2] One of the leading scholars advocating such a view, Professor Zephyr Teachout, has gone so far as to suggest that there is actually an "anticorruption principle" embedded in the Constitution, logically implying that political corruption rises to the level of a constitutional violation.[3] This principle posits that, as a matter of American history and constitutional law, "officeholders" are constitutionally obligated to act in the "public interest" and in pursuit of the "common good"; anything less is deemed to amount to "corruption."[4]

The Supreme Court's decision in *Citizens United v. Federal Election Commission* only intensified scholars' and jurists' concerns about the dangers of political corruption.[5] In *Citizens United*, the Court held that the section of the Bipartisan Campaign Reform Act (BCRA) limiting direct corporate political expenditures for expression during a presidential campaign violated the First Amendment.[6] In a strongly worded dissent, Justice Stevens relied on arguments grounded in the anticorruption principle as specifically fashioned by Professor Teachout to justify the BCRA's suppression of corporate political speech.[7] Justice Stevens's dissent, like Professor Teachout's version of the anticorruption principle, relied on a broad definition of corruption, one extending far beyond the simple act of bribery.[8] According to Justice Stevens, "There are threats of corruption that are far more destructive to a democratic society than the odd bribe."[9]

Justice Stevens's opinion in *Citizens United* is not the first time that members of the Court have sought to uphold restrictions on political speech in the name of anticorruption. In *Austin v. Michigan Chamber of Commerce*, the Supreme Court upheld a state law that restricted corporate political expenditures in state elections.[10] The *Austin* Court considered Michigan's law to be "aim[ed] at a different type of corruption in the political arena: the corrosive and distorting effects of immense aggregations of wealth that are accumulated with the help of the corporate form."[11] The Court's decision in *Austin*, as Justice Scalia observed in his dissent, "endorse[d] the principle that too much speech is an evil that the democratic majority can proscribe."[12] The *Austin* decision, he said, allowed for "anything the Court deem[ed] politically undesirable [to be] turned into political corruption—by simply describing it as politically 'corrosive.'"[13]

The anticorruption principle, as developed by Professor Teachout, seeks to provide important constitutional grounding for the theories relied on by the *Austin* majority and Justice Stevens's opinion in *Citizens United*. Under the anticorruption principle, if proposed legislation undermines the "public good," it is unconstitutional for members of Congress to vote for it, even if they believe it would benefit their constituents.[14] The anticorruption principle requires that members of Congress always be motivated by the goal of advancing the "public good."[15] Any political action not motivated by this goal is considered inherently "corrupt" and, therefore, unconstitutional.[16]

The most radical element of Professor Teachout's anticorruption principle is its conclusion that private citizens, as well as public officials, are to be treated as "officeholders" when they interact with the government.[17] As such, they—like public officials—are constitutionally restricted in what they can say and do in the political arena. Under the anticorruption principle, "Citizens must generally work for, and desire, the public good, at least in their political interactions."[18] Despite the First Amendment's guarantee to the contrary, under the anticorruption principle a private citizen may not petition the government for redress of grievances[19] if the grievance is designed to advance the citizen's personal interests at the expense of the public good.[20] Such a limitation on a private citizen's actions is an extraordinary leap beyond the regulatory framework of the Constitution, which, with the exception of the Thirteenth Amendment,[21] restricts only government action.[22]

Professor Teachout labels as "political corruption" any activity that brings about political "inequality," has the effect of "drowning out" other political voices, or gives rise to a "dispirited public" or a loss of "political integrity."[23] Under her definition of the term, "corruption" exists when those with financial means are allowed to use their wealth for political purposes.[24]

In examining the premise and rationale of Professor Teachout's anticorruption principle, it is important to understand its purported constitutional foundation. The principle is designed to be far more than merely a policy-based limitation on or counterweight to the First Amendment right of free expression. Rather, it is designed to function as a freestanding constitutional directive. It is not difficult to grasp the strategic goal of this characterization. If accepted, it would tend to equalize the constitutional weight of the competing interests. For reasons to be explained, however, as both a conceptual and historical matter it borders on the incoherent to characterize the anticorruption limits on private individuals as constitutionally dictated. In fact, the truth is quite the opposite: Not only is the anticorruption principle not constitutionally dictated, it is itself unconstitutional. The anticorruption principle categorically limits political speech by deeming political activity "corrupt" when it is not motivated by an altruistic interest in advancing the good of society as a whole.[25] Under the principle, contributing money to or purchasing advertising on behalf of candidates because their policies would benefit the private citizen's personal interests would necessarily be deemed an unconstitutional act.[26] There is little doubt that adoption of the anticorruption principle would have a dramatically negative impact on the free and open communication of valuable political expression.[27] In addition to the serious First Amendment implications raised by the anticorruption principle, however, the history, theory, and logic used to support the principle's existence are seriously flawed. The Constitution imposes no freestanding anticorruption principle. In fact, the word *corruption* appears only once in the documents, and that is in the context of treason.[28] What the Constitution does include are narrow, prophylactic provisions aimed at protecting the government from specific harms *caused by* corruption, not *a general prohibition* on corruption.[29]

Beyond its lack of any foundation in constitutional text, the anticorruption principle also lacks any basis in American historical practice.[30] Interest groups, which are often focused exclusively on advancement of the narrow interests of their members, have long been part of the American political experience.[31] Because the anticorruption principle rests on the theory that purely self-interested motivation—untied to pursuit of the common good—in the political process is inherently improper, virtually all interest group activity logically would have to be prohibited. This theory thus ignores the central role interest groups have always played in American politics.[32] Indeed, the Constitutional Convention itself was overwhelmingly influenced by special interests.[33] Coalitions formed and regrouped throughout the Convention.[34] Delegates were motivated to form coalitions by their states' local interests, not by some notion of a universal common good.[35] Moreover, interest group activity in the nation certainly did not cease when the Constitution was ratified. If anything, it steadily increased.

Perhaps most troublesome is the fact that the anticorruption principle stands in stark contrast to the foundational precepts of American political theory that were embodied in the First Amendment right of free expression.[36] As argued throughout this book, American democracy is largely adversarial in nature.[37] Thus, citizens are not required to pursue advancement of the common good in their personal political activities; to the contrary, it is generally understood that citizens may seek to influence the political process exclusively for the purpose of advancing their own personal interests.[38] To be sure, citizens may choose to pursue altruistic or ideological goals, rather than narrow, selfish ones. But central to the notion of self-determination is governmental "epistemological humility."[39] In regulating political advocacy, government may not superimpose its own normative perspective on its citizens. American democracy relies on individual self-determination as well as the interaction of adverse and competing interests. By confining the constitutional protection of free expression to a universal pursuit of the public good, the anticorruption principle contravenes the core premise of the American democratic system.

The next section of this chapter provides a detailed description of the anticorruption principle as its advocates—particularly Professor Teachout—have shaped it.[40] The section that follows explores the numerous historical and conceptual flaws in the premises that underlie the principle.[41] The final section examines the principle's inconsistency with a proper understanding of American democratic theory and its ominous implications for the First Amendment right of free expression.[42]

UNDERSTANDING THE ANTICORRUPTION PRINCIPLE

It is necessary to understand what the anticorruption principle entails before discussing its problematic premises and implications. Although a number of scholars and jurists have advocated some form of an anticorruption principle, Professor Teachout has provided its most detailed and enthusiastic explication. The fact that the leading anticorruption advocate on the Supreme Court has expressly relied on her scholarship adds further credibility to Teachout's version of the principle.[43] This discussion therefore focuses largely on her articulation of the anticorruption principle.

The Goals of the Anticorruption Principle

Although the prevention of both corruption and the appearance of corruption has been recognized by the Supreme Court as an appropriate limitation on the First Amendment's reach in the electoral process, that concern has been viewed solely as a subconstitutional competing government interest, not as a freestanding constitutional directive.[44] Professor Teachout, however, seeks to take anticorruption concerns out of the "competing government interest" category and place them on equal constitutional footing with the constitutional right with which it competes. As fashioned by Teachout, the anticorruption principle provides constitutionally grounded justification for any governmental action aimed at fighting corruption.

Under the anticorruption principle as Professor Teachout describes it, "Political virtue is pursuing the public good in public life."[45] Public officials, she asserts, must be motivated by an interest in pursuing the "public good" when using "the reins of power."[46] Her version of the anticorruption principle thus does far more than restrict public officials' actions; it also restricts their thoughts and motivations in taking those actions. For example, if an elected official votes against a bill solely because she is concerned about her reelection prospects without taking into account the bill's impact on the common good, presumably her vote would have to be deemed corrupt. Indeed, her vote would even have to be considered unconstitutional because it violated the anticorruption principle, which, according to Professor Teachout, is constitutionally dictated. But even commission of such a violation does not necessarily provide an express basis for impeachment.[47] Thus it is unclear what legal consequences would flow from a public officeholder's violation of the anticorruption principle. Whatever those consequences, however, under the anticorruption principle it would nevertheless be unconstitutional for an elected official to vote against a bill that would benefit the nation as a whole solely because it would result in fewer jobs in his district. An interest in one's own constituents does not necessarily translate into pursuit of the common good. Moreover, if an elected official's constituents advocate enactment of legislation because it would personally benefit them, the constituents' advocacy would also necessarily violate the anticorruption principle because, pursuant to Teachout's extremely broad definition of "officeholder," private citizens are subject to the stringent limits imposed by the anticorruption principle as much as government officials are, and their actions and motivations are similarly subject to constitutional scrutiny.

Under the anticorruption principle, according to Professor Teachout, the Constitution requires people to possess *civic virtue*—meaning that they must "put[] public good before narrow personal interests in [their] public actions."[48] In contrast, participants in the governing process who are tempted by narcissism, ambition, or luxury, to place private gain before public good in their public actions are deemed "corrupt."[49] Pursuant to her approach, when a private person executes his "public duties"—including any engagement in the political process or interaction with the government—he is constitutionally required to put the "public good" first.[50] As bizarre as all of these results undoubtedly seem, they are logically inescapable implications of Professor Teachout's constitutionally dictated version of the anticorruption principle.

Defining the Terms

One might reasonably wonder why a constitutionally based anticorruption principle is needed in the first place because we already have laws criminalizing corruption. As already seen, however, the "corruption" prohibited by the anticorruption principle reaches far beyond prevailing understandings of the term.[51] As shaped by Professor Teachout, the anticorruption principle prohibits "officeholders" from taking any political action motivated purely by self-interest.[52] Because the concept of the public good is presumably to be defined subjectively,[53] the anticorruption principle would seem to require only that officeholders *believe* that they are acting in the interest of the public good, as they understand it. Corruption, therefore, "is defined in terms of an attitude toward public service, not in relation to a set of criminal laws."[54] The anticorruption principle is premised on the notion that the concept of "corruption" sweeps within its reach political activities that, while not illegal in and of themselves, are rendered toxic by the actor's purpose in engaging in them.[55] A person is "corrupt," according to Professor Teachout, when "the public good does not motivate him."[56]

The public's use and understanding of the word *corruption* appears to be out of step with a definition of the term that encompasses otherwise legal activity solely because of the actor's improper motives. For example, the Wikipedia entry on the word *corruption* in the political context confines the definition to criminal acts, such as extortion and bribery.[57] Moreover, news stories on American corruption demonstrate that the term's modern understanding encompasses solely criminal behavior, not simply activity by public officials motivated by something other than pursuit of the public good. For example, a Google search for the word *corruption* revealed not a single story concerning Professor Teachout's noncriminal version of the term.[58] This suggests that the definition employed by Professor Teachout—at least when measured against common understanding—is at best exaggerated and at worst downright misleading.

The definition of *officeholder* under the anticorruption principle is also stretched well beyond common perceptions of the term. According to Professor Teachout, "Citizenship is a public office, like the public office of Senator or President."[59] Therefore, "All citizens—especially powerful citizens—are responsible for keeping public resources generally serving public ends."[60] This extreme definition of *officeholder* leads to the conclusion that private citizens, like government officials, are restrained by the Constitution's anticorruption principle. According to Teachout, private citizens may not "ignore a general commitment to the public at large."[61] Pursuant to this definition, a citizen is considered corrupt if her "interactions with government or with politics"[62] are motivated by self-interest. It is unclear, however, what would happen to a citizen under Teachout's framework if he were to violate the Constitution by not "working for, and desiring, the public good."[63] Presumably, a constitutionally dictated anticorruption principle must have some enforcement mechanism. Otherwise, people have no incentive to follow the principle's mandate. Yet Professor Teachout never discusses how the principle would be enforced against *any* officeholder, let alone against private citizens. Teachout's version of "corruption" and her enforcement of it in the Constitution thus place us into a constitutional fantasyland where the legal topography is, to say the least, unchartered.

Professor Teachout supports her claim that citizenship is a public office—and that citizens can therefore be deemed to have violated the Constitution—by noting that "people regularly call a local businessman 'corrupt' if he tries to get something out of government using political ties."[64] One might reasonably assume that is true of quid pro quo bribery, in which event it would fall quite naturally within the traditional realm of corruption. But because the public uses the term *corrupt* to refer to private citizens as well as elected officials, she reasons, the concept of citizenship as a public office will make sense to most people.[65] The logical implication of her definition of *officeholder* to include private citizens is that citizens are imbued with a "public trust" when they interact with government.[66] Professor Teachout argues that while citizens possess a constitutional right to petition the government, they are at the same time constitutionally obligated "to giv[e] credit and thought to the impact on others, and to using public channels for public ends."[67]

One of the key purposes of the anticorruption principle is the reduction, if not complete elimination, of the influence of wealth in political campaigns. Campaign expenditures result in corruption, Professor Teachout argues, when any of the following "modern conceptions of "corruption" arise: (1) criminal bribery, (2) political inequality, (3) "drowned voices," (4) a "dispirited public," or (5) "a lack of integrity" of the political process.[68] Quid pro quo bribery is described as being "the archetypal corruption."[69] Even the "criminal bribery" concept, however, includes "possibly legal" activities.[70] This is so, despite the fact that the Supreme Court has recognized a compelling government interest *only* in the prevention of "*quid-pro-quo* corruption."[71]

The "inequality" version of "corruption" equates the concept with unequal financial access to the political arena. Once money is involved in politics, Professor Teachout argues, "It creates unequal access and unequal voice."[72] It follows, then, that the anticorruption principle mandates the removal of the unequal impact of money. The anticorruption principle could thus be employed to uphold limitations on political expenditures by candidates for no reason other than to even the political playing field.

An extension of the political equality argument is the notion that corruption also occurs when the voices of powerful actors "drown out" other speakers' voices. The anticorruption principle would prohibit any communication found to suppress other speech by virtue of its volume, whether literal (speech that is audibly louder than other speech) or figurative (speech that is "louder" because more people hear it). Again, the anticorruption principle's purpose is to limit the use of money by those who have it to give those without money an equal shot at contributing to the American political colloquy.

The final two modern conceptions of "corruption" described by Teachout—a dispirited public and a lack of political integrity—are both tied to public perception. Anything that gives rise to the perception of corruption has a dispiriting impact on the public and therefore would be prohibited by the anticorruption principle, she argues. Integrity can be lost any time a person "leverage[s] the channels of power to tempt officials into non-public actions."[73] Under this formulation, a constituent who contacts her elected representative about a matter of personal importance threatens the integrity of the political process.

It is not difficult to recognize that Professor Teachout has expanded the concept of "corruption" to include anything that conflicts with an ideological model committed to notions of economic equality in the political process. Under her version of the concept, those who are ideologically opposed to such redistribution in the political arena are automatically characterized as supporters of corruption—with apparently nothing to distinguish support for such "corruption" from open support for criminalized bribery. To be sure, reasonable people can differ over the values of economic redistribution, both in the political arena and in society in general. But by characterizing the position of those with whom she differs as fungible with support for bribery, Teachout alters the nature of the debate in ominous ways. The very use of the word *corruption* triggers notions of evil and illegality that have no place in the modern debate over American political theory and campaign finance.

The Historical Origins of the Anticorruption Principle

Professor Teachout finds as the primary historical source of the modern anticorruption principle the debates at the Constitutional Convention. Madison's notes recorded mention of the word fifty-four times.[74] According to Teachout, the delegates' discussion of corruption focused on two specific concerns: (1) the potentially corrupting influence of wealth, greed, and ambition on the political process; and (2) the susceptibility of the nation to foreign corruption due to its small size.[75] The anticorruption principle must be found in the Constitution, she reasons, because concerns about the need to prevent corruption entered into "some of the most extensive debates in the Convention—those about emoluments and perquisites of civil office, who should have the power of appointment, and the size of relative bodies."[76] According to Teachout, the Framers' overarching concern with corruption led them to use "near-apocalyptic language and [to] search for tools to ward off its threats."[77] She also cites Madison's famed *Federalist No. 10* as support for the existence of the anticorruption principle.[78] Madison's concern about the dangerous influence of factions supposedly evinces his belief that the existence of factions should be eliminated or, at the very least, controlled.[79]

There are, as we shall see, numerous inaccuracies in Professor Teachout's understanding of the Framers' comments and writings.[80] It is important to note, however, that even were one for the moment to suspend historical disbelief and unquestioningly accept her understanding of the Framers' intentions, Teachout must make a far stronger showing than that to establish existence of a constitutionally dictated anticorruption principle. She must further demonstrate that the Framers intended to embody their understanding within the body of the document. It was, after all, the Constitution's text, not the disembodied understandings of the Framers, that was subjected to the formal procedures of the ratification process. In an effort to meet that burden, Teachout identifies twenty-three constitutional features that, she believes, support the existence of an overarching anticorruption principle.[81] She contends that a synthesis of the specific constitutional clauses aimed at fighting corruption amount to a freestanding constitutional anticorruption principle. She points to specific clauses in Articles I, II, and III to establish that the Framers intended to embed an anticorruption principle in the Constitution. Article I, she asserts "was shaped by concerns that the House [of Representatives] would be populated by men of weak will, easily corrupted to use their office for venal ends, and that the Senate would become corrupted by vanity and luxury."[82] Smaller groups, it was believed, "were easier to buy off with promise of money."[83] Smaller groups were also more likely to "find similar motives and band together to empower themselves at the expense of the citizenry."[84] Large groups supposedly "couldn't coordinate well enough to effectively corrupt themselves."[85] Because of this, "the delegates decided to make the House of Representatives . . . larger to prevent against corruption."[86]

In addition to the Framers' concerns about size, Teachout finds evidence of the anticorruption principle in the constitutional methods adopted for electing the legislature.[87] The Constitution was designed so that members of the House of Representatives would be elected "by the people" rather than "by the legislature" because of fears that "congressional dependency on state legislatures could allow local corruption to infect national corruption."[88] Fears of the influence of foreign power also supposedly infused the delegates' fears of corruption, leading to "the clause demanding seven years of residency in the United States in order to serve in Congress."[89]

The provision for regular elections was one of the most important checks on corruption, Teachout claims.[90] The concern was that "longer terms strengthened the bonds with the Executive and weakened them with the people."[91] The Framers "wanted to avoid financial dependency of one branch upon another," she notes.[92] But while "a short term would ensure accountability and make it difficult to run too far on the public purse . . . a long term would make it more likely that men of good character would undertake the commitment to service."[93] Elections, therefore, would ensure that those corrupted by power and wealth would not be reelected.[94]

The Framers also included provisions to ward off the threat of conflicts and temptations that might corrupt legislators. Teachout believes that the Framers were concerned "that members of Congress would use their position to enrich themselves and their friends, and that they would see public office as a place for gaining civil posts and preferences, instead of as a public duty."[95] Evidence of this concern is reflected in the Ineligibility and Emoluments Clauses, which were included in order to allay concerns that "wealthy non-residents would purchase elections."[96] These clauses "reflect a deep anxiety about the possibility of civil service corrupting governmental processes by enabling members of Congress to create and fund their own positions as civil servants."[97] The Foreign Gifts Clause, she notes, grew out of fears "that foreign interests would try to use their wealth to tempt public servants and sway the foreign policy decisions of the new government."[98]

Teachout also points to a number of anticorruption clauses in Articles II and III. Article II "contains several provisions to limit executive corruption."[99] The Presidential Emoluments Clause, which forbids the president from being paid by the United States beyond his general compensation,[100] is one such provision. The clause was adopted "to prevent the President from becoming overly dependent upon Congress (and thereby corrupted by them)."[101] Article II, Section 1, requiring Senate approval of judicial appointment, limits potential executive corruption of the judiciary. The constitutional provision for impeachment is described by Teachout as "clearly the strongest anti-corruption element of Section 1."[102] Lastly, like Article I, Article II also carefully prescribes an elections process designed "to guard against corruption."[103]

Teachout claims that the purpose of Article III is to keep the judiciary "independent of both 'the gust of faction' and corruption."[104] She interprets the clause that allows judges to hold office only "during good behavior" to mean in the "absence of corruption,"[105] thus supporting the existence of an anticorruption principle. Article III, section 2's jury trial requirement is also said to be the result of "the anti-corruption urge."[106]

The Constitution's structural commitments of power are, as Teachout asserts, "some of the strongest anti-corruption provisions in the Constitution."[107] Her claim that the separation of powers among the three branches of government was intended as a check on corruption is not new. For example, G. Edward White has written that the foundational "republican" principles of the American Republic included "the 'anticorruption' principle, embodied in the separation . . . of powers."[108] Structural features within the Senate and the House are also identified as being adopted to "protect[] against corruption."[109] The Framers believed that "the dignity of the elites might make those in the Senate resistant to corruption."[110] On the other hand, the House was thought to be resistant to corruption because, in light of its size, "it would be logically impossible for various representatives to all have similar interests that could be similarly exploited."[111]

The preceding discussion has described, in some detail, the scope and rationale of the anticorruption principle as it has been fashioned by its leading scholarly advocate. The section that follows explores the countless flaws in Teachout's analysis in considerably greater scope and detail.

THE ANTICORRUPTION PRINCIPLE'S
FUNDAMENTAL FAILINGS

Professor Teachout's version of a constitutionally dictated anticorruption principle suffers from numerous flaws. These flaws fall under one or more of the following headings: (1) linguistic, (2) textual, (3) historical, (4) theoretical, and (5) constitutional. The analysis has already explained the linguistic defects in Professor Teachout's wildly broad and counterintuitive use of the term *corruption*.[112] The analysis therefore now turns to explorations of the remaining defects in her theory.

The Anticorruption Principle's Inconsistency with Constitutional Text

The argument that an anticorruption principle is embedded in the Constitution relies heavily on a synthesis of individual clauses with the document's overall structure. It is indisputable that the Constitution was designed, among other things, to prevent corruption on the part of government officials. In fact, many of the Constitution's provisions, including many of the clauses cited to support the anticorruption principle's existence, were written to establish a federal government resistant to the dangers of corruption. But that fact, standing alone, fails to justify the anticorruption principle as Teachout has fashioned it, for two reasons. First, the type of corruption that the Framers sought to prevent was far narrower in scope than the sweeping version urged by Teachout. Second, the text reveals that the Framers quite consciously chose to fight corruption *incrementally* and *prophylactically*. In contrast, Teachout describes a *direct* and *categorical* prohibition on corruption—one that appears nowhere within the document's four corners. The fact that the Framers were quite clearly aware of the dangers of political corruption yet chose *not* to employ the methodology described by Teachout demonstrates their unambiguous rejection of the approach she advocates.

Initially, it is important to recognize that the corruption that the Constitution aims to prevent in no way extends to the anticorruption principle's far-reaching definition of the term suggested by Teachout. Corruption, as understood by the Framers, involved only the failure of elected officials to serve their respective electorates. It did not include an elected official's failure to pursue some vague notion of the common good. Corruption, properly understood, included the situation where a legislator, on his own, engages in an activity *solely to benefit himself*, at the expense of his constituents. It does not include situations where public officials choose solely to foster or protect the narrow interests of their constituents, even at the expense of the broader common good. The Constitution's Framers designed the government to ensure that elected officials acted in the best interests of their constituents, rather than in their own personal interests. It was failure to comply with this dictate that the Framers characterized as corruption.[113] Every one of the clauses to which Teachout points is explainable by the Framers' desire to assure that elected officials truly represent their constituencies, and nothing more than that.

Equally important is that Teachout has confused narrowly prophylactic structural protections designed to retard the growth of corruption with a direct, categorical prohibition of corruption—something the Constitution's text does not include. Virtually all of the provisions to which Teachout points unambiguously establish only the former, not the latter. For example, the Ineligibility and Emoluments Clauses[114] and the Foreign Gifts Clause,[115] which Teachout points to as Article I's strongest protections against corruption,[116] are classic illustrations of the Framers' limited prophylactic approach. The Foreign Gift Clause's strong, "almost petulant"[117] prohibition demonstrates that the Framers chose to put explicit prohibitions on *specific invitations to corruption* in the Constitution, rather than to ban corruption categorically. This was due to the Framers' recognition of the futility of attempting to outlaw "the fallibility of mortals."[118] Instead, they added to the Constitution "auxiliary precautions" against office holders' impropriety—precautions that lie "at the heart of the constitutional separation of powers."[119]

Articles II and III also include a number of clauses aimed exclusively at *stemming the threat of corruption*, rather than categorically banning the activity. The Presidential Emoluments Clause serves as a check on potential executive corruption by preventing the executive from receiving pay beyond his or her general compensation,[120] thus preventing dependency on either Congress or the states. The executive's ability to corrupt the judiciary was limited by Article II, section 1, which requires Senate approval for judicial appointments.[121] Despite providing for lifetime tenure, Article III prevents judicial corruption by providing that judges may hold their "Offices [only] during good Behaviour."[122] Clause after clause of the Constitution thus demonstrates that the Framers intended to create a government resistant to the dangers of corruption, as they understood the term.[123] This is a far cry, however, from the sweeping, direct ban on corruption that Professor Teachout has purported to glean from the Constitution's text.

Teachout does not even attempt to provide textual support for her claim that the anticorruption principle restricts private citizens. She would be hard pressed to do so, for the Constitution's almost universal limitation to governmental action is well established and understood. Indeed, the only constitutional provision that restricts private activities is the Thirteenth Amendment, which prohibits involuntary servitude.[124] There is no support in the Constitution for the proposition that citizenship is a public office and thus that private citizens are restrained in the same manner as public officials. To the contrary, the philosophical grounding of the Constitution in liberal political theory necessarily dictates recognition of a separation between the state and private citizens.[125]

The Anticorruption Principle and American Political History

In shaping the anticorruption principle, Teachout seeks to draw support from a gross misreading of American history. She relies heavily on the writings and debates of the Framers during and immediately following the Constitutional Convention.[126] But what the history of the framing really establishes is that the Framers themselves were committed to the pursuit of narrow special interests.

The Framers and the Founding
Contrary to the understanding of anticorruption principle advocates, American political thought at the time of the founding actually rejected the notion that a government could be centered on the pursuit of the common good and civic virtue. By the 1780s, according to one authority, "dozens of historical actors . . . came to doubt America's capacity for an overarching commitment to the public good."[127] Historian Gordon Wood has recounted the fundamental shift in American political thought from the focus on "individual self-sacrifice for the good of the state" to an emphasis on what was referred to as "public opinion."[128] America, according to Wood, was designed to "remain free not because of any quality in its citizens of Spartan self-sacrifice to some nebulous public good, but . . . because of the concern each individual would have in his own self-interest and personal freedom."[129] America, then, was a government grounded predominantly, if not entirely, in the pursuit of its citizens' self-interest and consent.[130]

The Framers' goal was to create a government that would resist the potential threat of corruption, by which they meant only the failure of elected representatives to pursue or advance the interests of their constituents.[131] The Framers wanted to "insulate the new government from . . . corruption . . . rather than promote virtue."[132] The Framers had come to realize that the notion of a coherent, overriding "public good," even if subjectively defined, was not viable in a large, heterogeneous society.[133]

It is important to note that the Framers did not seek to eliminate special interest groups or factions. Nor did they expect elected officials to forgo efforts to advance the regional interests of their constituents in the name of the "public good." Indeed, one need look no further than the Constitutional Convention itself to see regional interests and factions at work. Alignment among delegates, and thus among different states, was largely dictated by narrow state interests on the issues before the Convention. Political scientist Calvin Jillson has provided a model of factional politics at the Constitutional Convention.[134] By analyzing roll call data from the Convention, Jillson was able to distinguish the specific points in time when state delegates realigned their interests.[135] His findings show that "both the intellectual composition and the regional distribution of the ideas, values, and attitudes which formed the American political culture during the founding period" contributed to the various factional alignments that developed during the Convention.[136]

The roll call data from the Convention demonstrates the existence of four "very clear periods of coalition alignment."[137] Each period of alignment serves as an example of the central role of factions and regional interests in the creation of the Constitution. Delegates first demonstrated allegiance to regional interests during the Convention's opening days.[138] As with all coalitional splits during the Convention, alignment among delegates fell along state-based divides. The major alignments of states were the result of predictable disagreement on some of the most substantial issues before the delegates.[139] The question of representation split the delegates into factions based on the size of their states.[140] Debate over the projected role of the executive, on the other hand, resulted in a battle between middle state delegates and those delegates from the peripheral states.[141] The debate over slavery, not surprisingly, resulted in two distinct groups: the delegates from northern states, which did not allow slavery, and the delegates from southern states, which did have slavery.[142] Even among the southern states, however, there was disagreement among the delegates on the issue of slavery, which was largely rooted in the differing interests within each state.[143]

Teachout contends that corruption should be understood to include "the use of government power and assets to benefit localities or other special interests."[144] By her definition, however, virtually all of the delegates at the Convention were corrupt. According to Jillson, the delegates, instead of being united by some "assertedly moral norm"[145] or "public good," were "divided by their adherence to regionally distinct visions of the republican government that they all professed to desire."[146] It is impossible to reconcile Teachout's notion that the Framers were trying to create a government that would condemn the very acts that proved essential to the creation of that government: regional interests and factions.

The only general consensus among the delegates was the desire for some form of republican government.[147] But even "republicanism" was not a universally agreed-on concept. According to Jillson, "Different groups or factions in various sections of the nation defined 'republicanism' as they perceived it and could only view their opponents as dangerously anti-republican."[148] The delegates were well aware of the fact that they brought differing views to the table. No one expected mass agreement on how to form the new nation based on some generalized notion of the common good.[149] As Madison observed, "In general the members seem . . . averse to the temporizing expedients."[150]

Madison on Factions

Teachout's reliance on Madison's *Federalist No. 10* to support the existence of her version of a constitutional anticorruption principle is entirely misplaced.[151] She points to this famous document as evidence that Madison intended to create a government in which factions would be eliminated.[152] According to Teachout, Madison was concerned about the dangers of factions and "argued that a large, confederate republic was less likely to lead to faction and instability than a small one."[153] She therefore concludes that Madison opposed the corruption caused by the pursuit of narrow self-interest. Teachout fails to grasp, however, that Madison believed that a large country would decrease the danger that factions might bring to bear on the nation *because more factions would exist in a larger nation, thereby diluting the relative power of individual factions.*[154]

The most serious flaw in Teachout's reliance on Madison is her complete failure to acknowledge that Madison expressly rejected any effort to legally abolish factions—motivated by self-interest or otherwise—because any such effort would represent a serious threat to liberty.[155] He therefore accepted the presence of factions as necessary for the existence of a free society. Factions, according to Madison, occur when "a number of citizens, whether amounting to a majority or minority of the whole, . . . are united and actuated by some common impulse of passion, or of interest, adverse to the rights of other citizens, or to the permanent and aggregate interests of the community."[156] He recognized two conceivable ways to eliminate factions: "destroying the liberty which is essential to [their] existence . . . [or] by giving every citizen the same opinions, the same passions, and the same interests."[157] Madison considered both alternatives to present a serious threat to republican government. Most importantly, he concluded that "it could not be a less folly to abolish liberty, which is essential to political life, because it nourishes faction, than it would be to wish the annihilation of air, which is essential to animal life, because it imparts to fire its destructive agency."[158] Because ensuring liberty meant that factions would continue to exist, Madison was willing to tolerate them; eliminating liberty would be "worse than the disease."[159] To be sure, Madison saw potential dangers in any one faction gaining excessive political power. But it was by controlling them through the use of narrowly focused prophylactic structural devices, rather than by rendering them categorically illegal, that he sought to avoid this danger. And, as previously explained,[160] this is exactly what the Constitution's text does.

The anticorruption principle, as Teachout fashions it, clumsily (and dangerously) seeks to deem unconstitutional a private individual's pursuit of his own narrow special interest through the political process. She thus expects of society that which Madison recognized is impossible to achieve and dangerous to attempt. Far from enforcing Framers' practices and intent, then, Teachout advocates a policy in direct opposition to their goals. Rather than try to fight the inevitable, Madison accepted reality: "The latent causes of faction are thus sown in the nature of man."[161]

The Central Role of Interest Groups in the History of American Politics

The preceding discussion demonstrates the crucial role that factions played both at the Constitutional Convention and in the minds of the Framers. American history, both pre- and post-Convention, tells a similar story, with interest groups playing a central role in all facets of American political life. It is impossible to reconcile the central role played by interest groups throughout American history with Teachout's assertion that the Constitution was designed to eliminate the very existence of such groups. One need not be a serious student of American history to know that interest groups and self-promotion are embedded in this nation's social fabric.[162] Indeed, in the words of political scholars, "a group basis of American politics has been acknowledged since the founding."[163]

The period following the Constitution's ratification was marked by the continued prevalence of special interests' influence over governmental decision making. Commentators have long recognized the important dynamic of interest groups in American political history. "Groups of self-seeking individuals have ever importuned legislatures for special favors," observed one early-twentieth-century scholar.[164] In the words of a politician of the same era, "Groups, some of them actuated by the most patriotic motives, and others purely selfish, have maintained what are commonly called lobbyists in Washington, I presume since the foundation of the Government."[165]

Interest groups today continue to play a vital role in American democracy, as anyone who follows the news is aware. They have "become an integral part of our representative system of government."[166] Groups offer "more effective representation (than parties) and hence secur[e] overall public policy that better 'fits' citizens' preferences."[167] In addition, "the political and social experiences *within* groups are viewed as democratically relevant."[168]

The role of interest groups in American society has grown exponentially during the twentieth and twenty-first centuries, leading some to describe interest groups as "the stuff of which [American] politics is made."[169] From 1890 to 1899, 256 interest groups appeared before Congress.[170] By 1917, that number had grown to 1,301.[171] These national interest groups existed to "advance . . . their policy goals within the Washington establishment."[172] Members of Congress reportedly found national associations to be "valuable in enabling them to arrive at a clearer understanding of the facts concerning the opinion and interests of a specific group."[173] These associations, according to one scholar, "must be understood and their place in government allotted, if not by actual legislation, then by general public realization of their significance."[174] In 1929, representatives from over 500 national organizations came to Washington, D.C., "to watch legislation and speak for their membership."[175] These organizations were "as much a part of the actual government of the country as were other, now well-established units that have arisen outside of the formal legal framework of law and constitution."[176] Their purpose was to guard the interests of their respective groups.[177] These organizations typically employed two strategies when lobbying the federal government: "If they [were] not working to get something for themselves they [were] busily struggling to prevent an enemy organization from obtaining legislative favors."[178]

Interest group formation experienced a "veritable explosion" in the 1960s and 1970s.[179] Citizen groups that were organized around an idea or cause (sometimes called single-issue groups) saw significant growth during this period as well. Half of all citizen groups were formed after 1960.[180] By 1963, a survey of Americans showed that 57 percent "reported that they held membership in a voluntary association."[181] Although it is impossible to document the exact number of interest groups operating in America at any one time, in 1980 the *Encyclopedia of Associations* identified over 14,000 national nonprofit organizations.[182] While not all of these organizations could be labeled narrowly self-interested, there is no doubt that many were. Every labor union could be said to be seeking to promote the economic interests of its members, regardless of the impact of such actions on the interests of the nation as a whole. Moreover, most of us would likely find nothing immoral or corrupt in workers joining together to promote their personal economic interests through the political process. Indeed, there is little doubt that the First Amendment right of association, as shaped by Supreme Court decisions, would protect their right to do so.[183] Yet Teachout characterizes such political activity as corrupt and unconstitutional. It is difficult to take seriously a political and constitutional theory so inconsistent with the nation's accepted practices and normative perceptions.

No one could today reasonably doubt that interest groups remain a vital part of the American political scene. The American people are aware that they have a right to seek to influence the political process to advance their self-interest, whether it is through membership in the National Rifle Association or the National Organization for Women. Modern citizens would therefore no doubt be shocked to learn from Professor Teachout that the Constitution condemns their activities as inherently corrupt and would prevent them from taking action to protect and further their own interests. The modern citizen's involvement in the political landscape is highlighted by the number of organizations that continue to thrive. Today, a search for national organizations in the *Encyclopedia of Associations* generates 24,750 results.[184] A similar search for regional, state, and local organizations generates 103,334 results.[185] Yet the anticorruption principle, if accepted, would immediately call into question the constitutionality of many of the associations operating in the United States today.

THE ANTICORRUPTION PRINCIPLE AND AMERICAN DEMOCRATIC THEORY

The anticorruption principle, in its rejection of self-interest as a legitimate basis for political action, is irreconcilable with the foundations of liberal democratic theory and the American democratic tradition. Majority rule, electoral representation, and the concept of one-citizen/one-vote are central to American democracy.[186] As argued throughout this book, inherent in this formulation of American democracy is the assumption that citizens' interests may constantly be in conflict, leading to recognition of the centrality of the version of democratic theory called adversary democracy.[187] The anticorruption principle threatens the heart of America's adversarially based democratic system, which (short of quid pro quo bribery, of course) ensures a citizen's right to attempt to influence the political process to advance in her own best interest.

There are two ways individuals may seek, thorough exercise of their expressive or associational rights, to achieve their political goals: (1) by convincing those in power to take action on their behalf or (2) by attempting to elect candidates who share their political positions. Teachout's anticorruption principle severely impairs both opportunities whenever individuals seeks to advance their personal interests in either manner. To understand why the anticorruption principle is incompatible with adversary democracy, it is important to recall what this version of democratic theory encompasses. As explained in earlier chapters, adversary democracy recognizes that in any self-governing society people's interests will inevitably conflict.[188] Adversary democracy contemplates the existence of citizens' conflicting interests.[189] This is not to say, however, that all citizens must be able to exert equal power or influence. Rather, the equal protection of interests is accomplished through the equal distribution of power to representatives.[190] Citizens pursue their own interests by voting and lobbying their representatives "in proportion to the intensity of their feelings."

Adversary democracy "recognizes democracy as a system of collective self-government that manages conflict."[191] The conflict that exists in a system of collective self-government is the inescapable result of the inevitably competing interests and ideologies that motivate individuals.[192] It follows, therefore, that a large, heterogeneous society will rarely, if ever, share a singular vision of a substantive "public interest."[193] In fact, acceptance of the contention that a monolithic public interest exists apart from the interests of the individual citizens could enable the more powerful to mislead the less powerful into collaborating in ways that primarily benefit the former.[194]

Long before Professor Mansbridge coined the term *adversary democracy*, our democratic system recognized as a central tenet of political life the individual's ability to promote her self-interest as she determines it.

Liberal theory "holds that individuals establish political authority and engage in political activities to pursue their individually-defined purposes."[195] Hence, an individual's purpose may not be defined by a collective authority. To be sure, in most situations the individual must ultimately abide by the choices of the majority, or at least of its elected representatives. But American democracy is historically based on the expectation that the individual will be able to influence choices in ways that benefit him, as evidenced (in Gordon Woods's words) by the "total grounding of [American] government in self-interest."[196] As framed by Professor Teachout, the anticorruption principle would restrict any government-related activity motivated by the desire to promote individual self-interest at the expense of the common good—whatever that means, and whoever gets to define it. Citizens would be allowed to interact with the government only when motivated by an interest in advancement of the public interest. Her theory thus clashes with the premises of adversary democracy, which are dictated by the premise of liberal democracy and which have dominated the nation since its founding.

It would of course be naïve to suggest that adversary democracy is free of problems. Some no doubt believe that, at least in certain instances, promotion of one's own interest at the expense of, or at least without regard to, the interests of others is morally reprehensible.[197] But it is important to understand that there is nothing in the concept of adversary democracy that inherently precludes the individual from choosing to act on the bases of altruism, ideology, or abstract moral principle, rather than purely on the basis of narrow self-interest. The point of adversary democracy is simply that this moral choice must rest ultimately with the individual citizen, rather than be imposed by some externally derived moral force.

It is important to recognize how much we take for granted the moral legitimacy of self-interest promotion. Medicare recipients urging their representatives to increase their benefits despite the resulting increase in the nation's budget deficit is, after all, an example of self-promotion and therefore of adversary democracy. Yet many of those who attack self-interest in politics would likely consider such promotion not only acceptable but even desirable. At the very least, presumably no one would seriously suggest that such self-promotional efforts are not fully protected by the First Amendment right of free expression, despite their inescapable grounding in self-interest. Once one accepts that self-promotional group politics, as a matter of American political theory and practice, is both normatively legitimate and historically well established, one must logically accept the centrality of adversary democracy to American politics. And once one reaches that conclusion, one must reject any commitment to the mutually inconsistent anticorruption principle.

This is not to say, of course, that special interest group politics is immune to abuse. In *Federalist No. 10* Madison warned of the serious threat of factions to democratic rule. But as previously shown, rather than try to eliminate special interest groups altogether, Madison sought to establish prophylactic structural devices designed to prevent and control the potential for such abuse. The American experience leading up to the Constitution's creation, according to Gordon Wood, demonstrated that "no republic could be made small enough to contain a homogenous interest that the people could express through the voice of the majority."[198] In light of this, Madison recognized that a large republic was necessary so that no one special interest group would dominate. Madison believed that an "extended sphere of government" would encourage the creation of additional factions so that, in the end, the various special interests would balance each other out.[199] He sought to structure a government in which "no one common interest or passion will be likely to unite a majority of the whole number in an unjust pursuit."[200]

Under Professor Teachout's anticorruption principle, "civic virtue" is assumed to be the sole legitimate motivating force underlying the political choices of all "officeholders," a concept that encompasses both elected officials and private citizens.[201] But while the Framers included in the Constitution prohibitions against actions that a legislator might be tempted to undertake in furtherance of his own self-interest at the expense of his constituents, they never banned government decisions designed to benefit specific groups of constituents. And they most certainly did nothing to prevent private citizens from seeking to influence the political process in pursuit of their personal or economic interests.

THE ANTICORRUPTION PRINCIPLE'S OMINOUS IMPLICATIONS FOR THE FIRST AMENDMENT RIGHT OF FREE EXPRESSION

Above and beyond the concept's numerous theoretical and historical problems, the most serious concern to which the anticorruption principle gives rise is its extremely harmful impact on the First Amendment right of free expression. This is so as a matter of both First Amendment theory and doctrine. On a theoretical level, the anticorruption principle conflicts with the foundational premise of a system of free expression: commitment to the precept of epistemological humility. A concept of free expression confined *ex ante* by an externally derived normative dictate is effectively no right at all. As the Supreme Court has long recognized, the right to speak cannot be confined to expression of only one predetermined viewpoint.[202] Yet the anticorruption principle seeks to shape American governmental structure and the right of free expression to implement a commitment to only one normative political theoretical model—namely, a preference for pursuit of the common good, rather than the exclusive promotion of individual interest.

On a less abstract level, advocates of the anticorruption principle appear oblivious to the dramatically harmful impact that acceptance of the principle would have on free speech. For one thing, the necessary logical implications of a commitment to the anticorruption principle would be that political activities motivated by concern for the common good would receive First Amendment protection, while those motivated by pure self-interest would not. It is difficult to imagine a more invidious, viewpoint-selective gradation of First Amendment rights. Yet if that is not deemed the logical implication of the anticorruption principle, then the anticorruption principle would seem to serve no purpose at all.

In addition to ignoring its inherent viewpoint-based impact, anticorruption principle advocates completely ignore the simple fact that political communication costs money, and therefore a restriction on the use of money in political campaigns inevitably restricts the availability of information and opinion to the electorate. And there is no way to know, *ex ante*, that all or even most of that information and opinion will be worthless—if, indeed, a definitive definition of that term even exists. As the Supreme Court has recognized, the First Amendment assures that it is the individual, not the government, who determines a communication's worth. Thus, purportedly in an effort to abolish a form of corruption that our system has never sought to suppress, anticorruption principle advocates would substantially undermine something that has long been central to the American political tradition: free and open debate in the course of a political campaign.

Professor Teachout argues that the First Amendment should not "breathe[]" at the expense of political integrity."[203] However, it is by no means clear what her concept of "political integrity" is designed to include. The vagueness inherent in that phrase potentially allows for the suppression of virtually *any* political speech, as long as the speech is deemed to have occurred "at the expense of political integrity."[204] Teachout argues that political integrity is threatened by "the perception of people that they do not have the character or capacity to control the federal government."[205] But would this mean that First Amendment protection would turn on some sort of empirical assessment of voter attitudes, with the level of protection changing as the results of the surveys change? What if different surveys gave rise to conflicting results? And even if those were the public's perceptions, how could anyone know what specific acts or events had led to their existence? Would it matter whether those perceptions had any basis in reality? Or is the concern about public perception in reality nothing more than a rhetorical flourish, designed simply to justify sweeping suppression of free and open political communication? Either way, subjective voter preference is a dangerous basis on which to justify the suppression of valuable political expression. Presumably by the same questionable reasoning, suppression of the speech of Communists in the 1950s could have been justified on the bases of surveys showing that voters considered them a threat to American democracy. Surely, widespread restrictions on political speech cannot be grounded in so subjective and volatile a showing. The same is true, however, of the presumably well-meaning but sorely misguided advocates of the anticorruption principle.

Implicit in Teachout's argument is the notion that political speech may be suppressed when it results in anything that falls within Teachout's preposterously broad definition of *corruption*. Recall that, according to Teachout, there are four situations, in addition to criminal bribery, in which corruption arises: inequality, drowned voices, dispirited public, and loss of integrity.[206] The anticorruption principle would provide the constitutional basis for the elimination of potentially valuable political expression in all of these situations. Teachout appears to be totally oblivious to the serious costs that will be incurred if the anticorruption principle is used to remedy her wholly subjective versions of corruption. If the Court were to take such an approach, modern free speech protections would be seriously eroded—if not virtually destroyed—in the political process.

The statute invalidated in the Court's decision in *Citizens United* illustrates one danger of permitting anticorruption interests to trump First Amendment protections. In *Citizens United*, a nonprofit organization challenged the Bipartisan Campaign Reform Act of 2002 (BCRA)[207] on First Amendment grounds.[208] During the 2008 presidential primary season, the nonprofit corporation Citizens United released a film about then-

Senator Hillary Clinton, who was vying for the Democratic presidential nomination.[209] Citizens United received most of its funding from individual donors, but it also received a small amount of funding from for-profit corporations.[210] In light of this fear, Citizens United sought declaratory and injunctive relief against the Federal Election Commission, arguing that the BCRA prohibition was unconstitutional as applied to the film.[211]

The Court, in holding the BCRA's restrictions on corporate expenditures unconstitutional,[212] recognized the inherent problem with any law that restricted speech solely based on who the speaker was—in this case, a nonprofit organization that received some funding from for-profit corporations.[213] "Speech," the Court observed, "is an essential mechanism of democracy, for it is the means to hold officials accountable to the people."[214] The Court noted that "the right of citizens to inquire, to hear, to speak, and to use information to reach consensus is a precondition to enlightened self-government and a necessary means to protect it. The First Amendment 'has its fullest and most urgent application to speech uttered during a campaign for political office.'"[215] By restricting people's motivations when they engage in political discourse, the anticorruption principle threatens the "fullest and most urgent application" of the First Amendment—the protection political speech. The Court concluded that "political speech must prevail against laws that would suppress it, whether by design or inadvertence."[216]

It is important to understand that, if accepted, Teachout's principle would authorize suppression of speech well beyond the context of corporate political speech. The anticorruption principle would uphold laws that sweepingly suppress political speech. Presumably, under the anticorruption principle, a law need only purport to suppress political speech motivated by self-interest to survive a First Amendment challenge. As a result, citizens would be denied the information and opinion that may well prove essential to making their political choices. Logically many national associations whose purpose is to advocate on behalf of their members could constitutionally be prohibited from doing so in the political arena because, by their very nature, they are committed to the advancement of their membership's narrow self-interest. It is impossible to believe that the Constitution was designed to tolerate such devastating suppression.

Teachout seeks to rationalize the need for the anticorruption principle in terms of the causes of corruption, primarily "unequal access to political life, and political power."[217] According to Teachout, "basic intuition" tells us that "there must be some kind of equality in political access."[218]

Political access here takes on a much larger connotation than simply the right to vote. For Teachout, political access includes all forms of politically related speech, including campaign contributions and campaign expenditures. The problem, as Teachout sees it, is that money in politics generally results in unequal access and unequal voice.[219] The more that speakers are able to communicate their message to a political actor, the more likely the political actor is to decide in a fashion favorable to the communicator. Campaign contributions, which allow people to communicate messages to candidates, "are likely to warp [political actors'] decisions."[220] A political actor whose decisions are "warped" because of campaign contributions is considered corrupt. The individuals (or organizations) making the contributions are also considered "corrupt" if their contributions are motivated by a personal interest in the candidate's election, rather than an interest in advancing the "public good." Therefore, limitations on campaign contributions are deemed necessary to create political equality and stave off corruption.

Other scholars have also rationalized the anticorruption principle on the basis of equality concerns. David Strauss, for example, has argued that "'corruption' in the system of campaign finance is a concern . . . principally because of inequality."[221] Strauss questions the validity of the Court's statement in *Buckley v. Valeo*[222] that government restriction of "the speech of some elements of our society in order to enhance the relative voice of others is wholly foreign to the First Amendment."[223] He views campaign contributions as tantamount to votes and thus deserving of the same equality-preserving measures.[224] The primary flaw in the reasoning of these highly respected scholars is their failure to recognize the dangers to free and open political debate that would inevitably result from a reduction of would-be speakers to the lowest common economic denominator. A second fallacy is their false equation of expression with the exercise of the vote. Unlike expression, the vote has automatic and immediate legal consequences—the election of government officials.[225] In any event, the argument proves too much because it would reduce every speaker's legal ability to speak to the lowest common denominator—a truly preposterous restriction. But whichever way one comes out on this important question, it surely does not advance debate by labeling the prospeech position "corruption," with all of that term's linguistic baggage and associations.

The anticorruption principle is also designed to restrict well-funded speech when its effect is to "drown out" the speech of less economically powerful speakers. But neither Teachout nor any other scholar or court has provided any evidence to support the proposition that well-funded speech drowns out other points of view, nor could they, because in all but the most extreme cases (the existence of which has never been documented) the "drowning out" concept makes no logical sense. Except in the case of a truly "limited pie" of expressive resources (for example, when one candidate purchases all available television and radio advertising space), the scope and amount of Candidate *A*'s expression have no impact on Candidate *B*'s ability to communicate her message. Even if Candidate *A*'s expression were to be cut in half, that would have absolutely no impact on Candidate *B*'s ability to communicate to the electorate. It would mean solely that that *the relative position* of Candidate *B* would have improved. Telling those with money that they cannot spend it on political campaigns does not provide money and means for those who have none. The net result of an equality-based approach to corruption, then, is an equality of ignorance. Society is deprived of the information those with economic power would have shared, but the resultant expressive void is left unfilled.

CONCLUSION

Professor Teachout's arguments in support of the anticorruption principle were apparently persuasive enough to convince Justice Stevens, who expressly relied on her scholarship in his dissent in *Citizens United*.[226] This is truly puzzling, because her version of the anticorruption principle has absolutely nothing to recommend it—at least as a matter of American constitutional theory, political theory, or history. It is unsupportable in its assertions that the Constitution directly imposes a sweeping prohibition on political corruption and that the constitutional restriction extends to the political activities of private citizens, as well as elected officials. To complicate matters, she defines "corruption"—generally associated by the common person with quid pro quo bribery—to include pretty much anything that is inconsistent with the positions of one particular ideological perspective. Moreover, her theory is completely inconsistent with the reasoning and constitutional strategy adopted by the Framers, as well as with the nation's long history of interest group politics.

In an ideal world, it would be wonderful for constitutional scholars to be able to ignore text, Framers' understandings, well-established history, foundational principles of democratic theory, accepted linguistic usage, and principled legal reasoning to implement wholesale their own ideological perspectives under the guise of constitutional analysis. Professor Teachout has sought to do just that, and others seem to share at least much of her perspective. Thankfully, the Supreme Court to date has refused to indulge Professor Teachout's ideologically driven approach. One can only hope that such a principled constitutional analysis continues to prevail.

CHAPTER SIX

Adversary Democracy, Political Fraud, and the Dilemma of Anonymity

THE RIGHT NOT TO SPEAK AS THE RIGHT OF EXPRESSION

It has long been accepted, both doctrinally and theoretically, that the constitutional right to speak subsumes within it the constitutional right *not* to speak.[1] A traditionally recognized subcategory of the constitutional guarantee of silence is the right of anonymity—in other words, the right not to reveal one's identity when exercising one's affirmative right to express oneself.

In one important sense, of course, the right of anonymity qualitatively differs from the right not to speak. While the latter right could be construed to constitute a generic right to keep silent, the right of anonymity represents an expressive hybrid. It applies when and only when one first chooses to speak, write, or associate for political purposes. The right of anonymity, then, represents a *selective* form of expressive silence. Nor are the theoretical underpinnings of the right of anonymity identical to the rationale for a generic right to remain silent. While the right to remain silent is grounded primarily in the desire to avoid the individual's humiliation, demoralization, and cognitive dissonance that flows from being forced by the government to speak,[2] the right of anonymity is designed to avoid chilling the speaker's willingness to contribute fully and frankly to public discourse without fear of retaliation or retribution from either government or private power centers.

From one perspective, at least, it would be difficult to deny the beneficial impact on public debate that flows from the First Amendment right of anonymity. One need not be a trained psychologist to recognize that the speaker's ability to conceal her identity is likely to embolden her, resulting in an increase in contributions to public debate. It is therefore not surprising that anonymity has played an important role in American history[3] and has widely been recognized by the Supreme Court as a central element of First Amendment protection.[4]

Once one views the right of anonymity from the perspective of adversary democracy, its constitutionally protected status becomes far more complicated. Recall that the theory of anonymity, when applied in the First Amendment context, protects the right of individuals to advocate on behalf of their own personal, economic, or ideological agendas.[5] It recognizes that citizens who contribute to public debate are often something other than objective pursuers of the common good. Rather, on many occasions they selectively slant their expression to emphasize points that help their position and ignore or gloss over others that might hurt their position. Although this recognition accurately reflects the reality of the American political process and beneficially assures preservation of core precepts of individualism,[6] it also gives rise to the legitimate concern that, absent proper speaker identification, recipients of the expression conveyed by advocates on behalf of a particular position might be unable to recognize the speaker's personal agenda and therefore fail to judge the expression with an appropriate level of skepticism. The problem with the unbending protection of anonymity, then, is that while it may well avoid the chilling of speakers, it simultaneously denies information that might be of significant value to the recipients of that expression in judging the merits of the speakers' arguments. In this way the First Amendment right of anonymity risks distorting and undermining listener choices that have been influenced by anonymous advocacy. When applied in the political realm, a right of anonymous advocacy threatens to distort the electorate's democratic decision making by improperly influencing voter choices.

It is true that the Supreme Court has wisely recognized a First Amendment right not to speak, even though forced speech could conceivably provide valuable information to readers, viewers, or listeners. But anonymity gives rise to far more complex problems than does pure compelled speech because, unlike silence, by its very nature anonymity always accompanies an affirmative act of expression. When one chooses to remain *completely* silent, one is of course not misleading a reader or listener. In contrast, the danger of a right to anonymity applied to political expression centers around the risk of what amounts to political fraud: deception-induced political choices and behavior. This does not refer to the *commercial* fraud that, all agree, is uniformly unprotected by the First Amendment.[7] It refers, rather, to the conscious effort to deceive or mislead the public solely for political or ideological purposes. It is surely not uncommon for those who contribute to public discourse to distort or even fabricate information or opinion to induce the populace to undertake specific political acts (for example, voting for or against a particular candidate) or inducing the public to attempt to persuade government officials to take certain action. It is true, of course, that in many instances it will be impossible to separate goals of *political* gain from those of *financial* gain. Speakers often seek to manipulate the political process for purposes of their own financial interests.[8] But, in the case of political fraud, the connection to a speaker's financial gain is indirect; the immediate goal of the speaker is not to induce listeners to give him money, but rather to induce listeners to take specified political action that will ultimately benefit him. Under these circumstances, whether the speaker's ultimate motivation for seeking to induce listener action is ultimately economic or not is irrelevant. The potential for speaker anonymity to lead to political fraud has taken on even greater importance with the growth of the Internet in recent years. It is now possible to quickly reach enormous numbers of people with total and easily maintained anonymity, thereby enabling communicators to misrepresent themselves and their interests and, as a result, mislead recipients.

As harmful as political fraud may be to the functioning of the democratic system, it is by no means certain that in all cases such expression falls outside the scope of First Amendment protection. To be sure, in the line of cases growing out of *New York Times Co. v. Sullivan*,[9] the Supreme Court made clear that consciously false defamatory statements of public officials or public figures are, in fact, unprotected.[10] However, the Court recently held in the *United States v. Alvarez* that speech is not automatically excluded from the First Amendment's scope *merely* because it is false. Rather, it is only false speech *that gives rise to harm* that can be constitutionally punished.[11] While this decision clearly excludes traditional *commercial* fraud from the First Amendment's protection, it leaves open the question of whether *political* fraud (that is, alteration of listeners' political choices on the basis of intentional falsehoods) falls outside the scope of the First Amendment, because it leaves open whether such activity gives rise to what the court would characterize as "harm."[12]

The resolution of the dilemma of how to deal with political fraud is by no means easy or obvious. As an abstract matter, one could reasonably want to deter or punish such knowingly false statements. But vesting in government a freewheeling power to punish even intentionally deceptive statements beyond the narrow context of defamation could lead to serious erosion of First Amendment guarantees by stifling or deterring risk-averse speakers and inviting abuse of such far-reaching governmental power. This could happen in one of two ways. First, it would be relatively easy for government to abuse this power by stifling political opponents or suppressing unpopular expression under the guise of ferreting out, punishing, or deterring political fraud. Second, the First Amendment problem would become considerably greater were we to expand the category of unprotected speech to include not only consciously *false* statements but also those that are technically true but deemed to be intentionally *misleading*. Political advocates invariably provide only one side of a debate; it is all but inevitable and expected that they will omit data, evidence, or arguments that might undermine their position. One could arguably classify such truncated arguments, at least in a certain sense, as intentionally misleading. Yet it is virtually inconceivable that we could exclude such advocacy from the First Amendment's protection without seriously threatening the uninhibited nature of political debate.

The First Amendment dilemma in protecting false or misleading political speech arises because a refusal to protect such expression could seriously undermine the viability of the system of public communication, but protection of such expression could simultaneously threaten important First Amendment values. One possible resolution of the dilemma to which political fraud gives rise is to leave nondefamatory false or misleading political speech protected but simultaneously to revoke the constitutional protection of anonymity. In this way, government would be able to assure that readers or listeners are provided with information about the speaker's identity so that they can more effectively judge the merits of his speech. The theory underlying this compromise solution to the political fraud dilemma is that listener skepticism can serve as an effective antidote to deceptive political speech without risking the serious harm to First Amendment interests that would flow from total suppression. If recipients of expression know who the speaker is, in today's world of technology it will usually not be very difficult for them to discover any hidden political or economic agendas the speaker may have. Of course, it would be unrealistic to expect most listeners to take the time and effort to Google an individual speaker, but we can rest assured that at least a few will, especially those with competing interests. Those individuals will likely also have the incentive to publicize the connections, interests, and biases of the speaker. In this manner, recipients of speech will be better able to judge the persuasiveness of the speaker's arguments and information.

It is a reality of communication that who the speaker is will, in many instances, appropriately affect a listener's perception of and judgment about the expression. For example, the Supreme Court has upheld required revelation of the names and amounts of contributors to political campaigns, in most situations.[13] The Court found that the interest in avoiding political corruption justified whatever deterrent impact might result on campaign contributions (though it is true that the Court's recognition of such contributions as protected speech is somewhat limited).[14] It is also true, however, that knowing who has contributed to a candidate may tell the voters a great deal about the candidate.

It is thus appropriate to conclude that important competing First Amendment interests are implicated by the decision as to whether to protect speaker anonymity.[15] The question must therefore be asked, when the dust settles, whether the interests of free expression are more harmed than helped by an unwavering guarantee of a speaker's right to anonymity. The answer to that question, in light of the risks and rewards inherent in our nation's form of adversary democracy, is likely that the Supreme Court needs to recognize at least some limits on the First Amendment right of anonymity.

In resolving this First Amendment uncertainty, one may benefit by analogizing the situation to the adversary system, which has long served as the cornerstone of the Anglo-American judicial process. In litigation, both judge and jury are fully aware of the preexisting interests possessed by both the attorneys and witnesses. Of course, that the communicator is biased in the litigation context does not necessarily imply that what she says will be of no value to the adjudicator. However, if the judge and jury were not made aware of those preexisting interests and biases, they would likely fail to bring an appropriate degree of skepticism to their judgment of the communication's value. The recipient of the communication, in other words, is in a far better position to judge the value of the expression by knowing who the speaker is because that knowledge enables the recipient to place the expression in proper perspective. Though a First Amendment metaphor to our judicial system is by no means perfect, roughly the same beneficial dynamic could operate in public discourse were speakers required to reveal their identity.

It would be incorrect to assume that no harm to expressive values would result from the loss of speaker anonymity. However, it is important to understand that the harm need not be as severe as might first be thought. Initially, First Amendment anonymity can appropriately be subdivided into two categories: expressive anonymity and associational anonymity. The former includes direct expressive contributions, while the latter includes private associational choices that an individual makes. Although some of the important decisions concerning anonymity have concerned the expressive variety,[16] the large majority have involved associational anonymity. In the 1960s, for example, the Supreme Court decided a series of cases in which southern states sought the names of members of civil rights organizations in their state. The Court held that such efforts violate the First Amendment, on the grounds that they contravened the right of First Amendment anonymity possessed by the organization's members.[17] The specter of a governmental authority to ferret out the names of members of unpopular political associations should be frightening to anyone who values democracy and liberty, and the Court was clearly correct in blocking such efforts. It must be emphasized, however, that were the Court to revoke constitutional protection for anonymity in an effort to dilute the problems of political fraud, it would need only do so in the purely expressive context. One who wishes to privately join a political association could do so, without fear of governmental publicity or retribution.

More importantly, the greatest protection against ideologically grounded abuse of this new governmental power would be the First Amendment's prohibition on underinclusive viewpoint-based selectivity. Absent demonstration of some nonideologically grounded compelling interest, government would be allowed by the First Amendment to require either *all* expression to reveal the speaker's identity or none. Absent a showing of some viewpoint-neutral compelling interest, those in power would not be allowed selectively to designate only specified expression for the loss of speaker anonymity.

One must nevertheless concede the threat to robust public debate that could flow from a loss of speaker anonymity. However, if, for that reason, we were forced to seek some sort of further compromise between the two competing First Amendment concerns, we could possibly confine the loss of First Amendment anonymity rights to those situations in which speakers not only fail to reveal their true identity but actually adopt a false identity that is determined to affirmatively mislead the listener as to the speaker's interest in and relationship to the arguments made. The rationale for this more limited restriction on the anonymity right is that when a speaker claims total anonymity, the recipient of the expression is placed on notice to consider the information and arguments with a certain degree of caution, for the simple reason that the speaker chose not to identify herself. In contrast, when a speaker falsely identifies herself, the fraudulent nature of the expression has been compounded, doubly deceiving its recipient and further distorting its influence on the democratic process.

Whichever version of the limit on anonymity one chooses, the goal of this chapter is to raise awareness about this troubling dilemma of First Amendment theory. That is something that to this point—surprisingly— appears not to have been attempted by anyone. The first section of this chapter lays the theoretical groundwork for the analysis and proposals that will follow, by comparing and contrasting the speaker- and listener- focused theories of free expression.[18] The section that follows explores the elements and arguments in support of the doctrine of First Amendment anonymity, in both its expressive and associational varieties.[19] The third section explains the First Amendment dilemma of political fraud,[20] while the final section examines the intersection of the two categories of free speech doctrine. It proposes limitation of the anonymity right as the best available resolution of the political fraud dilemma.[21]

THE RIGHT NOT TO SPEAK, THE RIGHT OF ANONYMITY, AND THE THEORY OF FREE EXPRESSION

The Right Not to Speak and the Values of Free Expression

Before one can fully understand the First Amendment implications of the right of anonymity, it is first necessary to understand the expressive grounding of the right not to speak at all. To be sure, a right of anonymity and a right not to speak are by no means identical. But in an important sense anonymity functions as a subcategory of a right not to speak: The choice not to reveal one's name is a narrower exercise of a broader right to choose not to speak at all because it represents the decision of the speaker to selectively limit his expression. Thus, determination of whether one chooses to place a First Amendment value on a speaker's ability to remain anonymous must begin with an exploration of the theoretical grounding of the broader First Amendment right not to speak.

Numerous tomes have been written about the theoretical founda- tions of the guarantee of free expression. It is noteworthy, however, that relatively little of that theoretical inquiry has focused on the basis for an individual's right to choose not to express himself. In prior writing, I provided my own views on that issue. I argued that "compelled speech undermines the interests fostered by protection of free expression by giving rise to four distinct but related harms: confusion, dilution, humiliation, and cognitive dissonance."[22] By "confusion," I meant the risk of "confusing the populace as to the actual strength and popularity of substantive positions advocated by the government."[23] Were private individuals to parrot the positions of those in power despite their actual opposition to those positions, the populace could easily be misled as to the popularity of those positions. By "dilution" I meant the risk of "diluting the force of the speaker's persuasiveness in the eyes of the listeners"[24] because the force of a speaker's voluntary expression of a contrary viewpoint would be undermined by the speaker's parroting of government's positions. The risk of humiliation referred to the risk of "publicly humiliating the speaker [by forcing him to utter words with which he disagrees], thereby possibly demoralizing him and undermining his resolve to maintain his own positions . . . ."[25] Finally, "cognitive dissonance" referred to "a psychological process whereby an individual who has been forced to express a view contrary to her own eventually rationalizes her actions by subconsciously adopting the positions she has been forced to express."[26] All of these harms, I argued, explained the Supreme Court's long-established doctrine that forced expression contravenes the First Amendment.[27]

Not all theories of free expression provide unambiguous support for a categorical right not to speak. As explained more fully in an earlier chapter,[28] Alexander Meiklejohn viewed the First Amendment guarantee of free expression exclusively as a means of benefiting the listener. He saw the value of free speech to be the manner in which it facilitates the democratic process. His theory started with the premise that "governments . . . derive their just powers from the consent of the governed. If that consent be lacking, governments have no just powers."[29] He considered government officials in a democracy to be merely agents of the true governors—the electorate. Because the electorate exercises its governing function in the voting booth, it is necessary to guarantee free and open debate so that the citizens can benefit from all possible information and opinion in making their governing decisions.[30] However, the individual speaker's interest in communicating mattered not at all in Meiklejohn's philosophy. The function served by the speaker, instead, was solely as a communicator of information and opinion to the citizen, thereby facilitating the citizen's performance of the function of self-government.[31]

By no means have all free speech scholars concurred in Meiklejohn's view concerning the irrelevance of the speaker's interest. Indeed, there are respected scholars who place relatively little, if any, value on the listener's receipt of the expression, at least to the extent it is divorced from the speaker's right to communicate.[32] Nevertheless, if one were to follow Meiklejohn's reasoning to its logical conclusions, one might well choose to provide at best limited constitutional protection to the right not to speak. In those instances in which forced expression could reasonably be expected to benefit the listener's self-governing decision making (for example, where the speaker is required to reveal valuable information), not only would such speech appear not to violate the First Amendment, but under Meiklejohn's theory it would actually seem to further its listener-based values.

The Supreme Court appeared to echo Professor Meiklejohn when, in *Red Lion Broadcasting Co. v. FCC*,[33] it upheld against First Amendment attack the Federal Communications Commission's "fairness doctrine," which (prior to its subsequent repeal) "imposed on radio and television broadcasters the requirement that discussion of public issues be presented on broadcast stations, and that each side of those issues must be given fair coverage."[34] Justice White, speaking for the Court, found the doctrine to be consistent "with the First Amendment goal of producing an informed public capable of conducting its own affairs."[35] "It is," he wrote, "the right of the viewers and listeners, not the right of the broadcasters, which is paramount."[36] Yet mystifyingly, a few years later in *Miami Herald Publishing Co. v. Tornillo*[37] the Court declined to uphold a seemingly parallel legislatively imposed right of access to the print media, without ever attempting to distinguish *Red Lion*, thereby leaving the listener-focused version of First Amendment theory in a rather unsettled state.

It is important to note that, although both forms of compulsion are appropriately deemed unconstitutional, the First Amendment interests are by no means all one-sided in either the compelled speech or right-of-access contexts. Government's inability to require speech or to require private communicators to establish a private right of expressive access threatens to reduce the amount of information available to the populace and thereby undermine the democratic facilitation function that a listener-focused First Amendment theory seeks to achieve. But, when competing First Amendment interests are implicated, some "tragic choices" will have to be made.[38] On balance, it seems clear that the expressive harms of both compelled speech and a governmentally imposed obligation on unwilling private communicators to provide expressive access to other private speakers far outweigh what are concededly concrete competing expressive benefits. Whether the First Amendment calculus should reach the same conclusion when a right of speaker anonymity is at stake, however, is by no means clear. It is to that issue that the chapter now turns.

The Right of Speaker Anonymity as a Subcategory of the Right Not to Speak

Though they are not identical, the right against compelled speech possesses the same constitutional DNA as the right of anonymity. Much as it has protected the right against compelled speech, the Supreme Court has generally protected a speaker's right to keep his identity private. For example, in *Talley v. California*[39] the Court held unconstitutional a city ordinance prohibiting distribution of any handbill that did not have printed on it the name of the individual who prepared, distributed, or sponsored it. The Court reasoned that compelled speaker identification unduly chilled speakers. The Court's opinion pointed to numerous historical incidents of anonymous protests and calls for political action. In support of the ordinance's constitutionality, the city argued that the identification requirement was necessary to reveal those responsible for fraud, false advertising, and libel.[40] The Court rejected this argument, however, noting that the ordinance was not confined to such situations, so it need not consider the constitutionality of an ordinance so limited.[41]

In its subsequent decision in *McIntyre v. Ohio Election Commission*,[42] the Court held unconstitutional an Ohio statute that prohibited the distribution of any material "designed to influence the voters in any election . . . unless there appears in a conspicuous place the name and business address of the person who is responsible therefor." Writing for the majority, Justice Stevens stated: "'Anonymous pamphlets, leaflets, brochures and even books have played an important role in the progress of mankind.' Great works of literature have frequently been produced by authors writing under assumed names."[43]

There is certainly nothing inherently unreasonable in the Court's thinking. As a historical matter, we need only recall the *Federalist Papers*, where Hamilton, Madison, and Jay assumed obvious aliases, to recognize that anonymity has played an important role in assuring the robust and wide-open nature of our expressive framework. This history is not surprising because it is not difficult to predict that forced speaker identification would have a chilling effect on speakers who seek to contribute unpopular ideas to the expressive marketplace, for fear of private shunning or governmental retribution. But it would be a mistake to collapse the different categories of constitutional inquiries. In certain ways the First Amendment argument for anonymity is even stronger than the rationale for a right not to speak. When a private individual chooses not to speak, the First Amendment interests of the citizens in expanding their store of information are not advanced.[44] Under these circumstances, the populace is deprived of whatever benefit it might have received had the individual chosen (or even been forced) to communicate. In these instances, the Court has concluded that the First Amendment interest in allowing speaker expressive autonomy overrides the competing listener-centric First Amendment interest in providing the populace with information and opinion. Anonymity, in contrast, is inextricably linked to the affirmative exercise of a speaker's right to express herself. Indeed, a distinctive concept of anonymity is incoherent in the context of total silence; in such a situation, anonymity is simply subsumed by individuals' broader choice not to express themselves. Anonymity is valuable, then, when and only when speakers have initially chosen to express themselves, for it is only then that the issue of speaker identity even comes into question.

If it is true, as the Supreme Court has suggested, that a prohibition on anonymity almost inevitably chills unpopular or controversial expression, then a choice against allowing anonymity—unlike the choice not to permit silence under certain circumstances—may well reduce the sum total of information and opinion contributed to public debate. Recognition of a constitutional right to remain totally silent represents a speaker-centric First Amendment approach that, in certain circumstances,[45] may well undermine the values sought to be fostered by listener-centric First Amendment theory. In contrast, from one perspective at least, rejection of a right of anonymity arguably undermines *both* speaker-centric *and* listener-centric models of free expression. Viewed in this manner, the constitutional interest in protecting anonymity appears to be even more powerful than the constitutional interest underlying the well-established right not to speak at all. When a private individual or entity successfully resists coerced expression, that individual or entity may well choose to remain completely silent. For reasons already explained, however, that is not so in the case of speaker anonymity. In cases where a speaker seeks anonymity, the speaker is necessarily seeking to communicate, albeit anonymously.

Distinguishing the Expressive and Associational
Subcategories of Anonymity

The Supreme Court has construed the First Amendment right of anonymity to apply beyond the directly expressive context. In addition, it has recognized anonymity interests also when the right of expressive association is involved. The First Amendment right of association, it should be noted, finds no express grounding in the provision's text. By its terms, the First Amendment protects the rights of speech, press, and assembly, not a right to associate. But the Court has quite reasonably inferred a constitutionally protected right to associate from a synthesis of the rights of speech, press and assembly. In *NAACP v. Alabama ex rel. Patterson*, the Court reasoned that "effective advocacy of both public and private points of view, particularly controversial ones, is undeniably enhanced by group association."[46] In that case, the state attorney general had issued a subpoena demanding that the organization disclose the names of its Alabama members. The NAACP, the Court stated, "has made an uncontroverted showing that on past occasions revelation of the identity of its rank-and-file members has exposed those members to economic reprisal, loss of employment, threat of physical coercion, and other manifestations of public hostility. Under these circumstances we think it apparent that compelled disclosure of petitioner's Alabama membership is likely to affect adversely the ability of petitioner and its members to pursue their collective effort to foster beliefs which they admittedly have the right to advocate."[47]

Though both are rightly deemed protected by the First Amendment, in certain senses political association appears to be appropriately distinguishable from direct expression. While the latter involves a direct communication between speaker and listener, the former involves at most an indirect form of communication. As a general matter, association is a more private activity than is direct expression. It is true, of course, that often associational activity will function as a precursor to or facilitator of direct expression. It is in this sense that association can be seen as ancillary to and facilitative of the right of expression. However, the First Amendment associational right will apply just as much to settings in which no direct expression will result. In the case of association, the private individual joins with others in organizations that may or may not engage in widespread public communication. Yet the First Amendment right will apply as much in these contexts as when the association is unambiguously designed to give rise to contributions to public debate. For example, the First Amendment right of expressive association presumably applies to a private political organization in which the members distribute no leaflets and take out no advertisements but instead do nothing more than meet in private settings so that the members can exchange their private views on issues of the day. The First Amendment right is deemed applicable in such settings because individuals are furthering all of the values served by the expressive guarantee by communicating their views to others and learning of the views of others.[48]

Although conceptual distinctions between exercises of the rights of association and expression may exist, the rationale for guaranteeing the right of anonymity appears to be identical in both contexts. Whether the individual who is exercising his First Amendment right is doing so directly and publicly through expression or indirectly and privately through association, the reason for guaranteeing a right of anonymity is the same: A general awareness that the speaker holds unpopular views could easily lead to public shunning, governmental coercion, or other negative consequences. Loss of anonymity could therefore readily lead to the chilling or punishing of the exercise of either expressive or associational rights. However, when one includes as part of the constitutional calculus the negative consequences for First Amendment interests caused by protection of speaker anonymity, it may be necessary to draw a distinction between the levels of constitutional protection given to expressive and associational anonymity.[49]

Before one can understand the basis for this suggested distinction, one must first understand the constitutional dark side of the right of anonymity. To comprehend the First Amendment difficulties caused by the constitutional guarantee of anonymity, one must also understand a competing First Amendment concern: the harms to the healthy functioning of the democratic process caused by political fraud, defined as consciously false and deceptive contributions to public debate that are potentially as toxic to democratic decision making as subprime mortgages proved to be to banks. Once the significant First Amendment harms caused by political fraud are fully understood, we will then be in a position also to understand how constitutional protection of anonymity dangerously facilitates the perpetuation of that fraud.

THE FIRST AMENDMENT AND THE DILEMMA
OF POLITICAL FRAUD

Conscious Falsity and the First Amendment

In narrowly defined circumstances, falsity can conceivably advance First Amendment values, as when an author writes fiction or when two people exchange fantasies. However, when falsity is portrayed as truth, the expression's furtherance of the interests sought to be fostered by the First Amendment is questionable. Indeed, one could reasonably suggest that it actually undermines free speech values.[50] Despite this fact, the Supreme Court has chosen under certain circumstances to extend full First Amendment protection to unambiguously false statements. In the line of cases beginning with *New York Times Co. v. Sullivan*,[51] the Court held that much false and defamatory speech is to receive full First Amendment protection when it concerns public officials or public figures, reasoning "that erroneous statement is inevitable in free debate, and that it must be protected if the freedoms of expression are to have the 'breathing space' that they 'need to survive'"[52] The Court's concern, in other words, was that risk-averse speakers might well wish to make statements they believe to be true but would be deterred from doing so for fear that those statements might ultimately be found to be false—and therefore legally actionable—by a jury years later. It is therefore necessary, the Court reasoned, to protect a category of even false statements that cause harm, to avoid the chilling effect on true expression that would likely result from the opposite decision.[53]

While several justices disagreed,[54] the *New York Times* majority chose not to make the First Amendment protection of defamation of public officials absolute. Instead, it fashioned an exception for defamatory statements made with "actual malice," defined as statements made with knowledge that they are false or with reckless disregard for their truth or falsity.[55] Thus, while the First Amendment was construed to protect even false defamatory statements, it was not construed to protect *consciously* or *recklessly* false defamatory statements.[56]

If one were to ask *why* consciously false statements, represented by the speaker as truthful, should be categorically excised from the First Amendment's protective scope (a question, by the way, which the Court has never asked), two conceivable answers come to mind. First, it could be argued that such statements are inherently devoid of value—in other words, they foster no conceivable interest sought to be advanced by First Amendment protection. Second, it could be argued that such statements are so likely to be harmful that they can be categorically excluded, *ex ante*. In what way is a consciously false statement harmful? In the specific context of the *New York Times* doctrine, the answer should be obvious: Consciously false defamatory comments unfairly and unjustly harm individuals' reputations without any corresponding benefit to society. When the statements are uttered without knowledge of falsity, the *New York Times* Court did see a benefit in protecting them, as a means of providing the "breathing space" necessary to assure robust and wide-open public debate. However, when the speaker actually knows that what she is saying is false, the *New York Times* majority reasoned, the concern about chilling truthful speech is rendered irrelevant.[57] Absent this concern, consciously false defamatory statements appear to serve no First Amendment value.

Until quite recently, the issue of whether the *New York Times* doctrine's categorical exclusion of consciously false speech from constitutional protection applies as well in areas of expressive regulation other than defamation had received little attention.[58] To be sure, it was well established that commercial fraud—usually defined as the "use of deceit, a trick or some dishonest means to deprive another of his/her/its money, property or a legal right"[59]—is categorically deemed to fall beyond the scope of First Amendment protection.[60] However, it is clear that this exception has been confined to the context of commercial speech; in any event it applies as much to false commercial claims made without knowledge of falsity as it is to those made with such knowledge.[61] In the *Alvarez* decision referenced earlier,[62] the Court rejected the notion that consciously false speech is categorically excluded from the First Amendment's reach. But the Court so held only in the context of false speech that had no recognizable harm.[63] But what about nondefamatory, consciously false statements made in the context of political debate? Unlike the law invalidated in *Alvarez*, fraudulent political debate may give rise to significantly harmful consequences. Hardly any court has even touched on the issue, much less resolved it.

The only appellate decision to deal extensively with the issue is *State ex rel. Public Disclosure Commission v. 119 Vote No! Committee*,[64] where the Washington State Supreme Court refused to find exception for conscious falsity recognized by the line of cases beginning with *New York Times* to apply beyond the narrow confines of the defamation context of the *New York Times* doctrine itself. The statute held unconstitutional by Washington's Supreme Court imposed punitive civil penalties for, among other things, sponsoring, "with actual malice," "political advertising that contains a false statement of material fact."[65] Concerned with the sweeping chill on political speech that might result from such a statute,[66] the court hesitated to find *all* conscious falsehoods beyond the First Amendment's scope. The statute's inclusion of the "actual malice" requirement was presumably designed to confine its reach to consciously or recklessly false statements, thereby satisfying the *New York Times* test and rendering the statute constitutional. But the court held that the defamation context differed significantly from the case of general political advocacy: "The State's reliance on the law of defamation is misplaced. By its nature defamation concerns statements made by one person against another and is designed to protect the property of an individual in his or her good name."[67] The state had defended the statute on the grounds that its restrictions fostered an informed public, but the court disagreed. The state's argument, the court noted, "presupposes the State possesses an independent right to determine truth and falsity in political debate. However, the courts have 'consistently refused to recognize an exception for any test of truth . . .'"[68] Rather than relying "on the State to silence false political speech," the court reasoned, "the First Amendment requires our dependence on even more speech to bring forth the truth."[69] Therefore, "The preferred First Amendment remedy of 'more speech, not enforced silence' thus has special 'force.'"[70] No doubt, the Washington Supreme Court had its heart in the right place. It quickly turned to the well-known First Amendment precept that one appropriately responds to false speech with true speech, rather than with suppression. And why not? Surely that precept has a strong philosophical and constitutional pedigree, finding its most articulate advocacy in the works of such giants as John Stuart Mill[71] and Justices Holmes[72] and Brandeis.[73] It represents classic "marketplace-of-ideas" thinking, a well-known subset of free speech theory.

Despite its once-venerable origins in the theory of free expression, the marketplace-of-ideas approach has in modern times been subjected to blistering scholarly criticism.[74] In the words of one commentator, "It is naïve to think that truth will *always* prevail over falsehood in a free and open encounter, for too many false ideas have captured the imagination of man."[75] For present purposes, however, the validity of the marketplace-of-ideas theory is beside the point. Even if one were to suspend disbelief and accept its premises, the fact remains that the Washington Supreme Court still ignored a central consideration in relying on the marketplace-of-ideas theory to invalidate a statute punishing consciously false statements. The marketplace-of-ideas theory could conceivably justify invalidation of a governmental prohibition on the expression of *certain ideas* deemed by those in power to be "false." As the Supreme Court has stated, "There is no such thing as a false idea."[76] Used in this manner, the marketplace-of-ideas theory does no more than rationalize the constitutional prohibition on governmental suppression of unpopular viewpoints—an essential element of a viable democratic process. But a prohibition on suppression of the expression of *normative* viewpoints does not necessarily imply a similar suppression of the expression of *descriptive* or *historical* facts. Democracy may not be able to coexist with governmental ability to suppress ideas it deems distasteful, but it may well coexist with government's ability to punish someone for saying it is raining outside when it is not. More importantly, even were we to decide to protect false statements of fact out of fear that free expression would likely be chilled as a result, it still does not automatically follow that the expression of *consciously* false statements should be equally protected. One who makes a consciously false statement is not attempting to contribute in good faith to public debate; he is, rather, doing nothing more than attempting to deceive others. On this basis, one might reasonably conclude that consciously false statements—at least those proximately giving rise to perceptible harm—fall outside the First Amendment because they *fail to* contribute to the marketplace of ideas.

The Washington Supreme Court's distinction between suppression of consciously false statements in the defamatory and nondefamatory contexts turned on its assessment of the strength of the competing governmental interests: Defamation causes severe individual harm, while nondefamatory falsehoods in a political campaign have no comparably harmful impact on society. But the court was much too quick to dismiss the government's asserted compelling interest. Perhaps this resulted because the state failed to articulate the true harm to the First Amendment that flows from permitting the expression of conscious falsehoods in the political process. My analysis therefore now turns to this issue.

The First Amendment Harm of Conscious Falsehoods

No one would likely dispute the absence of First Amendment protection for the expression in the following situation: *A* tells *B* that he will sell him his car if *B* gives him $500. Relying on this representation, *B* gives *A* the money, and *A* tells him he will deliver the car later that afternoon. *A*, however, never had any intention of selling *B* his car and instead simply absconds with the money, never to be seen by *B* again. While *A* of course used words and voice in the process, it would be absurd to suggest that he was engaging in an expressive act in the sense contemplated by the First Amendment. He was, rather, employing words as part of a criminal act, much as a holdup man says to his victim, "Your money or your life." In neither case could it seriously be suggested that the concerns of free expression are implicated. The example of *A*'s fraudulent behavior would be dealt with by modern First Amendment doctrine under well-established principles of commercial speech protection: False commercial promotions are unprotected, whether they are said with knowledge of falsity or were merely honest mistakes. While one might reasonably question the categorical exclusion of nonintentionally false commercial speech from the First Amendment's protective scope, the absence of protection for intentionally false commercial communications should hardly be controversial.

Now imagine the following hypothetical in a political context: A candidate for Congress speaks to a group of Vietnam-era veterans and tells them that he understands what they went through in battle because he, too, served in combat in Vietnam. He is therefore in a better position than his opponent, he argues, to understand their needs and protect their interests in Congress. On the basis of this representation, he asks for and receives from audience members monetary contributions to his political campaign. In reality, the candidate never served in Vietnam but had instead been a draft resister and staunch antiwar activist. Though this expression takes place in a political, rather than a commercial, context, it is difficult to imagine that the candidate's words would receive any more First Amendment protection than *A*'s words did in my first hypothetical. Both cases, reduced to their simplest form, involve nothing more than the use of expression as part of a scheme to defraud victims out of their money. In both situations, words are employed as part and parcel of a criminal act of theft by deceit.

The final hypothetical involves a slight twist on the second example. Assume that, as in example number two, the candidate falsely represents to the veterans' group that he served in combat in Vietnam, just as they did. Now, however, assume that instead of seeking financial contributions, he simply asked for audience members' votes on Election Day. The Washington Supreme Court in *119 Vote No! Committee* tells us that in this situation, the "expression" of the candidate becomes part of the core of the First Amendment and therefore constitutionally immune from governmental punishment. Yet in virtually every sense, the candidate's behavior in example 3 parallels his behavior in example 2: In both, the candidate made a knowing misrepresentation on which his victims reasonably relied, causing them to give up something of value. It is true that in one hypothetical it was the listeners' money that was stolen while in the other case it was their votes. But if one were to adopt a Meiklejohnian listener-centric perspective on the First Amendment,[77] in a certain sense the loss of the victims' vote is at least as harmful as the loss of the victims' money. While it is appropriate to conclude that loss of the money is a compelling harm external to the First Amendment that justifies suppression (even assuming, for purposes of argument, that the fraudulent statements constitute "expression" in the first place), loss of the vote is a harm to core democratic functions—functions that are intertwined with the system of free expression.[78] If the sole or primary purpose of free expression is to facilitate citizens' performance of the self-governing function in the voting booth, as Meiklejohn posited, then protecting the candidate's knowingly false expression in the name of the First Amendment actually counterproductively undermines First Amendment values. And this is so, even if one does not believe, as Meiklejohn did, that the listener-centric model is the *only* proper way to view First Amendment interests.

Put simply, protecting consciously false statements made by candidates or their supporters in a political campaign amounts to what can be accurately labeled political fraud. Such fraudulent statements do more harm than simply retard development of an informed electorate, as the state apparently argued to the Court in *119 Vote No! Committee*. Rather, such expression affirmatively confuses and deceives the electorate, thereby distorting both public debate and democratic decision making. It makes no difference whether one rationalizes exclusion of fraudulent expression from the First Amendment on the grounds that it is conceptually to be characterized as an act (that is, the equivalent of theft) rather than expression, or on the grounds that the harm caused by fraud is categorically deemed sufficient to counterbalance whatever expressive interests are implicated. The end result, either way, is that fraud falls outside the bounds of constitutional protection. At least prima facie, the situations of commercial and political fraud would seem to be similar in this regard.

The Dilemma of Political Fraud

The problem with reaching the conclusion that political fraud lies beyond the scope of First Amendment protection may well center on the concern raised by the Washington Supreme Court in *119 Vote No! Committee*.

Categorical exclusion of political fraud from the First Amendment would place ominous power in the hands of those in authority to threaten or coerce those who oppose them. Although the example of the political candidate's blatant misrepresentation may be extreme, other examples of consciously false statements may involve more subtle misrepresentations that are part and parcel of the day-to-day political process. Where the proper line is to be drawn will naturally be difficult to determine.

These difficulties become even more troubling when one moves from openly false statements ("I served in Vietnam") to judgmental ("I was the best governor this state has ever seen") or factually accurate but misleading statements (a candidate stating that "I have great experience; I have been elected to high office twice," without revealing that both times he was impeached, convicted, and forcibly removed from office). On the one hand, it can be plausibly argued that a half-truth amounts to a whole lie. Strategically selective arguments will invariably mislead a listener as much as a directly false statement would. Therefore, if government is to regulate or suppress affirmatively false assertions in the political arena, it is equally necessary to do the same for statements deemed intentionally misleading due to their strategic incompleteness. On the other hand, to punish presentation of only one side of a political debate because it is misleading would threaten to undermine the very foundation of political advocacy. Under such a regulatory scheme every speaker would have to be transformed from an advocate for her position into an objective observer. Moreover, even if speakers wanted to avoid misleading listeners due to selectivity, it would often be difficult for them to know at what point they had actually included "enough" counterarguments or information to qualify her speech as nonmisleading. Surely, such a system could not survive in a world where expression is designed to be robust and wide open.

We are, then, presented with a very real constitutional dilemma: Either we protect consciously false expression in the political arena—expression that will often mislead its recipients and threaten to seriously distort performance of the democratic process—or we invite widespread chilling of potentially valuable expression and place a dangerous weapon of suppression in the hands of those in power. Both alternatives appear to give rise to seriously harmful consequences for important interests sought to be fostered by the constitutional guarantee of free expression. Neither result, then, seems particularly inviting from a constitutional perspective. Perhaps one can at least dilute the harm caused by political fraud by adjusting established constitutional doctrine on the speaker's right of anonymity. It is to this issue that the chapter now turns.

DILUTING POLITICAL FRAUD BY ADJUSTING THE RULES OF ANONYMITY PROTECTION

There can be little question that the constitutional guarantee of anonymity exacerbates the problem of political fraud, even if one proceeds on the assumption that political fraud is fully protected by the First Amendment. In many instances, it seems reasonable to predict, political fraud is substantially facilitated by a constitutional guarantee of a speaker's right to anonymity. Initially, speakers who are not permitted to hide their identity will probably be less likely to make flagrantly fraudulent statements for fear of public shunning. More importantly, concealment of the speaker's identity itself is often likely to function as an element of the fraud itself. For example, a speaker who advocates particular legislation that would benefit a certain interest group may not wish to reveal that he would be among the primary beneficiaries of that legislation. By retaining his anonymity, he can, if only by implication, falsely project himself as an objective observer.

Simply as a matter of common sense, it is appropriate for listeners, in judging the value, completeness, or sincerity of expression, to include as part of their calculus the possible interest of the speaker. They cannot do so if the speaker is allowed to preserve his anonymity. The statement that smoking does not cause heart disease is likely to be taken far more seriously if it is uttered by a heart specialist with no connections to tobacco companies than if it is made by a representative of the tobacco industry. And this is so, it should be emphasized, even if the substance of the expression itself is assumed to be uttered without speaker knowledge of the statement's falsity.

It might be responded that a listener's judgment concerning the merits of expression should be influenced not at all by the speaker's identity. Rather, the argument proceeds, the value of the expression should be deemed to stand or fall on its own: Either the speech is persuasive, or it is not. Who the speaker is, the argument posits, has no relevance to its proper impact. This argument is flawed, however, because it ignores the inescapable realities of the communicative process. Rarely does expression contain within its four corners arguments that are unambiguously dispositive. Instead, speech often contains assertions of fact or conclusory assessments of worth that are not easily verifiable. In either case, the listener's confidence in the speaker's expertise and objectivity will likely have enormous relevance as to how the listener assesses the value of the expression. This does not necessarily suggest that the speaker's identity is the *only* relevant factor in assessing the impact of expression. But it would be equally incorrect to suggest the total irrelevance of speaker identity to that assessment.

This does not mean that the speech made by a biased or interested party is necessarily false or intentionally deceptive. For example, as noted earlier, an attorney representing a client is not expected to make her opponent's case for him to the judge or jury; she naturally has a personal and professional interest in judicial acceptance of her arguments. Indeed, this personal and professional agenda has been built into the adversary system because it is thought that such investment will lead to more effective representation and, ultimately, to more accurate decision making.[79] It surely does not follow that what the attorneys say is necessarily false or fraudulent. Nevertheless, it would be folly to allow the attorneys to hide their identities or allegiances. Both judge and jury are placed in a far better position to measure the force of advocates' arguments by their awareness of the identity and allegiances of those advocates. Requiring revelation of speaker identity would facilitate the democratic decision making process in several important ways. First, the voters would be able to place the substance of the expression in far better perspective by knowing who the speaker is. As a result of this knowledge they will be able to shape their acceptance and understanding of the views expressed in light of the relative objectivity and expertise of the speaker, even if the speaker made no affirmative representations about either factor. Second, governmental prohibition of anonymity would make it far more difficult for the speaker to misrepresent the level of her personal interest or qualifications to comment. Third, in situations in which the speaker advocates election or appointment of another individual, the voters would be able to judge the candidate by who her supporters are.

It is true that revoking the right of anonymity will not cure all dangers of political fraud. Indeed, in the example of a speaker's misrepresentation about his military record, the identity of the speaker was presumed to be already known.[80] As those examples show, even when the speaker's identity is known, the expression may still be misleadingly incomplete—or even an outright lie. Moreover, even if the speaker's identity is known she may still conceal her preexisting political or financial connections and interests.[81]

Nevertheless, it is reasonable to predict that, at the very least, speaker identification will go a long way to deter extreme cases of political fraud. If nothing else, it would dilute the general impact of political fraud on the populace by enabling them to quickly determine the speaker's underlying agenda.

There is, of course, a potentially negative effect of the revocation of the constitutional guarantee of anonymity. For example, the thought of the Southern states of the 1950s and 1960s being allowed to employ the exposure of membership lists as a means of intimidating the NAACP and other civil rights organizations is both frightening and intolerable.[82] We must start from the premise that any construction of the First Amendment that would authorize such governmental intimidation must be rejected. But it is important to recall the distinction between *associational* anonymity and *expressive* anonymity.[83] The interest in avoiding political fraud could readily be confined to abolition of the right to anonymity that accompanies direct contributions to public debate, for it is such expressive activity that most proximately gives rise to the First Amendment harms to be avoided by the reduction in political fraud.

Even in the case of directly expressive anonymity, it must be conceded that certain First Amendment interests would be threatened by loss of constitutional protection. But it is important to note two important qualifying factors. First, revocation of the constitutional protection of expressive anonymity would not automatically deprive speakers of the opportunity to invoke anonymity. To prohibit anonymity, the majoritarian branches of either the state or federal governments would still have to take appropriate legal action to implement such a prohibition. Second, the majoritarian branches could not revoke the right to anonymity in an ideologically selective or discriminatory manner. For example, a law could not revoke anonymity exclusively for expression of specified political positions. The prohibition on viewpoint selectivity is a well-accepted precept of free speech doctrine.

This equal protection element of the right of free expression assures imposition of an important political restraint on government's ability to restrict expressive rights. Government is likely to be far more hesitant to impose a restriction when that restriction must reach all speakers than when it is permitted to limit the reach of its restriction to selected groups who are underrepresented among governmental decision makers. For example, in the case of southern states seeking NAACP membership lists in the 1960s, even were we to ignore the arguable difference between expressive and associational anonymity suggested earlier, revocation of a First Amendment right of anonymity would not necessarily imply the constitutionality of such forced exposure. The constitutional problem would no longer be forced exposure; rather, it would be discrimination in the regulation of expression based purely on ideological considerations. There exists a widely recognized First Amendment right to equal treatment: Government may not discriminate in its treatment of different speakers on the basis of ideology, even if there exists no freestanding right to engage in the regulated behavior.

One must acknowledge the difficulty in making the Solomonesque choice between the First Amendment interest in anonymity on the one hand and the competing interest in avoiding or deterring political fraud, on the other. To dilute the harms to democratic decision making that derive from rampant and otherwise unregulable political fraud, we would be forced to incur the risks of chilling the exercise of expressive rights in certain contexts. If one were ultimately to find the choice between those two alternatives intolerable, there does exist a possibly more limited, less invasive version of the loss of anonymity right. We could conceivably decide to remove the First Amendment right of speaker anonymity only in situations in which concealment of a speaker's true identity can be shown to be part of an affirmative effort to mislead. Thus, it would be only where a speaker, rather than choosing to remain anonymous, falsely identifies himself—either expressly or impliedly—as someone other than who he is in a way that would falsely induce material reliance by listeners that the right of anonymity would be deemed irrelevant. For example, assume that in a chat room for law firm associates a law firm's hiring partner not only fails to identify herself but also talks as if she were an associate at her firm and praises its treatment of younger lawyers. In this case, the speaker has done more than remain anonymous; she has affirmatively portrayed herself as someone she is not for the purpose of inducing detrimental reliance on the part of the recipient of her communication. In cases of pure anonymity, at least the listener is put on notice of the possible need to be skeptical of the speaker's arguments.[84]

The possible problem with this approach is that, while in one sense it seems more limited than a total prohibition on anonymity, in another sense it may open the very Pandora's box that is the general regulation of political fraud that we have sought to keep shut. However, one can reasonably excise the issue of anonymity from the constitutional thicket of political fraud because it is logically and practically separable from an inquiry into the substance of particular messages. Thus, exclusion of deceptive identification from the scope of First Amendment protection would not necessarily trigger all of the serious difficulties associated with any effort to regulate political fraud in general.

CONCLUSION

Ultimately, one must make a tragic First Amendment choice on the question of a speaker's right to anonymity. While one cannot summarily dismiss a choice different from the one advocated here, it is nevertheless reasonable to believe that abolition of the right of expressive anonymity is fully justified as a prophylactic means of deterring and diluting the serious First Amendment harms to the democratic process caused by political fraud. To be sure, some level of political fraud may well be an inescapable by-product of a system of adversary democracy. But those are simply the realities of political life in the United States—a cost of doing business—and likely could not be completely removed even if we tried to do so. In light of these political realities, it is appropriate to recognize that the only realistic mean of even reducing those inevitable harms is through limitation of a speaker's right of anonymity.

The possible resolutions of the dilemma of political fraud suggested here, much as Justice Holmes once said about the First Amendment itself in his most famous free speech opinion, would be "an experiment, as all life is an experiment."[85] Fortunately or unfortunately, we can demand no more of ourselves than this.

CHAPTER SEVEN

Conclusion: The Optimistic Skepticism of the Adversary First Amendment

There is, to be sure, something very skeptical about a theory of free expression grounded in notions of the adversary version of democratic theory. Superficially, at least, the theory lacks the moral attractiveness of a theory of free expression grounded in notions of the cooperative pursuit of the common good. In short, there seems to be something very selfish about adversary democracy—hardly an attractive quality in any normative theoretical framework. Who, then, wants to be placed in the position of defending a First Amendment theory grounded in selfishness? As this book has sought to demonstrate throughout, however, the issue is far from that simple.

The normative distaste for a theory grounded in selfishness can be dealt with in two ways. First, one need only point to the principle of epistemological humility that must underlie any coherent theory of free expression.[1] Any theory of free expression grounded in an *ex ante* preference for one particular normative view (a preference for cooperative pursuit of the common good, for example) is inherently flawed because it is grounded in a normative premise determined by means external to the choices made by the citizens, a result inherently inconsistent with the foundational premise of democracy.[2] In this regard, it is essential to keep in mind that, while cooperative theories logically protect only expression designed to pursue the common good,[3] a theory of free expression derived from precepts of adversary democracy leaves to the individual speaker the choice of whether to be motivated by concerns of selfishness or altruism.[4] It also leaves to the individual speaker the decision of whether to pursue whatever concerns she seeks to advance in a cooperative or confrontational manner. Second, instead of viewing the adversary First Amendment solely as a cynical means of fostering selfishness, the theory may just as easily be viewed from a far more optimistic perspective on human capacities and predilections.

The adversary First Amendment is appropriately derived from the following two premises: (1) Individual growth and development constitute foundational normative premises of any political system grounded in precepts of liberal democracy, and (2) there exists the never-ending danger that those in power will seek to suppress the individuality of those who reject the normative dictates of the current regime, usually under the guise of promotion of the common good. The adversary theory of free expression, then, is premised on a normative process-based commitment to individual growth and development and a never-ending effort to protect such individualist values from societal oppression. In pursuit of this effort, the theory rejects dangerous notions of paternalism that might threaten the individual's ability to protect himself through his speech. In this sense, the adversary First Amendment effectively combines the optimism of liberal individualism associated with Mill and Kant with the dark skepticism of the possessive individualists, who grounded their belief in individualism in a dark form of skepticism about the human condition.

Adversary democracy necessarily recognizes two key elements of the human condition: First, humans are not angels; and, second, this insight applies to both those presently in power and those who wish to acquire power. It is therefore necessary to be "streetwise" in bringing a healthy skepticism to the supposed good faith of either group. It is only in this manner that democracy can protect its continued existence and thereby protect the optimistic developmental values sought to be fostered by the initial commitment to democracy. Thus, by empowering individuals to employ the system of free expression as a means of protecting their own interests, the cynical form of adversary democracy effectively serves as a bodyguard for the optimistic branch of the theory. It would therefore be wrong to adopt a communitarian-like notion that commitment to a belief in individual integrity as an element of both free speech theory and democratic government will necessarily degenerate into a base form of possessive individualism.

In shaping the theory of adversary democracy, it is vitally important to distinguish the *process-based* version of individualism from a broader, more substantive *behavioral* version. As the application of adversary democracy to the right of free expression demonstrates, it is quite possible to confine democracy's commitment to individualism to activities inherently intertwined with the democratic process itself. Absent such a commitment, the theory of adversary democracy posits, it is impossible either to achieve the values sought to be attained by a commitment to democracy or even to assure that society's commitment to the process will continue. It surely does not necessarily follow from a commitment to this process-based libertarianism, however, that those chosen to govern are prohibited from restricting whatever form of activity in which individuals seek to engage—whether it is using drugs, not wearing seat belts, being free of taxes, or owning guns. A commitment to the value of individualism does not mean individuals live in a vacuum, untied to a surrounding society. Unlike expression or voting, those activities are not themselves central to participation in the democratic process or the means by which we persuade or decide.

Certain political theorists have questioned "the extent to which individuals are 'free' in contemporary liberal democracies."[5] For example, political theorist Carole Pateman has argued that "the 'free and equal individual' is, in practice, a person found much more rarely than liberal theory suggests."[6] David Held articulates the position in this manner:

> Liberal theory—in its classical and contemporary guises—generally assumes what has, in fact, to be carefully examined: namely whether the existing relationships among men and women, working, middle and upper classes, blacks and whites, and various ethnic groups allows [sic] formally recognized rights to be actually realized.[7]

He further notes that "if liberals or neo-liberals were to take these issues seriously, they would discover that massive numbers of individuals are restricted systematically—for want of a complex mix of resources and opportunities—from participating actively in political and civil life."[8]

The problems to which these scholars point are no doubt real ones. They have been left for discussion to this late point in the book simply because I have previously dealt with them in some detail in prior work.[9] Suffice it to say, at this point, that while I in no way dismiss the moral problems caused by the discrimination and poverty unfortunately tolerated within the democratic system, the critics have failed to point to a better alternative. To be sure, our system can be improved on, but ultimately democracy turns on the will of the electorate. Though in the American political system the majority is of course limited by the constraints of the countermajoritarian Constitution, to the extent that neither of those sources condemns those practices it is unclear what we should be doing to correct the problems. Should we simply impose a czar, empowered to right all moral wrongs perceived by a group of scholars, regardless of what our Constitution provides and the electorate prefers? That is exactly what authoritarian Marxist regimes attempted through much of the twentieth century—without the greatest success, judging by the near-universal collapse of the undemocratic Marxist regimes of Eastern Europe toward the close of that century. Neo-Marxist attacks on democracy took on something of a hollow ring following those events. Thus, while no one could rationally claim that democracy is free from moral problem or doubt, we would be well advised to recall the wisdom of Churchill's classic assertion that democracy is the worst governmental form—except for all the others.[10]

My quarrel with these political and constitutional theorists, however, has not been the focus of this book. Rather, my concern here has been with those theorists who, while committed to democracy in its broad outlines, advocate a collectivist or communitarian form of the theory that is designed to foster pursuit of "the public interest" or "the common good." On their face, these versions of democratic theory share a rejection of the notion that the primary goal of the protection of free speech is to foster individual development for its own sake. All of these theories are flawed because of their near-universal dismissal of the individual's value, other than as a political spoke in the communitarian wheel. Collectivist theories of democracy threaten meaningful individuality or creativity because they all filter such expression through the potentially stifling concepts of "civic virtue" and "the common good," however those in power happen to define those phrases. Adversary democracy accepts the view, expressed by a respected democratic theorist, that "a human being cannot be reduced to his or her citizenness. For us, a man is not merely a member of a collective. . . . Modern democracy is meant to protect the freedom of the individual as a person—a freedom that cannot be entrusted . . . to the 'subjection of the individual to the power of the whole.'"[11]

In addition to these serious theoretical deficiencies, collectivist democratic theories' greatest problem is not their broad theoretical outlines but rather the troublingly inconsistent means in which they apply them. Individuals' use of free expression as a means of fostering their own selfish interests is by no means universally condemned by collectivist theorists. Rather, all too often, either implicitly or explicitly, they immunize from such judgmental condemnation numerous categories of expressive activity that are invariably infected with promotion of personal interest. Thus, while Alexander Meiklejohn summarily excised from the First

Amendment's scope such expressive activities as commercial speech, radio, and lobbying because they are focused on narrow self-promotion rather than pursuit of the common good,[12] just as summarily he included within that scope the sale of books and newspapers, as well as any political speech motivated by self-interest.[13] Zephyr Teachout goes Meiklejohn one better by constitutionally *condemning*, rather than *protecting*, any expressive expenditures in the electoral process motivated by something other than "civic virtue"—whatever that means.[14] Robert Post offers the most intellectually sophisticated of the collectivist theories of free expression, but he, too, ultimately fails to justify his selective use of "common good" pursuit as a test for the protection of expression.[15] His suggested explanation for providing substantially reduced constitutional protection for commercial speech is that it is not motivated by a desire to participate in public debate in pursuit of the common good.[16] But he provides no empirical basis on which to assume that all noncommercial speech is so motivated or that all commercial speech is not so motivated. Nor does he adequately explain why, as a matter of coherent constitutional or political theory, anything should turn on such an inquiry.[17] Because he simultaneously overvalues the participatory aspect of expression to democratic theory and undervalues the informational aspect of expression, his theory is fatally underinclusive.

Adversary democracy, to be sure, is not always pretty. To the contrary, it is often rough-and-tumble and not designed for the faint of heart. But the keys to adversary democracy are important to keep in mind. First, if nothing else it reflects the reality of citizens' motivation and political behavior. Any democratic theory of free expression that ignores these realities is largely useless at best and harmful at worst. Second, it limits and controls adverseness in ways designed to avoid violence and preserve the democratic process.

By requiring adherence to the First Amendment's principle of epistemological humility,[18] adversary democracy effectively incorporates a type of Rawlsian "veil of ignorance."[19] When those of us in the mythical state of nature seek to establish our governmental structure, none of us knows who in society will be a part of which moral faction or which moral faction will be politically or militarily more powerful than the others. We are therefore sufficiently risk averse to leave the ultimate moral choice to some form of the expression of popular will. But in doing so we require that those who do exercise political power not be permitted to suppress or—even worse—destroy those who disagree. This bet-hedging form of reasoning does not represent a commitment to a firmly held substantive moral perspective so much as an instrumental construct designed to prevent society from degenerating into an authoritarian form of government—whichever faction happens to hold authoritarian power.

Even at its worst, a First Amendment grounded in principles of adversary democracy is far preferable to a logically flawed or deceptively manipulative appeal to democratic and expressive theories grounded in some vague notion of the pursuit of "the common good" as a basis for the selective suppression of unpopular ideas. Collectivist democratic theories of free expression, then, are invariably underinclusive. They underprotect the expression that is essential to the flourishing of a democratic system founded on principles of free political choice, made by the people, and a commitment to the foundational values of self-determination and individual development.

Reference Matter

Notes

CHAPTER ONE

1. *See* U.S. Const. amend. I ("Congress shall make no law . . . abridging the freedom of speech").

2. See, for example, Alexander Meiklejohn, *Free Speech and Its Relation to Self-Government* (1948).

3. See, for example, Robert C. Post, *Constitutional Domains: Democracy, Community, Management* 7 (1995) [hereinafter Post, *Constitutional Domains*].

4. See Robert H. Bork, Neutral Principles and Some First Amendment Problems, 47 *Ind. L. J.* 1, 23 (1971).

5. See David Held, *Models of Democracy* 2 (1987) ("The history of the idea of democracy is complex and is marked by conflicting conceptions. There is plenty of scope for disagreement"); and James G. March and Johan P. Olsen, *Democratic Governance* 1 (1995) ("'Democracy' has become a term of such general legitimacy and indiscriminate use as to compromise its claim to meaning").

6. See Robert A. Dahl, *Democracy and Its Critics* 3 (1989). Dahl explains that the word *democracy* comes from the Greek word *demokratia*, which combines the Greek root *demos*, meaning "the people," with the root *kratia*, meaning "rule or authority." Id.

7. *Cf.* Dan M. Kahan, Democracy Schmemocracy, 20 *Cardozo L. Rev.* 795, 795 (1998) (making the same point with regard to so-called democratic theories of congressional delegation).

8. Of course, individuals in a constitutional democracy may ratify a constitution as a "precommitment" or "entrenchment" device that places certain decisions beyond the grasp of majoritarian decision making. See Steven G. Calabresi, The Tradition of the Written Constitution: A Comment on Professor Lessig's Theory of Translation, 65 *Fordham L. Rev.* 1435, 1455 (1997) (describing the Constitution as an "entrenchment" device); and John O. McGinnis and Michael B. Rappaport, The Constitutionality of Legislative Supermajority Requirements: A Defense, 105 *Yale L. J.* 483, 510 n.126 (1995) ("The Constitution is itself a societal

precommitment to limit the range of future choices"). Thus, scholars have long suggested that the Constitution creates a "countermajoritarian difficulty": To the extent the Constitution prevents the majority from making self-governing decisions that conflict with its provisions, it interferes with self-rule. See, for example, Alexander Bickel, *The Least Dangerous Branch* 16 (2d ed., 1962) (coining the term *countermajoritarian difficulty*). A constitutional democracy remains a democracy, though, because the people themselves choose to limit their decision-making authority according to the norms they adopt and continue to retain in their constitution and retain the authority, by recourse to a supermajoritarian process, to alter or abandon that constitution.

9. See Martin H. Redish, Product Health Claims and the First Amendment: Scientific Expression and the Twilight Zone of Commercial Speech, 43 *Vand. L. Rev.* 1433, 1435 (1990) (coining the term *epistemological humility*).

10. *W. Va. State Bd. of Educ. v. Barnette*, 319 U.S. 624, 641 (1943).

11. Letter from Thomas Jefferson to Colonel Yancey (Jan. 6, 1816), in 6 *The Writings of Thomas Jefferson: Being His Autobiography, Correspondent, Reports, Messages, Addresses and Other Writings, Official and Private* 517 (H. A. Washington, ed., 1859). Jefferson continued, "The functionaries of every government have propensities to command at will the liberty and property of their constituents. There is no safe deposit for these but with the people themselves; nor can they be safe with them without information." Id.

12. See Meiklejohn, *Free Speech and Its Relation to Self-Government, supra* note 2, at 14–15.

13. Robert C. Post, Viewpoint Discrimination and Commercial Speech, 41 *Loy. L. A. L. Rev.* 169, 175 (2008).

14. Id. at 176 (quoting Jürgen Habermas, 2 *The Theory of Communicative Action* 81 [Thomas McCarthy, trans., 1987] [1981]).

15. See Meiklejohn, *Free Speech and Its Relation to Self-Government, supra* note 2, at 39, 57, 62–63. Compare id. at 46 (describing the First Amendment as "offer[ing] defense to men who plan and advocate and incite toward corporate action for the common good"), with id. at 94 (describing the First Amendment as not protecting "men . . . engaged . . . in argument, or inquiry, or advocacy, or incitement which is directed toward our private interests, private privileges, private possessions").

16. Post, *Viewpoint Discrimination, supra* note 13, at 176 (internal quotation omitted).

17. Note that in arguing that the First Amendment "reaches" all such expression, the book does not necessarily intend to suggest that all such expression is to receive protection in all contexts, regardless of the strength of the competing governmental interest. It means only that all such expression is to receive the protection of the strict scrutiny traditionally afforded fully protected expression by the First Amendment.

18. See, generally, Chapter Three.

19. See, generally, Chapter Four (concerning commercial speech protection).

20. See, generally, Chapter Three (critiquing theories of Alexander Meikljohn and Robert Post).

21. See Chapter Two.

22. See Chapter Three.
23. See Chapter Four.
24. See Chapter Six.
25. See Chapter Five.

CHAPTER TWO

1. *See* Jane Mansbridge, *Beyond Adversary Democracy* 18 (1982) ("Because interests often conflict in the modern nation-state, a fundamentally adversary system of electoral representation based on competing interests, equally weighted votes, and majority rule is probably the least dangerous method of managing these conflicting interests"); *see also* Ian Shapiro, *The State of Democratic Theory* 3 (2003) ("The central task for democracy is to enable people to manage power relations so as to minimize domination").

2. This of course is not to suggest that all political choices are grounded exclusively in self-interest. Altruistic concerns may be relevant to political motivation as well. *See* discussion below at 16. But this is likely the exception rather than the rule. Moreover, even when an individual's or group's motivation is purely altruistic, that individual or group will often proceed in a strategically adversarial manner in pursuit of its altruistic goals.

3. *See, generally*, Mansbridge, *Beyond Adversary Democracy, supra* note 1.

4. Ian Shapiro has proposed a "less demanding" definition of the "common good"—"that which those with an interest in avoiding domination share." *See* Shapiro, *The State of Democratic Theory, supra* note 1, at 3. This definition is consistent with adversary democracy because it rejects any definition of the "common good" that excludes particular individual or group interests. In this regard it seems to be more of a procedural definition of the common good rather than a substantive one.

5. *See* Mansbridge, *Beyond Adversary Democracy, supra* note 1, at 18 ("Because interests often conflict in the modern nation-state, a fundamentally adversary system of electoral representation based on competing interests, equally weighted votes, and majority rule is probably the least dangerous method of managing these conflicting interests"); Chantal Mouffe, *On the Political* 2 (2005) ("Envisaging the aim of democratic politics in terms of consensus and reconciliation is not only completely mistaken, it is also fraught with political dangers").

6. *See* Mansbridge, *Beyond Adversary Democracy, supra* note 1, at 17.

7. Chantal Mouffe describes this as the distinction between "agonism" and "antagonism." See Mouffe, *On the Political, supra* note 5, at 9. She argues that democracy must manage conflict so that it does not "destroy the political association" but that managing conflict, in turn, requires the recognition of the "the permanence of the antagonistic dimension of conflict." See *id.* at 20. As a result, she rejects theories of democracy that suggest that conflict can be "reconciled through deliberation" because they ignore the permanence of conflict. *Id.* As an alternative, she suggests a theory of democracy based on "agonism":

> While antagonism is a we/they relation in which the two sides are enemies who do not share any common ground, agonism is a we/they relation where the conflicting parties,

although acknowledging that there is no rational solution to their conflict, nevertheless recognize the legitimacy of their opponents. They are "adversaries" not enemies. This means that, while in conflict, they see themselves as belonging to the same political association, as sharing a common symbolic space within which the conflict takes place. We could say that the task of democracy is to transform antagonism into agonism.

This is why "the adversary" is a crucial category for democratic politics. . . . [I]t allows democratic politics to transform antagonism into agonism.

Id.

8. Mansbridge, *Beyond Adversary Democracy, supra* note 1, at 17.

9. *Cf.* Elias Canetti, *Crowds and Power* 189 (Carol Stewart, trans., 1962) ("The member of an outvoted party accepts the majority decision, not because he has ceased to believe in his own case, but simply because he admits defeat").

10. Stuart Hampshire, *Justice Is Conflict* 37–38 (2000).

11. *Cf.* George H. Sabine, *A History of Political Theory* 579 (3d ed., 1961) (arguing that democracy based on the "morality of rational self-interest . . . presumes freedom of private judgment" and therefore furthers personal liberty, while a democracy that stresses common "sentiments . . . equally native to all men" implies "very little personal autonomy because it attaches only slight important to individual preeminence").

12. Mansbridge, *Beyond Adversary Democracy, supra* note 1, at 15–16: "It is a commonplace that Hobbes was the first theorist systematically to legitimate self-interest as the cornerstone of political life." According to Mansbridge, "The new [capitalistic] economic order required a new political ethos, for which Thomas Hobbes obligingly provided a rationale. Hobbes's seventeenth century England was fraught with conflict. Disbanded private armies roamed the highways. Unlanded peasants became begging vagabonds on the highways or squatted in camps outside city walls." *Id.* at 15. Hobbes developed his political theory for these "masterless men." *Id.*

13. *Id.* at 17.

14. Joseph H. Carens, Possessive Individualism and Democratic Theory: Macpherson's Legacy, in *Democracy and Possessive Individualism: The Intellectual Legacy of C. B. Macpherson* 2 (Joseph H. Carens, ed., 1993).

15. *Id.* at 2–3.

16. According to political theorist C. B. Macpherson, for example, possessive individualism is fundamentally flawed for two reasons. First, it generates an impoverished view of life, making acquisition and consumption central and obscuring deeper human purposes and capacities. The possessive view of life distorts the democratic ideal, which Macpherson described as a commitment to "provide the conditions for the full and free development of the essential human capacities of all the members of the society." *Id.* at 3 (quoting C. B. Macpherson, *The Real World of Democracy* 37 [1966]).

17. John Stuart Mill, *On Liberty* (1859). *See also* John Stuart Mill, *Considerations on Representative Government* (1861). Another real-world example of the intersection between pluralistic and liberal democratic adversary theory, in addition to the one mentioned in the text, is the much earlier political activity of the Levellers in England of the 1640s, who argued that the poor needed an equal vote in order to

defend their own interests. Mansbridge, *Beyond Adversary Democracy, supra* note 1, at 16.

18. Shapiro, *The State of Democratic Theory, supra* note 1, at 275.

19. David Held, *Models of Democracy* 89 (1987).

20. For a detailed discussion of this point, see Martin H. Redish, Freedom of Expression as Freedom of Thought: Criminal Sentencing Enhancement and First Amendment Theory, 11 *Crim. J. Ethics* 29 (1992).

21. Jack L. Walker, A Critique of the Elitist Theory of Democracy, 60 *Am. Pol. Sci. Rev.* 285, 288 (1966) (emphasis in original).

22. *See*, for example, C. Edwin Baker, *Human Liberty and Freedom of Speech* 47 (1989). The liberty model holds that the free speech clause

> protects not a [Millian/Holmesisan] marketplace, but rather an arena of individual liberty from certain types of governmental restrictions. Speech or other self-expressive conduct is protected not as a means to achieve a collective good but because of its value to the individual. The liberty theory justifies protection of expression because of the way the protected conduct fosters individuals' self-realization and self-determination without improperly interfering with the legitimate claims of others.

Id.

23. Held, *Models of Democracy, supra* note 19, at 89.

24. *See*, for example, Joseph A. Schumpeter, *Capitalism, Socialism and Democracy* 269 (1942):

> Suppose we . . . make the deciding of issues by the electorate secondary to the election of the men who are to do the deciding. To put it differently, we now take the view that the role of the people is to produce a government, or else an intermediate body which in turn will produce a national executive or government. And we define: the democratic method is that institutional arrangement for arriving at political decisions in which individuals acquire the power to decide by means of a competitive struggle for the people's vote.

Id. While Schumpeter is often identified with pluralistic adversary theory, he was not an advocate of widespread citizen participation in the everyday aspects of the political process. Other developmental theorists would see such participatory activity as valuable to both moral and individual growth. *See* Benjamin Barber, *Strong Democracy: Participatory Politics for a New Age* 8 (1984).

25. U.S. Const. arts. I, II, III.

26. See Martin H. Redish & Elizabeth J. Cisar, "If Angels Were to Govern": The Need for Pragmatic Formalism in Separation of Powers Theory, 41 *Duke L. J.* 449, 451 (1991).

27. *See generally* Chapter Three *infra*.

28. *See* Chapter Three *infra*.

29. *Altruism* has been defined as "behavior promoting another's welfare that is undertaken for a reason 'independent of its effects on [one] own welfare.'" Jane J. Mansbridge, On the Relation of Altruism and Self-Interest, in *Beyond Self-Interest* 142 (Jane J. Mansbridge, ed., 1990) (emphasis and citation omitted).

30. *Id.* at 45. Elster correctly notes that "some of the excesses of the Chinese cultural revolution illustrate the absurdity of universal altruism. All Chinese

citizens were told to sacrifice their selfish interests for the interests of the people—as if the people were something over and above the totality of Chinese citizens." *Id.*

31. *Id.*

32. U.S. Const. art. IV, § 1, cl. 2.

33. The same logic arguably applies to the Dormant Commerce Clause. However, I have long held the view that this concept is both contra- and extratextual
because it appears nowhere in the text of the Constitution and in fact undermines
the carefully structured federalistic balance embodied in the text. See Martin H.
Redish & Shane V. Nugent, The Dormant Commerce Clause and the Constitutional Balance of Federalism, 1987 *Duke L. J.* 569, 571–72.

34. See Mansbridge, *Beyond Adversary Democracy, supra* note 1, at 17.

35. *Id.*

36. *See* Cass R. Sunstein, Beyond the Republican Revival, 97 *Yale L. J.* 1539,
1592–1597 (1988).

37. Mansbridge concedes that "no political scientist . . . has adopted this model
in its entirety. Contact with political reality makes it clear that self-interest provides
too weak a support for the kinds of negotiations and development of skills that a
functioning democracy requires." Mansbridge, *Beyond Adversary Democracy, supra*
note 1, at 340n32. For works that come close, see generally Schumpeter, *Capitalism, Socialism and Democracy, supra* note 24; and David Truman, *The Governmental
Process: Political Interests and Public Opinion* (1959). Both emphasize the centrality
of the bargaining process as a means of reconciling competing individual interests.

38. *See* Mansbridge, *Beyond Adversary Democracy, supra* note 1, at 10:

> For mainstream political scientists, pluralism, ethical relativism, trade-offs, and adjust-
> ments among competing selfish desires posed an ethically attractive, egalitarian alterna-
> tive to a potentially totalitarian single view of the public interest . . . . For Marxists and
> others on the Left, talk of a public interest obscured underlying class, race, or gender
> conflict in a way that kept the less powerful from understanding or acting on their
> interests.

39. *See*, for example, Robert D. Cooter and Daniel L. Rubinfeld, Reforming
the New Discovery Rules, 84 *Geo. L. J.* 61, 65 (1995): "The requesting party will
conduct additional discovery as long as the cost to her falls short of the expected
increase in the value of her legal claim . . . . As long as the complying party bears
part of the cost of compliance, the requesting party has an incentive to make inef-
ficient, abusive discovery requests."

40. It may well be the case that, in certain instances, a private individual or
public officeholder would, in fact, seek to protect another's private interests despite the lack of any direct benefit to herself. However, in structuring the American system, the Framers clearly proceeded on worst-case scenarios concerning
human motivations and behavior, as the prophylactic concepts of separation of
powers illustrates. See Martin H. Redish, *The Constitution as Political Structure* 99
(1995). It would be impossible to know, *ex ante*, in which situations the entrusted
party would in fact act out of altruistic or benevolent motivations untied to self-
beneficial consequences.

41. John Stuart Mill found the concept of a benevolent dictator to be oxymoronic because the individual would be unable to develop his faculties absent the opportunity to control or influence life-affecting decisions. John Stuart Mill, *Beyond Considerations of Representative Government* (1861). *See also* Peter Bachrach, *The Theory of Democratic Elitism: A Critique* (1967) (asserting that democratic theory should be based in part on the principle that "the majority of individuals stand to gain in self-esteem and growth toward a fuller affirmation of their personalities by participating more actively in community decisions").

42. *See*, for example, Sunstein, Beyond the Republican Revival, *supra* note 36, at 1555.

43. Mansbridge, *Beyond Adversary Democracy, supra* note 1.

44. *See* discussion *infra* at 18–22. For a detailed discussion of the role played by adversary theory in American political history, see Chapter Five, *infra* at 134–141.

45. Gordon S. Wood, *The Creation of the American Republic 1776–1787*, at 502 (1969) (quoting letter from Madison to Jefferson, Oct. 24, 1787) (internal quotation marks omitted).

46. *Faction* is defined in *The Federalist No. 10* as "a number of citizens, whether amounting to a majority or a minority of the whole, who are united and actuated by some common impulse of passion, or of interest, adverse to the rights of other citizens or to the permanent and aggregate interest of the community." *The Federalist No. 10* (James Madison) 48 (J. R. Pole, ed., 2007).

47. Wood, *The Creation of the American Republic 1776–1787, supra* note 45, at 610 (citing Noah Webster, *Sketches of American Policy* 25 [1785]).

48. Wood, *The Creation of the American Republic 1776–1787, supra* note 45 at 612.

49. *The Federalist No. 10* (James Madison), supra note 46.

50. *Id.* at 53.

51. *The Federalist No. 51* (James Madison), *supra* note 46, at 283.

52. Michael S. Gross, *Ethics and Activism: The Theory and Practice of Political Morality* 24 (1997).

53. Hannah Fenichel Pitkin, *The Concept of Representation* 196 (1967).

54. Mansbridge, *Beyond Adversary Democracy, supra* note 1, at 16.

55. *The Federalist No. 10* (James Madison), *supra* note 46, at 281.

56. Thomas Sowell, *Knowledge and Decisions* 317 (1980) (quoting *The Federalist No. 10* [James Madison]).

57. Indeed, the subtle irony of democratic theories of the First Amendment—and perhaps the clearest example of the contingency of the term "democracy"—is that the Framers of the American Constitution equated "democracy" with the system of government in ancient Athens, a system they thought neither practicable nor desirable for imitation on American soil. *See*, for example, *The Federalist No. 14* (James Madison), *supra* note 46, at 69 ("A democracy . . . must be confined to a small spot. A republic may be extended over a large region"); *The Federalist No. 48* (James Madison), *supra* note 46, at 269 ("In a democracy, where a multitude of people exercise in person the legislative functions, and are continually exposed, by their incapacity for regular deliberation and concerted measures, to the ambitious intrigues of their executive magistrates, tyranny may well be apprehended, on some favorable emergency, to start up in the same quarter").

58. Robert A. Dahl, *Democracy and Its Critics* 16–17 (1989). Citizens were not required to attend the Assembly's approximately forty annual meetings. *Id.* Indeed, some have noted the unlikelihood that all citizens could attend, as the Assembly's gathering place held only 6,000 people. See Nadia Urbinati, Representation as Advocacy: A Study of Democratic Deliberation, 28 *Pol. Theory* 758, 763 (2000) (citing Mogens Herman Hansen, *The Athenian Democracy in the Age of Demosthenes* 130–132 [J. A. Crook, trans., 1993]. Nonetheless, civic participation was considered an absolute duty. In the words of Pericles, a prominent Athenian citizen, "We do not say that a man who takes no interest in politics is a man who minds his own business; we say that he has no business here at all." Held, *Models of Democracy*, *supra* note 19, at 17 (internal quotation marks omitted).

59. *See id.* at 18, 21.

60. Mansbridge, *Beyond Adversary Democracy*, *supra* note 1, at 13–14; *see also id.* at 336n14 ("Popular morality as well as political philosophy in ancient Greece maintained that the good citizen was bound to put public above private interest").

61. *The Federalist No. 14* (James Madison), *supra* note 46, at 69.

62. *See* Edward L. Rubin, Getting Past Democracy, 149 *U. Pa. L. Rev.* 711, 716 (2001).

63. *The Federalist No. 10* (James Madison), *supra* note 46, at 51.

64. Wood, *The Creation of the American Republic 1776–1787*, *supra* note 45, at 409–410 (describing state legislatures' tendency during the 1780s toward "popular despotism"); id. at 595 (describing the Framers' awareness that the democracy they established was unique from "pure" democracies of the past because of its system of electoral representation and accountability).

65. *The Federalist No. 10* (James Madison), *supra* note 46, at 51–52.

66. *See* Urbinati, Representation as Advocacy, *supra* note 58, at 762–764.

67. Held, *Models of Democracy*, *supra* note 19, at 27 (noting that elite politicians came "from wealthy and well-established families, who had ample time to cultivate their contacts and pursue their interests").

68. Mansbridge, *Beyond Adversary Democracy*, *supra* note 1, at 13 (noting that Athenian citizens "used the rhetoric of the common good to further their own interests").

69. *See* Dahl, *Democracy and Its Critics*, *supra* note 58, at 21.

70. *See* Mansbridge, *Beyond Adversary Democracy*, *supra* note 1, at 13 and 335–336n13. Those clubs met before Assembly meetings to "test and select" the most effective speakers to deliver a particular message and sought to influence other citizens' votes by persuasion, bribery, and even threats. *See id.* at 335–336n13; *see also* Peter Riesenberg, *Citizenship in the Western Tradition: Plato to Rousseau* 21 (1992) (arguing that, even after reforms to create more political equality between ancient and new citizens, "inequalities persisted" and were an "accepted" part of Athenian citizenship). Thus, "despite the contemporary myth of the polis as the place of a disinterested and dialogic exercise of public reason, private and class interests" did in fact influence Athenian democracy; Urbinati, Representation as Advocacy, *supra* note 58, at 764.

71. *See* Josiah Ober, *Mass and Elite in Democratic Athens: Rhetoric, Ideology, and the Power of the People* 168 (1989) (describing "universal consensus" as an ideal "that seldom could be achieved in practice").

72. *See* Held, *Models of Democracy, supra* note 19, at 21.

73. *The Federalist No. 10* (James Madison), *supra* note 46, at 52.

74. *The Federalist No. 55* (James Madison), *supra* note 46, at 301.

75. *See* Letter from Madison to Jefferson (Oct. 17, 1788) (suggesting that "it is much more to be dreaded that the few will be unnecessarily sacrificed to the many" rather than the many to the few), quoted in Gordon S. Wood, *The Creation of the American Republic 1776–1787* at 413 (1969).

76. Sowell, *Knowledge and Decisions, supra* note 56, at 317.

77. *The Federalist No. 10* (James Madison), *supra* note 46 (describing the potential of democracy to deteriorate into a tyranny of the majority).

78. *See* Joseph A. Schumpeter, *Capitalism, Socialism and Democracy* 269–273 (5th ed., 1976) (describing the interaction between political competition and public opinion).

79. *See* Shapiro, *The State of Democratic Theory, supra* note 1, at 6–7.

80. *See* Mouffe, *On the Political, supra* note 5, at 20–21.

81. It is for this reason that I later argue against a broad First Amendment right of speaker anonymity. *See generally* Chapter Six, *infra*.

82. Robert J. Kutak, The Adversary System and the Practice of Law, in *The Good Lawyer* 172, 174 (David Luban, ed., 1983).

83. Stephan Landsman, *The Adversary System: A Description and Defense* 45 (1984).

84. *Baker v. Carr*, 369 U.S. 186, 204 (1962).

85. *Valley Forge Christian Coll. v. Am. United for the Separation of Church and State, Inc.*, 454 U.S. 464, 472 (1982) (quoting *Gladstone Realtors v. Vill. of Bellwood*, 441 U.S. 91, 99 [1979]).

86. *Baker*, 369 U.S. at 204.

87. *See id.*

88. *See* José Luis Martí, The Epistemic Conception of Deliberative Democracy Defended: Reasons, Rightness and Equal Political Autonomy, in *Deliberative Democracy and Its Discontents* 27, 27–29 (Samantha Besson and José Luis Martí, eds., 2006). In reality, there are numerous theories of deliberative democracy; the summary here emphasizes what those theories share in common. See *id.* at 27 (describing deliberative democracy as "a family of views according to which the public deliberation of free and equal citizens is the core of legitimate political decision making and self-government" [quoting James Bohman, Survey Article: The Coming Age of Deliberative Democracy, 6 *J. Pol. Phil.* 400, 401 (1998) (internal quotation marks omitted)]). Thus, the goal of deliberation is "neither toleration nor reaching coherent, binding, and stable decisions in the face of disagreement, but rather 'collective moral progress.'" Andrew Sabl, Deliberation in Its Place, 4 *Election L. J.* 147, 147 (2005) (citing Amy Gutmann and Dennis Thompson, *Democracy and Disagreement* 62 [1996]) (critiquing deliberative democracy).

89. Jon Elster, The Market and the Forum: Three Varieties of Political Theory, in *Deliberative Democracy: Essays on Reason and Politics* 3, 12 (James Bohman and

William Rehg, eds., 1997) (arguing that it is "conceptual[ly] impossib[le]" to express self-interested arguments in "a debate about the public good" and that purging "private and idiosyncratic wants" from public discussion about the common good allows "uniquely determined rational desires [to] emerge").

90. Amy Gutmann and Dennis Thompson, *Why Deliberative Democracy?* 144–150 (2004).

91. *See generally* Martin H. Redish, *Freedom of Expression: A Critical Analysis* 9–86 (1984).

92. *See* Jane Mansbridge, Conflict and Self-Interest in Deliberation, in *Deliberative Democracy and Its Discontents, supra* note 88, at 108, 117 (recognizing the necessity of deliberation for understanding one's own interest, especially for minorities).

93. *See* discussion *supra* at 24.

94. Lon L. Fuller, The Forms and Limits of Adjudication, 92 *Harv. L. Rev.* 353, 361–362 (1978).

95. *Id.* at 361.

96. *Id.* at 362.

97. *See*, for example, Schumpeter, *Capitalism, Socialism and Democracy, supra* note 24, at 269.

98. *See*, for example, Anthony Downs, *An Economic Theory of Democracy* 297–300 (1957). Data indicate this thesis accurately captures the explanation for low participation: people desire their elected officials to solve political problems for them so they can tend to other matters. *See* John R. Hibbing and Elizabeth Theiss-Morse, *Stealth Democracy: Americans' Beliefs about How Government Should Work* 114–121 (2002).

99. *See generally* Peter Bachrach, *The Theory of Democratic Elitism: A Critique, supra* note 41.

100. *See* Andrea Louise Campbell, Self-Interest, Social Security, and the Distinctive Participation Patterns of Senior Citizens, 96 *Am. Pol. Sci. Rev.* 565, 571 (2002) (noting that "researchers often have difficulty detecting self-interested behavior" when studying political participation); Carolyn L. Funk, The Dual Influence of Self-Interest and Societal Interest in Public Opinion, 53 *Pol. Res. Q.* 37, 53 (2000) ("Those with a direct self-interest in a policy can be mobilized to support or oppose a policy on the basis of that self-interest").

101. Sidney Verba, Kay Lehman Schlozman, Henry Brady, and Norman H. Nie, Citizen Activity: Who Participates? What Do They Say? 87 *Am. Pol. Sci. Rev.* 303, 312 (1993).

102. *Id.* at 314.

103. Campbell, *supra* note 100, at 565.

104. Indeed, it was precisely for its potential to promote this kind of political mobilization that James Madison defended the form of government the Constitution created. *See* discussion *supra* at 20–21.

105. *See* Diana C. Mutz, The Consequences of Cross-Cutting Networks for Political Participation, 46 *Am. J. Pol. Sci.* 838, 849–850 (2002).

106. *Id.* at 852.

107. The level of First Amendment protection to be given to unlawful advocacy is beyond the scope of this inquiry. For a detailed exploration of the issue, see

Martin H. Redish, *The Logic of Persecution: Free Expression and the McCarthy Era* 63–131 (2005).

CHAPTER THREE

1. See U.S. Const. amend. I ("Congress shall make no law . . . abridging the freedom of speech").

2. *See*, for example, Alexander Meiklejohn, *Free Speech and Its Relation to Self-Government* (1948).

3. *See*, for example, Robert C. Post, *Constitutional Domains: Democracy, Community, Management* 7 (1995) [hereinafter Post, *Constitutional Domains*].

4. *See* Robert H. Bork, Neutral Principles and Some First Amendment Problems, 47 *Ind. L. J.* 1, 23 (1971).

5. *See* David Held, *Models of Democracy* 2 (1987) ("The history of the idea of democracy is complex and marked by conflicting conceptions. There is plenty of scope for disagreement"); James G. March and Johan P. Olsen, *Democratic Governance* 1 (1995) ("'Democracy' has become a term of such general legitimacy and indiscriminate use as to compromise its claim to meaning").

6. *See* Robert A. Dahl, *Democracy and Its Critics* 3 (1989). Dahl explains that the word *democracy* comes from the Greek word *demokratia*, which combines the Greek root *demos*, meaning the people, with the root *kratia*, meaning rule or authority. *Id.*

7. *See* Dan M. Kahan, Democracy Schmemocracy, 20 *Cardozo L. Rev.* 795, 795 (1998) (making the same point with regard to so-called democratic theories of congressional delegations).

8. *See* Chapter One, *supra* at 2. However, as explained in Chapter One, *supra* note 8, individuals in a *constitutional* democracy may ratify a constitution as a "precommitment" or "entrenchment" device that places certain decisions beyond the grasp of majoritarian decision making. *See* Steven G. Calabresi, The Tradition of the Written Constitution, A Comment on Professor Lessig's Theory of Translation, 65 *Fordham L. Rev.* 1435, 1455 (1997) (describing the Constitution as an "entrenchment" device); John O. McGinnis and Michael B. Rappaport, The Constitutionality of Legislative Supermajority Requirements: A Defense, 105 *Yale L. J.* 483, 510n126 (1995) ("The Constitution is itself a societal precommitment to limit the range of future choices"). Thus, scholars have long suggested that the Constitution creates a "countermajoritarian difficulty": That is, to the extent the Constitution prevents the majority from making self-governing decisions that conflict with its provisions, it interferes with self-rule. *See* Chapter One, note 8.

9. *See* Martin H. Redish, Product Health Claims and the First Amendment: Scientific Expression and the Twilight Zone of Commercial Speech, 43 *Vand. L. Rev.* 1433, 1435 (1990) (coining the term *epistemological humility*).

10. *W. Virginia State Bd. of Educ. v. Barnette*, 319 U.S. 624, 641 (1943).

11. Letter from Thomas Jefferson to Colonel Yancey (Jan. 6, 1816), in 6 *The Writings of Thomas Jefferson: Being his Autobiography, Correspondent, Reports, Messages, Addresses and Other Writings, Official and Private*, at 517 (H. A. Washington,

ed., 1859). Jefferson continued, "The functionaries of every government have propensities to command at will the liberty and property of their constituents. There is no safe deposit for these but with the people themselves; nor can they be safe with them without information." *Id.*

12. Meiklejohn, *Free Speech and Its Relation to Self-Government, supra* note 2, at 26.

13. *See id.*

14. *See* discussion *infra* at 34–43.

15. *Cf.* Meiklejohn, *Free Speech and Its Relation to Self-Government, supra* note 2, at 26.

16. *Id.* at 26.

17. Robert C. Post, Meiklejohn's Mistake: Individual Autonomy and the Reform of Public Discourse, 64 *Colo. L. Rev.* 1109, 1115–1123 (1993) [hereinafter Post, Meiklejohn's Mistake] (contrasting his theory with "collectivist" theories of the First Amendment such as Meiklejohn's that sacrifice individual autonomy to ensure that public discourse achieves a "specific 'objective'").

18. *Id.* at 1120; *see also*, Robert C. Post, Equality and Autonomy in First Amendment Jurisprudence, 95 *Mich. L. Rev.* 1517, 1524 [hereinafter Post, Equality and Autonomy] ("Individual autonomy . . . is intrinsically connected to democratic self-governance").

19. Post, Meikeljohn's Mistake, *supra* note 17, at 1123.

20. Post, Equality and Autonomy, *supra* note 18, at 1523. Post's suggestion that this conviction must be "warranted" suggests that he is not focused exclusively on the individual's subjective understanding of democratic legitimacy. Indeed, it even seems to suggest that the objective reality of democratic self-determination is a necessary condition for democratic legitimacy. Even so, Post's participatory theory is strangely dismissive of democratic processes that promote the objective reality of democratic self-determination. *See* discussion *infra* at 34–50.

21. Post, Equality and Autonomy, *supra* note 18, at 1524.

22. *See* discussion *infra* at xx.

23. *See*, for example, Post, *Constitutional Domains, supra* note 3, at 7.

24. See Post, Equality and Autonomy, *supra* note 18, at 1525 (distinguishing the "constitutional interest" in informed decision making from that in collective self-determination and concluding that the former is an interest in the production of truth whereas the latter is an interest in furthering the "value of democratic self-governance").

25. *See* Robert C. Post, The Constitutional Status of Commercial Speech, 48 *UCLA L. Rev.* 1, 14 (2000) [hereinafter Post, Commercial Speech] (suggesting that the availability of information is relevant to democratic decision making but not to democratic legitimation).

26. *See*, for example, *id.* at 12 (describing public discourse as a "necessary [but not sufficient] precondition for democratic legitimation").

27. *See*, for example, Post, Equality and Autonomy, *supra* note 18, at 1528 ("I do not mean to deny, of course, that voting is an important means of participation in a democratic polity. I only claim that voting is not by itself sufficient to realize the value of democratic self-governance").

28. *See* Robert C. Post, Reconciling Theory and Doctrine in the First Amendment, 88 *Cal. L. Rev.* 2353, 2373 (2000) [hereinafter Post, Reconciling].

29. *See* Post, Commercial Speech, *supra* note 25, at 7.

30. It should be noted at the outset that there is no small amount of confusion in the manner in which Post treats the listener's interest in the receipt of information for First Amendment purposes. In virtually all of his scholarship to date, Post (as stated in text) has treated the listener's interest in receiving information as lexically inferior to the speaker's interest in contributing to public discourse. However, in his recently published book, *Democracy Expertise, Academic Freedom: A First Amendment Jurisprudence for the Modern State* (2012) [hereinafter Post, *Democracy*], Post appeared to alter his approach to the receipt of information. Now, rather than ranking information as of *lower* value, Post appears to view it simply as a *different* value, one he places under the heading of "democratic competence." He contrasts it with the more familiar "democratic discourse," which he treats quite differently. While at a later point I critique Post's new "democratic competence" model [*see* discussion *infra* at 58–59], for the most part I confine my analysis of his theory to the more established version of lexical inferiority.

31. *Cf. W. Virginia State Bd. of Educ. v. Barnette*, 319 U.S. 624, 641 (1943) (recognizing that democracy requires that "authority . . . is . . . controlled by public opinion, not public opinion by authority").

32. *See* discussion *infra* at 43–69.

33. *See* discussion *infra* at 43–69.

34. Robert C. Post, Viewpoint Discrimination and Commercial Speech, 41 *Loy. L. A. L. Rev.* 169 (2008).

35. *Id.* at 9 (quoting Jürgen Habermas, *The Theory of Communicative Action* 81 (Thomas McCarthy, trans., 1987)).

36. *See* Meiklejohn, *Free Speech and Its Relation to Self-Government, supra* note 2, at 39, 57, 62–63; *compare id.* at 46 (describing the First Amendment as "offer[ing] defense to men who plan and advocate and incite toward corporate action for the common good"), *and id.* at 94 (describing the First Amendment as not protecting "men . . engaged . . . in argument, or inquiry, or advocacy, or incitement which is directed toward our private interests, private privileges, private possessions").

37. Post, Viewpoint Discrimination, *supra* note 34 at 176 (internal quotation omitted).

38. Meiklejohn, *Free Speech and Its Relation to Self-Government, supra* note 2, at 26–27. Zechariah Chaffee criticized Meiklejohn for linking the First Amendment to the principle of "universal suffrage" because, at the time of the First Amendment's framing, the right to vote was anything but universal. *See* Zechariah Chafee Jr., Book Review, 62 *Harv. L. Rev.* 891, 896 (1949).

39. Alexander Meiklejohn, The First Amendment Is an Absolute, 1961 *Sup. Ct. Rev.* 245, 263 (1961).

40. Meiklejohn, *Free Speech and Its Relation to Self-Government, supra* note 2, at 25–26.

41. *See id.* at 26.

42. *Id.* at 25.

43. *Id.*

44. Alexander Meiklejohn, *Political Freedom: The Constitutional Powers of the People* 55 (1960).

45. Meiklejohn, *Free Speech and Its Relation to Self-Government*, *supra* note 2, at 26.

46. *Id.*

47. *Id.*

48. *Id.*

49. *See id.* at 23 ("The meeting has assembled, not primarily to talk, but primarily by means of talking to get business done. And the talking must be regulated and abridged as doing of the business under actual conditions may require").

50. *Id.* at 22–23.

51. *See id.* at 23–24 ("These speech-abridging activities of the town meeting indicate what the First Amendment to the Constitution does not forbid").

52. *Id.* at 27.

53. *See* Redish, *supra* note 9, at 1435.

54. *Cf.* Meiklejohn, *Free Speech and Its Relation to Self-Government*, *supra* note 2, at 26 ("When men govern themselves, it is they—and no else—who must pass judgment upon unwisdom and unfairness and danger").

55. *See id.* at 71 (criticizing Justice Oliver Wendell Holmes's First Amendment jurisprudence for its basis in a "philosophy of . . . excessive individualism"); *id.* at 75 (as part of this critique, arguing that Justice Holmes "does not pay attention [to] the Constitution itself" because he says nothing about the "fundamental agreement among us" to be a "self-governing community").

56. *See*, for example, *id.* at 62–63.

57. *See*, for example, Martin H. Redish and Gary Lippman, Freedom of Expression and the Civic Republican Revival in Constitutional Theory: The Ominous Implications, 79 *Cal. L. Rev.* 267, 291–292 (1991) (arguing that the New England town meeting is an inapt analogy to modern society); Ronald A. Cass, The Perils of Positive Thinking: Constitutional Interpretation and Negative First Amendment Theory, 34 *UCLA L. Rev.* 1405, 1419 (1987) (suggesting that by "idealiz[ing] the town meeting, Meiklejohn underestimates the array of self-governing speech); Kenneth Karst, Equality and the First Amendment, 43 *U. Chi. L. Rev.* 20, 40 (1975) (criticizing Meiklejohn for the assumption that the state can be an impartial moderator that determines when "'everything worth saying'" has been said.

58. *See* Meiklejohn, *Free Speech and Its Relation to Self-Government*, *supra* note 2, at 37–41.

59. *See id.* at 39, 57, 62–63; *compare id.* at 46 (describing the First Amendment as "offer[ing] defense to men who plan and advocate and incite toward corporate action for the common good"), *and id.* at 94 (describing the First Amendment as not protecting "men . . . engaged . . . in argument, or inquiry, or advocacy, or incitement which is directed toward our private interests, private privileges, private possessions").

60. *Id.* at 95.

61. *Id.*

62. *Id.* at 25.

63. *Id.* at 46.

64. *Id.* at 94.

65. *Cf.* Chafee, *supra* note 38, at 899–900 (describing the premise of a boundary between private and public speech as "the most serious weakness" of Meiklejohn's theory). Meiklejohn himself recognized that public and private interests are "curiously intermingled"; Meiklejohn, *Free Speech and Its Relation to Self-Government*, *supra* note 2, at 40. For more detailed criticism of his theory due to the impossibility of separating private and public speech, see Martin H. Redish, The First Amendment in the Marketplace: Commercial Speech and the Values of Free Expression, 39 *Geo. Wash. L. Rev.* 429, 434–438 (1971).

66. *See* Martin H. Redish, The Value of Free Speech, 130 *U. Pa. L. Rev.* 591, 606–607 (1982) (arguing that the same level of protection should be afforded to speech that facilitates individual decision making as that afforded to speech that facilitates collective decision making because "whether . . . decisions are made collectively or by the individual, in a democracy we assume the moral value of self-rule").

67. *See* discussion *supra* at 34–36.

68. On occasion Meiklejohn does actually appear to adopt this perspective. At one point, he argues that

> such books as Hitler's *Mein Kampf,* or Lenin's *The State and the Revolution,* or the *Communist Manifesto,* or Engels and Marx, may be freely printed, freely sold, freely distributed, freely read, freely discussed, freely believed, freely distributed throughout the United States. And the purpose of that provision is not to protect the need of Hitler or Lenin or Engels or Marx to "express his opinions on matters vital to him if life is to be worth living." We are not defending the financial interests of a publisher, or a distributor, or even of a writer. We are saying that the citizens of the United States will be fit to govern themselves under their own institutions only if they have faced squarely and fearlessly everything that can be said in favor of those institutions, everything that can be said against them.

Meikeljohn, *supra* note 2, at 91 (quoting Zechariah Chafee Jr., *Free Speech and Its Relation to the United States* 33 [1942]); *see also id.* at 94 [concluding that First Amendment protection extends to "speech which bears, directly or indirectly, upon issues with which voters have to deal—only, therefore, to matters of public interest"]).

69. Thus, Robert Post's participatory theory of the First Amendment adopts something approaching this perspective in defining "public discourse" because his theory posits that the principal democratic value of free speech is its potential to engender democratic legitimacy in the speaker. For a full discussion of this point, see discussion *infra* at 49–50.

70. Though it does not suggest that speech be classified according to a public/private dichotomy, the adversarial theory of free expression proposed in this book falls into this category to the extent it recognizes democratic value both in the individual's full access to information relevant to her self-determination and in the individual's full ability to advocate to influence the self-determination of others. *See* discussion *infra* at 70–74.

71. For an example of a conjunctive definition of public speech, see Cass Sunstein, Free Speech Now, 59 *U. Chi. L. Rev.* 255, 304 (1992) (classifying speech as "political speech" when *"it is both intended and received as a contribution to public deliberation about some issue"*). Such a hybrid is illogical for a theory of free speech that recognizes the value of free speech to accrue *either* to listeners *or* speakers. If the theory posits that the value of free speech accrues to listeners, it is underinclusive to the extent it excludes speech that might to be relevant to listener's self-governing interests because it is not democratically significant to its speaker. If the theory posits that the value of free speech accrues to speakers, it is underinclusive to the extent it excludes speech that might be democratically significant to the speaker because it is not relevant to its audience's democratic decisions.

72. See Meiklejohn, *Free Speech and Its Relation to Self-Government, supra* note 2, at 104 ("[Radio] is not entitled to First Amendment protection. It is not engaged in the task of enlarging and enriching human communication. It is engaged in making money. And the First Amendment does not intend to guarantee men freedom to say what private interest pays them to say for its own advantage. It intends only to make men free to say what, as citizens, they think . . . about the general welfare").

73. *See id.* at 39; *cf.* Cass, *supra* note 57, at 1419–1420 (finding it "baffling" that Meiklejohn would exclude the paid lobbyist's speech from the First Amendment because his speech is not "unimportant to political debate nor useless to individuals interested in influencing public policies that affect them"); Chafee, *supra* note 38, at 899 ("If discussing public questions with money in sight is outside the First Amendment, how about speeches by aspirants to a $75,000 job in Washington or editorials in newspapers or books on Free Speech?"). Also relevant is Meikeljohn's discussion of the clause of the First Amendment that forbids the government from "abridging . . . the right of the people . . . to petition the government for a redress of grievances." U.S. Const. Amend. I. Such claims by individuals are "public" and deserving of the unqualified protection of the First Amendment, Meiklejohn argued, because those who petition the government for redress "are not saying 'We want this; please give it to us.' They are saying to officials who are their agents, 'You have made a mistake; kindly correct it.'" Meiklejohn, *Free Speech and Its Relation to Self-Government, supra* note 2, at 40-41.

74. See *New York Times Co. v. Sullivan*, 376 U.S. 254, 266 (1964); *Smith v. California*, 361 U. S. 147, 150 (1959) (books); *Joseph Burstyn, Inc. v. Wilson*, 343 U. S. 495, 501 (1952) (motion pictures); and *Murdock v. Pennsylvania*, 319 U.S. 105, 111 (1943) (religious literature).

75. *See* Meiklejohn, *Free Speech and Its Relation to Self-Government, supra* note 2.

76. This discussion ignores the obvious and insurmountable difficulty that Meiklejohn's regime would encounter in seeking to have a reviewing court attempt to discern a speaker's subjective motivation in the individual case.

77. *See* Meiklejohn, *Free Speech and Its Relation to Self-Government, supra* note 2, at x–xiv.

78. *See* discussion *supra* at 34–36.

79. *See* Meiklejohn, *Free Speech and Its Relation to Self-Government, supra* note 2, at 91.

80. History alone provides ample reason to question this viewpoint. Consider the role economic self-interest played in demands for democratic political institutions in the first place. *See* Theodore Draper, *A Struggle for Power: The American Revolution* (1996) (arguing that the British "economic exploitation" of American colonists was a "root" cause of the Revolution). Some historians have gone even further to argue that the Constitution itself reflects the framers' economic self-interest. *See*, for example, Charles A. Beard, *An Economic Interpretation of the Constitution of the United States* 17 (2004) (1913) (arguing that the Constitution "was not the product of an abstraction known as 'the whole people,' but of a group of economic interests which must have expected beneficial results from its adoption"). *See generally* Chapter Five, *infra*.

81. Martin H. Redish and Clifford W. Berlow, The Class Action as Political Theory, 85 *Wash. U. L.* Rev. 753 (2007) (describing these antecedent decisions as "process-based autonomy" decisions).

82. *Cf.* Meiklejohn, *Free Speech and Its Relation to Self-Government*, *supra* note 2, at 26.

83. *See*, for example, Post, Commercial Speech, *supra* note 25, at 2367–2368 (describing two "historically . . . competing accounts of the practice of self-determination").

84. Post, Viewpoint Discrimination, *supra* note 34.

85. *See*, for example, Post, *Constitutional Domains*, *supra* note 3, at 6. Post argues, for instance, that majority rule is significant only because it is a "mechanism to realize the value of collective self-determination." *Id.* Treating majority rule as "an end in itself," he suggests, is a mistake. *Id.*

86. *See* Meiklejohn, *Free Speech and Its Relation to Self-Government*, *supra* note 2, at 26.

87. Post, Equality and Autonomy, *supra* note 18, at 1524.

88. *See* Post, *Constitutional Domains*, *supra* note 3, at 6–7; *see also* Post, Reconciling, *supra* note 28, at 2367 (describing democracy as those processes that permit individuals to "identify a government as their own"); and Post, Community and the First Amendment, 29 *Ariz. St. L.J.* 473, 480 (1997) (describing democracy as those processes that all individuals to "sense that the decisions and actions of their nation are responsive to their will").

89. Post, Equality and Autonomy, *supra* note 18, at 1523. Post's suggestion that this conviction must be "warranted" suggests that he is not focused on the individual's subjective understanding of democratic legitimacy only. Indeed, it even seems to suggest that the objective reality of democratic self-determination is a necessary condition for democratic legitimacy. Even so, Post's participatory theory is strangely dismissive of democratic processes that promote the objective reality of democratic self-determination. *See* discussion *infra* at 50–53.

90. *See*, for example, Post, Reconciling, *supra* note 28, at 2368 ("Democracy requires that citizens experience their state as an example of authentic self-determination").

91. Post, Commercial Speech, *supra* note 25, at 7; *see also* Post, *Constitutional Domains*, *supra* note 3, at 7 (describing "reconciliation" between individual and collective self-determination to be a necessary condition for democratic legitimacy).

92. Post, Reconciling, *supra* note 28, at 2368.

93. *Id.* at 2367.

94. *Id.* at 2368 (noting that how "citizens experience their state as an example of authentic self-determination" is a "puzzle" because "citizens can expect to disagree with many of the specific actions of their government").

95. *See id.* at 2368.

96. Post, Commercial Speech, *supra* note 25, at 7 (emphasis added).

97. Post, Equality and Autonomy, *supra* note 18, at 1524 (emphasis added).

98. Post, *Constitutional Domains*, *supra* note 3, at 7 ("The essential problematic of democracy . . . lies in the reconciliation of individual and collective autonomy").

99. Id. at 9 (quoting Jürgen Habermas, *The Theory of Communicative Action* 81 [Thomas McCarthy, trans., 1987]).

100. *See* discussion *infra* at 48–50.

101. *See* Post, Reconciling, *supra* note 28, at 2368; *see also* Post, *Constitutional Domains*, *supra* note 3, at 7 ("If public discourse is kept free for the autonomous participation of all individual citizens, and if government decisionmaking is subordinated to the public opinion produced by public discourse, there is the possibility that citizens will come to identify with the state as representative of their own collective self-determination").

102. Post, Equality and Autonomy, *supra* note 18, at 1524.

103. *See*, for example, Post, *Constitutional Domains*, *supra* note 3, at 7.

104. Post, Reconciling, *supra* note 28, at 2368; *see also id.* ("The participatory approach understand the First Amendment . . . as safeguarding the ability of individual citizens to participate in the formation of public opinion").

105. Post, Equality and Autonomy, *supra* note 18, at 1523.

106. *See*, for example, Post, Reconciling, *supra* note 28, at 2368 ("Democracy requires that citizens experience their state as an example of authentic self-determination").

107. *Cf.* Post, Commercial Speech, *supra* note 25, at 7 (describing the effect the opportunity to participate in public discourse has on an individual's sense of democratic legitimacy).

108. Post, Equality and Autonomy, *supra* note 18, at 1523 (emphasis added).

109. *See*, for example, Post, *Constitutional Domains*, *supra* note 3, at 7.

110. *See* Post, Reconciling, *supra* note 28, at 2373–2374.

111. *See*, for example, Post, Meiklejohn's Mistake, *supra* note 17, at 1114–1116.

112. *See* Post, Equality and Autonomy, *supra* note 18, at 1523–1524.

113. *Id.* at 1524.

114. Post provides absolutely no empirical support for the claim that voting does not support democratic legitimacy. He rests his position simply on the conclusion he draws from his hypothetical, "undemocratic" society. For the argument that voting, in reality, *does* advance democratic legitimacy as Post defines it, see discussion *infra* at 50–53. In any event, voting is itself an *exercise* of self-government, regardless of how individuals perceive it.

115. Of course, this is an enormous stipulation: Part of the point of the vote in the first place is that, without it, we could never expect government to have such honorable motives.

116. In other words, both majoritarianism and public discourse are necessary but insufficient conditions for democratic legitimacy.

117. Post seems to suggest as much to the extent that he believes that censorship of "information relevant to the voting of wise decisions" does not "endanger the process of democratic legitimation." Post, Commercial Speech, *supra* note 25, at 14–15. Post might respond that his hypothetical construct is not designed to demonstrate the irrelevance of voting but rather the emptiness of voting absent complementary participation. But, while his hypothetical construct conceivably *could* be employed to make this point, it is not the point Post ultimately makes. Rather, as will be demonstrated, Post concludes that the value of voting and the corresponding free speech interest in making the citizen's vote more informed is "lexically inferior" to the free speech value of participation. *See* discussion *infra* at 57–60. Thus, the criticism is fully justified.

118. Post, Equality and Autonomy, *supra* note 18, at 1523.

119. *Reynolds v. Sims*, 377 U.S. 533, 555 (1964); *see also Burson v. Freeman*, 504 U.S. 191, 198 (1992) (recognizing the vote as "a right at the heart of our democracy" and upholding under strict scrutiny a state statute that prohibited some forms of public discourse—the solicitation of votes and the display of campaign materials—in the vicinity of polling places because of its potential to interfere with the right to vote); *Wesberry v. Sanders*, 376 U.S. 1, 17 (1964) ("No right is more precious in a free country than that of having a voice in the election of those who make the laws under which, as good citizens, we must live. Other rights, even the most basic, are illusory if the right to vote is undermined").

120. Thus, the emphasis in the *Federalist Papers*, for instance, that the "electors" in the American republic would be "not the rich more than the poor; not the learned more than the ignorant; not the haughty heirs of distinguished names, more than the humble sons of obscure and unpropitious fortune." *The Federalist*, No. 57, at 308–309 (James Madison) (J. R. Pole, ed., 2005). Indeed, *Federalist* No. 54 emphasizes that the vote facilitates political equality and the procedural fairness not simply when the people vote in elections but also when their representatives vote in Congress. "Each vote whether proceeding from a larger or smaller state, or a state more or less wealthy or powerful, will have an equal weight and efficacy; in the same manner as the votes individually given in a state legislature, by the representatives of unequal counties or other districts, have each a precise equality of value and effect; or if there be any difference in the case, it proceeds from the difference in the personal character of the individual representative, rather than from any regard to the extent of the district from which he comes." *The Federalist* No. 54, at 298 (James Madison).

121. *See* discussion *supra* at 43–49.

122. Post *did* adopt this approach to determine that public discourse, but not voting, is necessary for democratic legitimacy. Recall his hypothetical in which

he posited a society with full voting rights but no public discourse. There he concluded that the absence of public discourse would destroy democratic legitimacy. *See supra* notes 108–109 and accompanying text. However, after making the negative inference from this hypothetical that public discourse must create democratic legitimacy, he never applies the same logic to recognize the role information and democratic decision making via the vote have for democratic legitimacy.

123. For a full discussion of Post's First Amendment theory, see discussion *infra* at 53–69. Briefly, in the First Amendment context, Post suggests that certain forms of informational speech that admittedly assists individuals in their democratic decision making may not qualify as public discourse if the speech was not spoken as part of an effort to engage public opinion. The speech is not public discourse, the argument goes, because the speech has no effect on the speaker's sense of democratic legitimacy. Post never considers, however, the effect governmental regulation of such speech will have on the *audience*'s sense of democratic legitimacy. In other words, concluding that the existence of certain speech does not create democratic legitimacy for the speaker, Post overlooks the extent to which its governmentally enforced absence will destroy democratic legitimacy for the audience.

124. *See*, for example, Post, Commercial Speech, *supra* note 25, at 12 (describing public discourse as a "necessary [but not sufficient] precondition for democratic legitimation"); Post, Equality and Autonomy, *supra* note 18, at 1528 ("I do not mean to deny, of course, that voting is an important means of participation in a democratic polity. I only claim that voting is not by itself sufficient to realize the value of democratic self-governance").

125. *Id.* at 1524.

126. Post, *Constitutional Domains*, *supra* note 3, at 7.

127. *See* Robert C. Post, Racist Speech, Democracy, and the First Amendment, 32 *Wm. & Mary L. Rev.* 267, 283 (1991) [hereinafter Post, Racist Speech] ("The very purpose of [public discourse] is the practice of self-determination. The goal is 'agreement' [or the attainment of 'a common will'] because in such circumstances the individual will is by hypothesis completely reconciled with the general will. . . . this goal is purely aspirational"). In this regard, Post's participatory concept of democracy most clearly reflects shared assumptions with the political theory of deliberative democracy. That connection, and the underlying theory of deliberative democracy, was discussed in Chapter Two. *See* discussion *supra* at 24–26.

128. *Id.* at 283.

129. *See*, for example, *id.* at 283 ("Absolute agreement can never actually be reached"); Post, Meiklejohn's Mistake, *supra* note 17, at 1115 (noting that the postulate of a "determinate fusion of individual and collective will" is "unconvincing under modern conditions of heterogeneity").

130. Robert Post, Democracy, Popular Sovereignty, and Judicial Review, 86 *Cal. L. Rev.* 429, 436 (1998).

131. *See*, for example, *id.* at 436 (If democratic self-government requires that citizens identify with a system of open participation in the formation of public opinion, democratic legitimacy is correspondingly rendered independent of the particular legislative outcomes of that system. This independence allows demo-

cratic legitimacy to fit more or less comfortably with the 'irreparable reasonable disagreement' that characterizes modern heterogeneous states. [quoting John Rawls, *Political Liberalism* 35 (1993)]); Post, Racist Speech, *supra* note 127, at 2368 (describing public discourse as facilitating democratic legitimacy so long as all citizens are permitted to participate in it and so long as it does not "reflect the values and priorities of some vision of collective identity"); and Post, Meiklejohn's Mistake, *supra* note 17, at 1116 ("Although citizens may not agree with all legislative enactments, although there may be no determinate fusion of individual and collective will, citizens can nevertheless embrace the government as rightfully 'their own' because of their engagement in these communicative processes").

132. Post, Commercial Speech, *supra* note 25, at 7.

133. Post, Meiklejohn's Mistake, *supra* note 17, at 1116.

134. *See* discussion *supra* at 51–52.

135. Post, Reconciling, *supra* note 28, at 2368; *see also id.* ("The participatory approach understand the First Amendment . . . as safeguarding the ability of individual citizens to participate in the formation of public opinion").

136. As an example, consider Post's argument that censorship of speech that facilitates informed decision making does not "endanger the process of democratic legitimation." Post, Commercial Speech, *supra* note 25, at 14–15.

137. *See* Post, Reconciling, *supra* note 28, at 2372 ("Where the doctrinal implications of different prominent theories of the First Amendment collide, courts will tend to give priority to the participatory theory of democracy").

138. *Id.* at 2373.

139. *See* Post, *Democracy, supra* note 30.

140. *See*, for example, *Debs v. United States*, 249 U.S. 211 (1911); *Gitlow v. New York*, 268 U.S. 652 (1925); and *Dennis v. United States*, 341 U.S. 494 (1951).

141. *See Brandenburg v. Ohio*, 395 U.S. 444 (1969); and *Hess v. Indiana*, 414 U.S. 105 (1973).

142. *See*, for example, Post, Recuperating First Amendment Doctrine, 47 *Stan. L. Rev.* 1249, 1272 (1995) ("The search for any general free speech principle is bound to fail. Were the Constitution to recognize and impose a single general value for speech, it would in a Procrustean way force the entire spectrum of state regulation of forms of social interaction into conformity with the particular social practices required by that single value. . . . All of life is not about truth-seeking; nor is it about democracy"); *id.* at 1274 (criticizing the Court for attempting to "craft a doctrine that would reflect a universal and general constitutional value for speech").

143. *See*, for example, Post, Reconciling, *supra* note 28, at 2371–2372 (noting the "priority" of the participatory theory over other free speech theories).

144. *See id.* at 2372 ("First Amendment jurisprudence contains several operational and legitimate theories of freedom of speech, so that it is quite implausible to aspire to clarify First Amendment doctrine by abandoning all but one of these theories").

145. *See id.* at 2373 ("The rules of the Meiklejohnian perspective will be imposed when required by that perspective and not incompatible with the participatory theory").

146. *See id.* at 2372–2373 (recognizing that the First Amendment may also protect speech for its truth-seeking value under the marketplace of ideas theory, or for its self-realization value); and Post, Equality and Autonomy, *supra* note 18, at 1521 ("To attribute to the First Amendment the purpose of facilitating collective self-determination is not necessarily to deny that the First Amendment can also serve other, distinct purposes").

147. *See* Post, Reconciling, *supra* note 28, at 2373.

148. *See* Post, Commercial Speech, *supra* note 25, at 5 (explaining that commercial speech has "subordinate" constitutional status because it "inform[s] an audience . . . about matters pertinent to democratic decision making" rather than "participat[ion] in the process of self-governance"). Of course, as Post admits and the preceding discussion of Meiklejohn's theory demonstrates, suggesting that commercial speech is protected under a Meiklejohnian theory is quite ironic because Meiklejohn believed commercial speech is not protected under the First Amendment at all. *See id.* at 13n55 (recognizing the irony); Meiklejohn, *Free Speech and Its Relation to Self-Government*, *supra* note 2, at 39 ("The constitutional status of a merchant advertising his wares . . . is utterly different from that of a citizen who is planning for the general welfare").

149. *See*, for example, Post, Commercial Speech, *supra* note 25, at 26–33 (describing how certain speech regulations that would be prohibited under the participatory theory may be entirely acceptable under the Meiklejohnian theory).

150. *See*, for example, *id.* at 26–32 (explaining why compelled speech, overbroad speech regulation, and prior restraints are unconstitutional under the participatory theory but may not be under the Meiklejohnian theory and arguing, therefore, that such regulations are unconstitutional when applied to public discourse but constitutional when applied to commercial speech).

151. For full discussion of this point, see discussion *supra* at 49–53.

152. *See*, Post, Commercial Speech, *supra* note 25, at 32. Post explains:

> To chill commercial speech is to lose information. On other constitutional value is at stake. Information is fungible. The central insight of Meiklejohnian analysis is that it does not matter which speaker provides information, so long as it is provided. If a particular speaker is chilled, therefore, it is quite possible that equivalent information will become available from other sources.

Id.

153. *See* Meiklejohn, *Free Speech and Its Relation to Self-Government*, *supra* note 2, at 25 ("If . . . at a town meeting, twenty like-minded citizens have become a 'party,' and if one of them has read to the meeting an argument which they have all approved, it would be ludicrously out of order for each of the others to insist on reading it again. No competent moderator would tolerate that wasting of the time available for free discussion. What is essential is not that everyone shall speak, but that everything worth saying shall be said").

154. This attitude, of course, goes back to the premise of the participatory theory that voting is merely a "mechanism" of democratic decision making. *See* discussion *supra* at 43–53.

155. *See*, for example, *Edenfield v. Fane*, 507 U.S. 761, 766 (1993) (recognizing that commercial solicitation may have "considerable value" because the "seller has a strong financial incentive to educate the market and stimulate demand").

156. *Virginia Bd. of Pharmacy v. Virginia Citizens Consumer Council*, 425 U.S. 748, 757n15 (1976) ("We are aware of no general principle that freedom of speech may be abridged when the speaker's listeners could come by his message by some other means. . . . Nor have we recognized any such limitation on the independent right of the listener to receive the information sought to be communicated"). *See also Schneider v. State*. For a more detailed examination of commercial speech protection viewed through the lens of adversary democracy, see generally Chapter Four, *infra*.

157. Post, Reconciling, *supra* note 28, at 2368.

158. *See id.* ("To the extent that the state cuts off particular citizens from participation in the public discourse it pro tanto negates its claim to democratic legitimacy with respect to such citizens"); *see also* Post, Commercial Speech, *supra* note 25, at 32 ("Democratic legitimation is not fungible; it is earned, speaker by speaker. A person who participation within public discourse has been chilled has by hypothesis become that much more alienated from the state").

159. Post, Reconciling, *supra* note 28, at 2368. If the state regulates the public discourse in such a manner, Post correctly argues, "It preempts the very democratic process by which collective identity is to be determined." *Id.*

160. *See* discussion *supra* at 36–43.

161. The point is that the listener derives legitimacy directly from her status as an audience member in the public discourse, and thus listening should be considered a valued form of "participation" under the terms of the participatory theory. It is distinct, then, from the separate argument that that the listener derives legitimacy from the decision-making process, and therefore listeners' rights to access public discourse must be protected as incident to that decision making. This second argument for listeners' rights is based on the contention that the participatory model has an underinclusive understanding of the conditions for democratic legitimacy, which is developed at length in the preceding discussion. *See* discussion *supra* at 49–50. The argument for listener autonomy here sets that critique aside, assumes that participation in the public discourse is *the* source of democratic legitimacy, and argues that Post has an unduly narrow idea of "participation."

162. It should be noted that for purposes of the present discussion, the analysis suspends disbelief on the correctness of Post's choice to assume democracy as the normative foundation of free speech analysis, rather than to ask why we choose a democratic system in the first place and, by this process of reverse engineering, glean more foundational normative values underlying the commitment to both democracy and free expression.

163. *See* discussion *supra* at 56–57.

164. For a more detailed exploration of the inseparability of information and opinion, see discussion *infra* at 58–59.

165. *See generally*, Post, *Democracy, supra* note 30.

166. For an explanation as to why Post's description of the protected speaker category is unduly narrow, see discussion *infra* at 62–69.

167. Post, *Democracy, supra* note 30, at 23–24; 41–43.

168. *Id.*

169. *See* discussion *supra* at 34–43. As Post recognizes, however, Meiklejohn would not have extended this logic to commercial expression, which Post does. Thus, Post employs Meiklejohn's reasoning purely as an analogy. Post, Democracy, *supra* note 30, at 16 and 41.

170. 376 U.S. 254 (1964). Meiklejohn suggested the decision was an occasion for "dancing in the streets." Harry Kalven, The New York Times Case: A Note on "The Central Meaning of the First Amendment," 1964 *Sup. Ct. Rev.* 191, 221n125.

171. Compare *Virginia Board; see generally* Chapter Four, *infra.*

172. *See generally* Redish, Product Health Claims, *supra* note 9.

173. Post, Commercial Speech, *supra* note 25, at 5 (emphasis added).

174. Post's protection of the audience's interest in the informational value of speech within a secondary, lexically inferior theory of the First Amendment does not ameliorate his wholesale indifference here to the legitimation listener's gain from their participation in public discourse.

175. Of course, to the extent the listener does so ultimately by voting according to her own self-determined choices, Post would consider this participation to be less important than participation in the public discourse. By Post's unsupported hypothesis, voting does not facilitate democratic legitimacy in the way that participation in public discourse does. *See* discussion *supra* at 45–53.

176. This is nothing more than a categorical judgment on Post's part, one that is wholly unsupported. For further analysis of the point, see discussion *infra* at 61.

177. *See* discussion *supra* at 56–59.

178. *See* discussion *supra* at 58–59.

179. The irrationality of this distinction may reasonably raise questions about the role that ideological hostility could conceivably play in the shaping of scholarly arguments against commercial speech protection. *See generally* Chapter Four, *infra.*

180. Post, Reconciling, *supra* note 28, at 2368. If the state regulates the public discourse in such a manner, Post correctly argues, "It preempts the very democratic process by which collective identity is to be determined." *Id.*

181. Post, Meiklejohn's Mistake, *supra* note 17, at 1120.

182. Meiklejohn, *Free Speech and Its Relation to Self-Government, supra* note 2, at 23.

183. Post, Meiklejohn's Mistake, *supra* note 17, at 1120.

184. *See* Robert C. Post, The Constitutional Concept of Public Discourse: Outrageous Opinion, Democratic Deliberation, and *Hustler Magazine v. Falwell,* 103 *Harv. L. Rev.* 601, 683–684 [hereinafter Post, Concept of Public Discourse] (recognizing that the definition of the boundaries of public discourse is itself a form of speech regulation).

185. *Cf.* Post, Meiklejohn's Mistake, *supra* note 17, at 1118 ("The state ought not to be empowered to control the agenda of public discourse of the presentation and characterization of issues within public discourse, because such control would necessarily circumscribe the potential for collective self-determination").

186. Post, Reconciling, *supra* note 28, at 2368. Post admits this, for instance, when he says that the "ultimate fact of ideological regulation" that comes with defining the boundaries of public discourse cannot "be blinked." Post, Concept of Public Discourse, *supra* note 184, at 683. Post suggests that such "ideological regulation of speech is deeply distasteful." *Id*. Yet, as this section suggests, he only encourages more ideological regulation of speech by devising inconsistent definitions of public discourse and contradictory standards for evaluating speech.

187. Post, Racist Speech, *supra* note 127, at 288–289 (describing the difficulty of defining the boundaries of public discourse).

188. *Id*. at 288.

189. *Id*. (internal quotation marks omitted).

190. Post, Equality and Autonomy, *supra* note 18, at 1521n15. In other words, Post is arguing that speech that creates common ground among individuals is protected as public discourse because "wide circulation of 'shared social stimuli'" allows individuals who otherwise would be "strangers" to share a "public communicative sphere" in which they can "forge" a "common will." Post, Recuperating, *supra* note 142, at 1276.

191. *Id*. at 11–12.

192. *Id*. at 17.

193. *See* Commercial Speech, *supra* note 25, at 18.

194. The restrictive definition, then, follows from Post's equation of participation in the public discourse with speaking in the public discourse. *See* discussion *supra* at xx.

195. *See*, for example, Post, Equality and Autonomy, *supra* note 18, at 1521n15 (describing why abstract art and wordless music are public discourse).

196. Like analysis of the "effort" behind the speech, analysis of whether the specific speech act "intrinsically" represents "participation" also shifts the First Amendment focus to the speaker and excludes reference to any possible participatory motive of a listener. See Post, Commercial Speech, *supra* note 25, at 20. This is because the listener's participatory motive is extrinsic to the speech itself.

197. *Id*. at 20 ("To include speech within public discourse is to signify that it is constitutionally valued not merely for the contribution it may make to public discussion, but also, intrinsically for the engagement it represents in the public life of the nation").

198. *See id*. at 13 (admitting that commercial speech affects the "formation of public opinion . . . as a by-product of the effort to sell goods" but nonetheless concluding that commercial speech is not public discourse). Post concedes, for instance, that commercial advertising "deeply influences our sense of ourselves as a nation" and provides information that is "highly relevant to the formation of democratic public opinion" but still concludes that commercial speech is not public discourse. *See id*. at 11–15.

199. Others scholars who propose democratic theories of the First Amendment invoke speaker motive as an explicit criterion in classifying speech. *See*, for example, Sunstein, *supra* note 71, at 304 (classifying speech as "high value," "political speech" when "*it is both intended and received as a contribution to public deliberation about some issue*").

200. *See* Post, Racist Speech, *supra* note 127, at 324n253 ("As a matter of policy . . . it is always dangerous to make the legality of speech depend primarily upon an assessment of speaker's intent, for there is a powerful tendency to attribute bad motives to those with whom we fundamentally disagree").

201. Post, Commercial Speech, *supra* note 25, at 12 ("This is not ultimately a judgment about the motivations of particular persons, but instead about the social significance of a certain kind of speech").

202. *Id.*

203. Of course, any evaluation of speech's "significance" invites judges to determine that speech they dislike is "insignificant" and therefore unprotected. Post's concept of "social significance" has the added tendency of inviting judges to discriminate against disfavored speakers, as well as disfavored speech.

204. *Id.* at 19.

205. *See* discussion *supra* at 34–36.

206. Indeed, in other contexts, Post actually recognizes that a participatory motive and a profit motive are not mutually exclusive, and that they can exist in the same speech and often do. "Many forms of public discourse," he suggests, "are fueled by an intense and hardy search for profits: motions pictures, books, magazines, and newspapers to mention a few." *Id.* at 31–32.

207. *Id.* at 20 ("To include speech within public discourse is to signify that it is constitutionally valued not merely for the contribution it may make to public discussion, but also, intrinsically for the engagement it represents in the public life of the nation").

208. *Id.* at 15–16, 16n68.

209. *Id.* at 32 (making this distinction in the context of distinguishing commercial speech from public discourse) (emphasis added).

210. *Id.* at 12.

211. Post, Concept of Public Discourse, *supra* note 184, at 680.

212. Post, Commercial Speech, *supra* note 25, at 18.

213. *Id.* at 20.

214. *Id.* at 27.

215. *Id.* at 4 (emphasis added).

216. Post, Reconciling, *supra* note 28, at 2368 (arguing that regulations of public discourse based on one "vision of collective identity" are illegitimate).

217. Post, Concept of Public Discourse, *supra* note 184, at 680.

218. Post, Meiklejohn's Mistake, *supra* note 17, at 1116–1119.

219. Post has argued that the courts fix the boundaries of the public discourse through reference to community social norms that "form part of our cultural inheritance" and determine "when we instinctively perceive speech as 'public.'" Post, Concept of Public Discourse, *supra* note 184, at 680–681. To perceive and apply these social norms effectively, judges must exercise their "moral tact" to recognize the "socially determined variability" of community norms based on their context. *Id.* In a more recent article, Post has argued that the Court should consider the "constitutional culture" of nonjudicial actors in a variety of contexts, including its determination of the "social significance" of speech. In considering the Court's

shift from excluding movies from the First Amendment in 1915 to including movies within the core of the First Amendment in 1952, Post writes:

> The social significance of movies may have altered so as to bring film within the ambit of an otherwise 'changeless' constitutional protection. . . . At what point in time the communicative significance of movies sufficiently changed as to bring film within the protection of the First Amendment . . . will be an inevitably disputed question. Because culture is always in motion, because its meaning is never entirely stable or fixed, there will always be differences of cultural interpretation.

Robert C. Post, Foreword: Fashioning the Legal Constitution: Culture, Courts and Law, 117 *Harv. L. Rev.* 4, 81–83 (2003). Thus, rather than suggest that the Court originally erred in not affording movies First Amendment protection, Post suggests "the common sense of the country" and "contemporary cultural practices" supported the conclusion that movies did not implicate First Amendment values so as to warrant their constitutional protection in 1915 but did by 1952.

220. Post recognizes this at least in principle, suggesting that a pure fidelity to community norms may "hegemonically establish the dominance of the perspectives of a particular community." Post, Concept of Public Discourse, *supra* note 184, at 681.

221. Post, Reconciling, *supra* note 28, at 2368.

222. *See* discussion *supra* at 34–43 (Meiklejohn); *supra* at 56–57 (Post). Of course, each is vastly underinclusive in this regard—both seem to exclude self-interested speech only when it is motivated by economic profit, and Post excludes only speech motivated by economic profit when it is commercial speech.

223. *See* discussion *supra* at 36–41 (Meiklejohn); *supra* at 45–53 (Post).

224. *See* Meiklejohn, *Free Speech and Its Relation to Self-Government, supra* note 2, at 14–15.

225. *See* Post, Viewpoint Discrimination, *supra* note 34, at 175.

226. Id. at 9 (quoting Jürgen Habermas, *The Theory of Communicative Action* 81 [Thomas McCarthy, trans., 1987]) (emphasis added).

227. *See* Meiklejohn, *Free Speech and Its Relation to Self-Government, supra* note 2, at 39, 57, 62–63; *compare id.* at 46 (describing the First Amendment as "offer[ing] defense to men who plan and advocate and incite toward corporate action for the common good") *and id.* at 94 (describing the First Amendment as not protecting "men . . engaged . . . in argument, or inquiry, or advocacy, or incitement which is directed toward our private interests, private privileges, private possessions").

228. Post, Viewpoint Discrimination, *supra* note 34 at 176 (internal quotation omitted).

229. *Id.*

230. Jane Mansbridge, *Beyond Adversary Democracy* (2d ed., 1983). *See generally* Chapter Two, *supra*.

231. *See* Chapters One and Two, *supra*. Political theorist Jane Mansbridge first coined the term *adversary democracy* and elaborated on its meaning. *See generally* Mansbridge, *Beyond Adversary Democracy, supra* note 230.

232. It should be emphasized that the form of autonomy referred to here is confined to process-based, or what or can appropriately be called "meta" autonomy,

meaning autonomy on decisions as to how to participate in the broader decision-making process. Thus, I in no way intend to adopt wholesale the views of libertarian theorists who extend individual autonomy to include much substantive decision making, thereby insulating it from collective control. *See* Redish and Berlow, The Class Action, *supra* note 81.

233. Even when individuals choose to pursue their notions of the common good, it should be emphasized, they will be required to employ adversary strategies in their efforts against those who have a very different notion of the common good. *See* Chapter Two, *supra*.

234. *See* discussion *supra* at 39.

235. *See* discussion *supra* at 61–62.

236. For my critique of Post's reliance on tradition, *see* discussion *supra* at 61–62.

CHAPTER FOUR

1. *See*, for example, *Valentine v. Chrestensen*, 316 U.S. 52, 54 (1942) (summarily rejecting First Amendment protection for commercial speech). For a description of the early history of the commercial speech doctrine, see Ronald D. Rotunda, The Commercial Speech Doctrine in the Supreme Court, 1976 *U. Ill. L.F.* 1080.

2. 425 U.S. 748, 770–773 (1976) (holding that truthful commercial speech is protected by the First Amendment).

3. *See*, for example, *Bd. of Trustees of the State Univ. of N.Y. v. Fox*, 492 U.S. 469, 477 (1989) (keeping the protection afforded to commercial speech subordinate to that afforded to noncommercial speech by refusing to impose a "least restrictive means" standard); and *Ohralik v. Ohio State Bar Ass'n.*, 436 U.S. 447, 456 (1978) ("[C]ommercial speech [enjoys] a limited measure of protection, commensurate with its subordinate position in the scale of First Amendment values . . .").

4. *See*, for example, *Thompson v. Western States Med. Ctr.*, 535 U.S. 357, 377 (2002), and *Lorillard Tobacco Co. v. Reilly*, 533 U.S. 525, 566 (2001).

5. For example, false commercial speech is automatically excluded from the scope of the First Amendment. *Compare Cent. Hudson Gas & Elec. Corp. v. Pub. Serv. Comm'n*, 447 U.S. 557, 566 (1980) (stating that for commercial speech to come within the First Amendment's protection, it "must concern lawful activity and not be misleading"), *with N.Y. Times Co. v. Sullivan*, 376 U.S. 254, 279–780 (1964) (explaining that certain categories of false noncommercial speech receive the protection of the "actual malice" test).

6. *See*, for example, C. Edwin Baker, Realizing Self-Realization: Corporate Political Expenditures and Redish's The Value of Free Speech, 130 *U. Pa. L. Rev.* 646, 652–657 (1982).

7. *See*, for example, Robert Post, The Constitutional Status of Commercial Speech, 48 *UCLA L. Rev.* 1, 27 (2000) (discussing the difference between public discourse and commercial speech).

8. The only possible exceptions to my critique are those free speech theorists who exclude protection of commercial speech because they believe that the First Amendment protects only purely political expression and who, therefore, exclude

all forms of nonpolitical speech, including literature, art, and science, as well as commercial speech. While I believe that such an approach is grossly underprotective as a matter of First Amendment theory, it would be incorrect to view it as a form of viewpoint regulation. *See infra* at 78–79.

9. Herbert Wechsler, Toward Neutral Principles of Constitutional Law, 73 *Harv. L. Rev.* 1, 15–16 (1959).

10. *Id.*

11. *See* note 8, *supra*.

12. *See*, for example, *Bolger v. Youngs Drug Prods. Corp.*, 463 U.S. 60, 66–67 (1983).

13. *See* discussion *infra*, at 85.

14. *See* discussion *infra*, at 104–114.

15. *See* discussion *infra*, at 114–120.

16. *See Valentine v. Chrestensen*, 316 U.S. 52, 54 (1942) (summarily rejecting First Amendment protection for commercial speech).

17. Thomas I. Emerson, *The System of Freedom of Expression* 414 (1970) ("The rule that communications in the 'commercial sector' of our society are outside the system of freedom of expression . . . has been widely observed, [but] has never been fully explained").

18. Much of that scholarship has been my own. *See* Martin H. Redish, *Money Talks: Speech, Economic Power, and the Values of Democracy* 14–62 (2001) [hereinafter Redish, *Money Talks*]; Martin H. Redish, The First Amendment in the Marketplace: Commercial Speech and the Values of Free Expression, 39 *Geo. Wash. L. Rev.* 429, 431–448 (1971); *see also* Alex Kozinski and Stuart Banner, Who's Afraid of Commercial Speech? 76 *Va. L. Rev.* 627, 648–652 (1990) (arguing that commercial speech should be afforded the same protection as noncommercial speech).

19. See, for example, C. Edwin Baker, Commercial Speech: A Problem in the Theory of Freedom, 62 *Iowa L. Rev.* 1, 3 (1976) ("A complete denial of first amendment protection for commercial speech is not only consistent with, but is required by, first amendment theory").

20. *See* discussion *infra* at 85–96.

21. *See Bolger v. Youngs Drug Prods. Corp.*, 463 U.S. 60, 66–67 (1983) (holding that an advertisement does not constitute commercial speech merely because of its form, references to a product name, or because it derives from economic motivation, but rather because of a combination of all of these characteristics); and *Cent. Hudson Gas & Elec. Corp. v. Pub. Serv. Comm'n*, 447 U.S. 557, 561–562 (1980) (defining commercial speech as "expression related solely to the economic interests of the speaker" and "speech proposing a commercial transaction"). *Compare Valentine*, 316 U.S. at 54 (defining commercial advertising as commercial speech), *with Pittsburgh Press Co. v. Pittsburgh Comm'n on Human Relations*, 413 U.S. 376, 384 (1973) ("Speech is not rendered commercial by the mere fact that it relates to an advertisement").

22. This was the definition of commercial speech that I assumed when, prior to the Court's extension of meaningful First Amendment protection to commercial speech, I argued that commercial speech deserved such protection. *See* Redish, The First Amendment in the Marketplace, *supra* note 18.

23. *See*, for example, *Lorillard Tobacco Co. v. Reilly*, 533 U.S. 525, 553–554 (2001) (stating that courts have recognized the "distinction between speech proposing a commercial transaction, which occurs in an area traditionally subject to government regulation, and other varieties of speech" [quoting *Cent. Hudson*, 447 U.S. at 562]).

24. The issue becomes significantly more problematic, of course, once the debate begins to concern possible government regulation of the actual sale of commercial products or services because at that point the speech could arguably be deemed political in nature. This fact, however, simply underscores the difficulty of attempting to segregate commercial speech as a self-contained category.

25. *See Va. State Bd. of Pharmacy v. Va. Citizens Consumer Council, Inc.*, 425 U.S. 748, 785 (1976) (Rehnquist, J., dissenting); and *Bolger*, 463 U.S. at 66–67 (explaining that because speech is part of the promotion of a sale it is relevant to the determination of commercial speech).

26. *See Thompson v. Western States Med. Ctr.*, 535 U.S. 357, 366–368 (2002).

27. It should be noted that, unless otherwise specified, when I refer to "commercial speech" in the course of this chapter I intend to include only truthful, nonmisleading expression. There are a number of significant arguments growing out of the question of First Amendment protection for false or misleading commercial expression. *See*, for example, Post, The Constitutional Status of Commercial Speech, *supra* note 7, at 37–41; Martin H. Redish, Product Health Claims and the First Amendment: Scientific Expression and the Twilight Zone of Commercial Speech, 43 *Vand. L. Rev.* 1433, 1443 (1990). In prior writing, I have argued that false commercial speech, much like most false political speech, should be measured by the "actual malice" test of *New York Times Co. v. Sullivan*, 376 U.S. 254, 280 (1964). *See* Redish, *Money Talks*, *supra* note 18, at 55–56. Thus, for reasons I have explained elsewhere, I ultimately conclude that even false commercial speech is to be treated fungibly with false noncommercial speech. *See id.* at 53–56. For purposes of intellectual simplicity, however, my critique in this chapter is aimed exclusively at arguments made for providing reduced or no First Amendment protection for even wholly truthful commercial speech.

28. *See*, for example, Baker, Commercial Speech, *supra* note 19, at 3.

29. *See* discussion *infra*, at 87–90; 94–95.

30. Wechsler, Toward Neutral Principles of Constitutional Law, *supra* note 9, at 16.

31. For example, Arthur S. Miller and Ronald F. Howell, The Myth of Neutrality in Constitutional Adjudication, 27 *U. Chi. L. Rev.* 661 *passim* (1960); Jon O. Newman, Between Legal Realism and Neutral Principles: The Legitimacy of Institutional Values, 72 *Cal. L. Rev.* 200, 202–208 (1984); and Benjamin F. Wright, The Supreme Court Cannot Be Neutral, 40 *Tex. L. Rev.* 599 *passim* (1962).

32. *See generally* Wechsler, Toward Neutral Principles of Constitutional Law, *supra* note 9, at 11–19 (arguing that courts should rely on principled analysis that transcends the immediate case but providing no criteria for courts to follow).

33. *Id.* at 15.

34. *See Planned Parenthood of Se. Pa. v. Casey*, 505 U.S. 833, 979–984 (1992) (Scalia, J., concurring in part and dissenting in part).

35. *See Barenblatt v. United States*, 360 U.S. 109, 127–128 (1959).

36. Note that in shaping these rationales, I draw on the analysis first developed in my book, *Money Talks*. *See* Redish, *Money Talks, supra* note 18, at 31–53.

37. Daniel A. Farber, Free Speech without Romance: Public Choice and the First Amendment, 105 *Harv. L. Rev.* 554, 562 (1991). At the very least, he is incorrect to the extent that I am included among the description of "everyone." *See generally* Martin H. Redish, The Value of Free Speech, 130 *U. Pa. L. Rev.* 591 (1982) (arguing that nonpolitical speech, like political speech, fosters self-realization value). Other commentators who reject the view described by Farber also seem not to fall within Professor Farber's description of "everyone." *See generally* C. Edwin Baker, Scope of the First Amendment Freedom of Speech, 25 *UCLA L. Rev.* 964, 966 (1978) ("Speech is protected not as a means to a collective good but because of the value of speech conduct to the individual"); and Kozinski and Banner, Who's Afraid of Commercial Speech?, *supra* note 18 (arguing that the commercial/noncommercial distinction "makes no sense").

38. *See generally* Alexander Meiklejohn, *Free Speech and Its Relation to Self Government* 93–94 (1948) (arguing that the First Amendment protects only "speech which bears, directly or indirectly, upon issues with which voters have to deal— only, therefore, to the consideration of matters of public interest"); and Robert Bork, Neutral Principles and Some First Amendment Problems, 47 *Ind. L.J.* 1, 27– 28 (1971) (advocating constitutional protection only to expressly political speech).

39. *See* Redish, *Money Talks, supra* note 18, at 22–29.

40. *Id.*

41. *See* Martin H. Redish, *Freedom of Expression: A Critical Analysis* 19–29 (1984).

42. *See id.* Professor Shiffrin has asserted that the key to the democratic process is participation, rather than self-government. Steven Shiffrin, *Remarks at the Loyola of Los Angeles Law Review Symposium: Commercial Speech: Past, Present & Future* (Feb. 24, 2007) [hereinafter Shiffrin, *Symposium Remarks*]. However, it is difficult to comprehend what possible value participation could have completely divorced from the interest in self-determination. Participation is a rather hollow activity, absent some say in the final choice. For more detailed discussion of this issue, *see generally* Chapter Three, *supra*.

43. *See*, for example, *Bolger v. Youngs Drug Prods. Corp.*, 463 U.S. 60, 66–67 (1983); *see supra* note 12 and accompanying text.

44. Even this assertion is questionable because it assumes that somehow we are able to separate expression into neat, severable units in which we can easily distinguish between political and commercial speech. This ignores the fact that expression about commercial products and services often simultaneously implicates traditionally protected expressive categories such as political or scientific speech.

45. *Va. State Bd. of Pharmacy v. Va. Citizens Consumer Council, Inc.*, 425 U.S. 748, 772n24 (1976).

46. *Id.*

47. Farber, Free Speech without Romance, *supra* note 37, at 562.

48. *Id.* at 565 (footnote omitted).

49. *Id.* at 566.

50. Indeed, one can see this simply by a casual examination of the Supreme Court's commercial speech decisions. In virtually none of them was the primary or exclusive subject of regulation false or misleading commercial speech. *See*, for example, *Thompson v. W. States Med. Ctr.*, 535 U.S. 357, 368 (2002) (prohibition on advertising of compound drugs); *Lorillard Tobacco Co. v. Reilly*, 533 U.S. 525, 556 (2001) (restrictions on tobacco advertising); and *Greater New Orleans Broad. Ass'n v. United States*, 527 U.S. 173, 185 (1999) (restrictions on advertising of gambling).

51. Farber, Free Speech without Romance, *supra* note 37, at 565.

52. *See*, for example, *Schenck v. United States*, 249 U.S. 47, 52 (1919) (explaining that unlawful advocacy can be suppressed only when it gives rise to a clear and present danger of illegal harm).

53. *See*, for example, *Brandenburg v. Ohio*, 395 U.S. 444, 448–449 (1969) (per curiam).

54. Baker, Realizing Self-Realization, *supra* note 6, at 652.

55. *Id.*

56. The theory that free speech values should be viewed from a listener's perspective is associated primarily with the writing of Alexander Meiklejohn. *See*, for example, Meiklejohn, *Free Speech and Its Relation to Self Government*, *supra* note 38, at 60. See generally Chapter Three.

57. *See* U.S. Const. amend. I.

58. *See* C. Edwin Baker, *Human Liberty and Freedom of Speech*, 225–249 (1989).

59. Martin H. Redish, Good Behavior, Judicial Independence, and the Foundations of American Constitutionalism, 116 *Yale L.J.* 139, 146–147 (2006); *see also* Robert W. Bennett, Objectivity in Constitutional Law, 132 *U. Pa. L. Rev.* 445, 449 (1984).

60. According to Professor Hovenkamp,

> The two greatest classical *legal* institutions in the United States—the modern business corporation and the constitutional doctrine of substantive due process—are both distinctively Jacksonian products. The modern business corporation had its origin in the general corporation acts, one of the most important legal accomplishments of a regime bent on democratizing and deregulating American business.

Herbert Hovenkamp, *Enterprise and American Law, 1836–1937*, at 2 (1991). Thus, the modern business corporation is a product of the Jacksonian period, a point in American history long after the framing of the Constitution.

61. *See* Vincent Blasi, The Pathological Perspective and the First Amendment, 85 *Colum. L. Rev.* 449, 480 (1985).

62. *See*, for example, Judith Miller, Defectors Bolster U.S. Case against Iraq, Officials Say, *N.Y. Times*, Jan. 24, 2003, at A11; and Judith Miller, Disarming Saddam Hussein: Teams of Experts to Hunt Iraq Arms, *N.Y. Times*, Mar. 19, 2003, at A1.

63. Martin H. Redish, The Adversary System, Democratic Theory, and the Constitutional Role of Self-Interest: The Tobacco Wars, 1953–1971, 51 *Depaul L. Rev.* 359, 362–363 (2001) [hereinafter Redish, Adversary System].

64. *See* discussion *infra* at 94–95.

65. *See* Ronnie Dugger, The Corporate Domination of Journalism, in *The Business of Journalism* 27, 27, 34–35 (William Serrin, ed., 2000) ("Corporate censorship

now shapes the whole mainstream media process . . . . The reporter, for the dissemination of whose honest work the press is supposed to be free, is subordinated now to the nature of the corporation itself and to the mass-audience requirements, ideological restraints, profit-making imperatives . . . of those same advertising and entertainment corporations").

66. *See* discussion *supra* at 90–92.

67. This argument, it should be noted, is distinct from an argument that posits that while commercial speech is deserving of First Amendment protection in the abstract, false and misleading commercial speech is not deserving of such protection. This argument, in contrast, assumes the *inherently* misleading nature of commercial speech because of its inherent advocacy.

68. *See* discussion *infra* at 134–141.

69. As previously noted, acceptance of the appropriateness of strategic incompleteness in expression provides the foundation for our commitment to the adversary system. *See* discussion *supra* at 23. *See generally* Redish, Adversary System, *supra* note 63, (discussing the concept of adversary theory in the context of free speech and due process).

70. Puzzlingly, this inherent incentive to suppress the competition appears to have been largely ignored by certain members of the Supreme Court in the area of campaign finance regulation. On occasion the Court has urged, for example, greater-than-normal deference to legislative choices in campaign finance regulation, due to the supposed "expertise" of a governing legislative body. *See Randall v. Sorrell*, 548 U.S. 230, 248 (2006); *McConnell v. Fed. Election Comm'n*, 540 U.S. 93, 137 (2003). He does so, despite the obvious fact that sitting legislators have an inherent interest in confining the ability of opponents to equalize the advantages traditionally associated with incumbency.

71. *See* U.S. Const. art. II, § 2; *id.* art. III, § 2; *id.* art. V.

72. *See The Federalist* No. 51, at 118 (James Madison) (J. and A. McLean, eds., 1788).

73. *See id. See generally* Martin H. Redish and Elizabeth Cisar, "If Angels Were to Govern": The Need for Pragmatic Formalism in Separation of Powers Theory, 41 *Duke L. J.* 449 (1991) (discussing the doctrine of separation of powers and the various models used to resolve separation of powers disputes).

74. *See generally* Steven Kelman, "Public Choice" and Public Spirit, 87 *Pub. Int.* 80 (1987) (arguing that the practice of public choice itself is essentially immoral); Cass Sunstein, Beyond the Republican Revival, 97 *Yale L. J.* 1539 (1988) (advocating that a republican approach to the First Amendment offers reasons to reform many areas of modern law); and Cass Sunstein, Interest Groups in American Public Law, 38 *Stan. L. Rev.* 29 (1985) (suggesting that courts should use principles of republicanism to assess political processes).

75. *See*, for example, Theodore J. Lowi, *The End of Liberalism: The Second Republic of the United States*, 77–78 (2d ed. 1979).

76. *See* Martin H. Redish, The Proper Role of the Prior Restraint Doctrine in First Amendment Theory, 70 *Va. L. Rev.* 53, 76 (1984) ("Nonjudicial administrative regulators of expression exist for the sole purpose of regulating; that is their raison d'etre"); *see also* Thomas I. Emerson, The Doctrine of Prior Restraint, 20

Law & Contemp. Probs. 648, 659 (1955) ("The function of the censor is to censor. He has a professional interest in finding things to suppress").

77.   *See*, for example, *Rubin v. Coors Brewing Co.*, 514 U.S. 476, 491 (1995) (finding a law that prohibits beer labels from displaying alcohol content violates the First Amendment).

78.   It might be suggested that even if I were correct in my assertion that none of these six posited justifications provides rational support for reduced protection for commercial speech, the six of them combined may do so. I have a great deal of trouble understanding this argument; adding six losing lottery tickets together does not equal one winning lottery ticket. I have demonstrated that each, on its own terms, is false, illogical, inconsistent, or otherwise invalid. It is therefore difficult to see how each could be transformed into a necessary-but-insufficient condition for the proposition that commercial speech is undeserving of protection.

79.   *See*, for example, Daniel A. Farber & Philip P. Frickey, Practical Reason and the First Amendment, 34 *UCLA L. Rev.* 1615, 1639–1656 (1987).

80.   Professor Farber's scholarship, for example, has included both rationalist and antirationalist arguments for reduced protection of commercial speech. As for rationalist arguments, see Farber, Free Speech without Romance, *supra* note 37, at 562–568, wherein he asserts a public choice version of what I have labeled a motivational hardiness argument. *See* discussion *supra* at 87. On the other hand, Professor Farber's work on commercial speech (coauthored with Professor Frickey) is characterized by reliance on a quasi-intuitionist form of "practical reason" and a rejection of heavily rationalist arguments in support of commercial speech protection. *See* Farber and Frickey, Practical Reason and the First Amendment, *supra* note 79, at 1639–1656.

81.   *See* Farber and Frickey, Practical Reason and the First Amendment, *supra* note 79, at 1622.

82.   Thomas H. Jackson and John Calvin Jeffries Jr., Commercial Speech: Economic Due Process and the First Amendment, 65 *Va. L. Rev.* 1, 2–6 (1979).

83.   Thomas I. Emerson, *The System of Freedom of Expression*, 414–417, 477 (1970).

84.   Professor Shiffrin has explicitly employed the term *intuitionism* to describe his approach to First Amendment interpretation. *See* Steven Shiffrin, The First Amendment and Economic Regulation: Away from a General Theory of the First Amendment, 78 *Nw. U. L. Rev.* 1212, 1254 (1984).

85.   Farber and Frickey, Practical Reason and the First Amendment, *supra* note 79, at 1640.

86.   *Id.* at 1641.

87.   *Id.*

88.   I have examined this issue in Martin H. Redish, Unlawful Advocacy and Free Speech Theory: Rethinking the Lessons of the McCarthy Era, 73 *U. Cin. L. Rev.* 9 (2004) (exploring contexts in which danger of harm should be found to restrict speech rights).

89.   Farber and Frickey, Practical Reason and the First Amendment, *supra* note 79, at 1641.

90.   *Id.* at 1646.

91. *Id.* at 1647–1648.

92. *See id.* at 1622.

93. *See id.* at 1622–1624.

94. *Id.* at 1641. Note that in a subsequent article, Farber does resort to a more rationalist form of argument to justify reduced protection for commercial speech. *See generally* Farber, Free Speech without Romance, *supra* note 37. However, I have already demonstrated the flaws in his argument. *See* discussion *supra* at 87–89.

95. Daniel A. Farber, The Inevitability of Practical Reason: Statutes, Formalism, and the Rule of Law, 45 *Vand. L. Rev.* 533, 538 (1992).

96. *See id.* at 542 ("Whatever practical reason may be, it is neither deduction nor intuition").

97. Professor Farber states, for example, that "practical reason does not mean— as is sometimes mistakenly thought—an embrace of ad hoc decisionmaking." *Id.* at 538–539.

98. *Id.* at 539.

99. *Id.*

100. *Id.*

101. *Id.*; *see also id.* at 541 ("Adherents to practical reason have not fully explained what cognitive processes in addition to deductive logic they view as legitimate").

102. *See,* for example, Post, *supra* note 7, at 34–41.

103. *See,* for example, *id.* at 20. *See also* Chapter Three, *supra.*

104. *See* U.S. Const. art. III, § 2 (providing federal judges with life tenure and protections of their salary during good behavior); *see also* U.S. Const. art. II, § 2 (providing the president with authority to nominate federal judges, subject to confirmation by the Senate).

105. The point is explained in greater detail in the critique of Post's theory of free expression contained in Chapter Three, *supra.*

106. *See Abrams v. United States,* 250 U.S. 616, 630 (Holmes, J., dissenting) (criticizing the majority's imposition of its views by means of censoring expression of minority views).

107. *See,* for example, *Brandenburg v. Ohio,* 395 U.S. 444, 448–449 (1969) (per curiam).

108. Note that it is my view that free expression does, in fact, serve ultimately only one value—self-realization—of which all other conceivable values are merely logical subvalues. *See* Redish, The Value of Free Speech, *supra* note 37, at 593. However, reconsideration of that issue is unnecessary for present purposes because even if one were to accept the notion of a synthesis of multiple free speech values, the application of traditional legal reason could still be employed.

109. Jackson and Jeffries, Commercial Speech, *supra* note 82, at 14.

110. *See,* for example, R. George Wright, *Selling Words: Free Speech in a Commercial Culture* 7 (1997).

111. *Id.*

112. *Id.* at 6.

113. Thomas Hobbes, *The Leviathan* 185 (C. B. MacPherson, ed., 1968) (1651).

114. *See* discussion *supra* at 85–96.

115. *Compare N.Y. Times Co. v. United States*, 403 U.S. 713, 720 (1971) (Douglas, J., concurring) (First Amendment is absolute), *and* Alexander Meiklejohn, The First Amendment Is an Absolute, 1961 *Sup. Ct. Rev.* 245, 246–248 (First Amendment protection of political speech is absolute), *with* Wallace Mendelson, On the Meaning of the First Amendment: Absolutes in the Balance, 50 *Cal. L. Rev.* 821, 825 (1962) (First Amendment requires use of a balancing approach).

116. Post has noted that presumably President Bush could fire Secretary of State Rice for suggesting the Iraq War was a mistake without violating the First Amendment, even though it would have, of course, been due to the expression of her viewpoint. Robert C. Post, *Remarks at the Loyola of Los Angeles Law Review Symposium: Commercial Speech: Past, Present & Future* (Feb. 24, 2007) [hereinafter Post, *Symposium Remarks*]. I fully concede the point. However, losing the position of secretary of state because of expression of one's viewpoint implicates an entirely distinct area of First Amendment analysis concerning government subsidies and benefits—a subject on which both Dean Post and I have written. *See* Redish, *Money Talks, supra* note 18, at 196–231; Robert C. Post, Subsidized Speech, 106 *Yale L. J.* 151, 152–153 (1996). I refer here solely to the more traditional and prevalent First Amendment context of directly coercive government regulation of expression. Surely the fact that a president can fire a cabinet officer for expressing unpopular views does not in any way imply that government can place a private citizen in jail for expressing a similarly unpopular view. I cannot imagine that Dean Post would disagree with this uncontroversial assertion.

117. Post has suggested that numerous regulations of viewpoint are permitted, consistent with the First Amendment. Post, *Symposium Remarks, supra* note 116. In attempting to support his assertion, however, Dean Post evinced substantial confusion over the nature of the viewpoint discrimination concept. *Id.* For example, he pointed to the fact that a doctor may be penalized for incorrectly reporting to a patient that a lesion was not cancerous. *Id.* This example, however, has absolutely nothing to do with the concept of viewpoint discrimination as employed in First Amendment analysis. That concept is confined to governmental penalizations of expression for no reason other than disagreement with or disdain for the normative ideological, economic, or sociopolitical views expressed.

118. *See* Henry Mayo, *An Introduction to Democratic Theory* 103 (1960) ("Everything necessary to [democratic] theory may be put in terms of (a) legislation [or decision-makers] who are (b) legitimated or authorized to enact public policies, and who are (c) subject or responsible to popular control at free election"); J. Roland Pennock, *Democratic Political Theory* 310 (1979) ("Elections are thought to constitute the great sanction for assuring representative behavior, by showing what the voters consider to be their interests by giving them the incentive to pursue those objectives").

119. *See* U.S. Const. art. V.

120. Meiklejohn, *Free Speech and Its Relation to Self Government, supra* note 38, at 24–25. Note that many commentators, including myself, believe the First Amendment does far more than this. *See generally* Redish, *The Value of Free Speech, supra* note 37 (First Amendment fosters self-realization). However, at the very least, the First Amendment must be deemed to protect the expression that influ-

ences and facilitates the voter's democratic choice in the voting booth. For present purposes, we need not take the argument further. For a more detailed critique of Meiklojohn's theory, see Chapter Three, *supra* at 37–43.

121. *See* discussion *supra* at 82–85.

122. In his response to an earlier version of these arguments, Dean Post contends that the concept of viewpoint discrimination, as I describe it, is too vague and convoluted to be of much help in First Amendment analysis. Post, *Symposium Remarks, supra* note 116. I find the assertion puzzling, to say the least. While it is true that Dean Post appears to have difficulty getting his arms around the concept, *see supra* note 116, the concept of viewpoint discrimination is both well-established and well-understood in First Amendment theory. *See* Farber, Free Speech without Romance, *supra* note 37, at 577 ("In First Amendment jurisprudence, restrictions based on viewpoint are especially suspect").

123. *Village of Skokie v. Nat'l Socialist Party of Am.*, 313 N.E.2d 21, 22 (Ill. 1978).

124. *Id.* at 26; *Collin v. Smith*, 578 F.2d 1197, 1207 (7th Cir. 1978).

125. *See*, for example, *Schacht v. United States*, 398 U.S. 58, 62–63 (1970) (holding unconstitutional a congressional ban on the unauthorized wearing of American military uniforms in a manner calculated to discredit the armed forces); *see also Good News Club v. Milford Cent. Sch.*, 533 U.S. 98, 107 (2001) (holding that a school's exclusion of a Christian children's club from meeting after hours at school, based on its religious nature, was unconstitutional viewpoint discrimination); *Legal Servs. Corp. v. Velazquez*, 531 U.S. 533, 549 (2001) (finding as unconstitutional a restriction that prohibited funding to organizations that represented clients seeking to challenge existing welfare laws); and *Rosenberger v. Rector & Visitors of the Univ. of Va.*, 515 U.S. 819, 835–837 (1995) (holding that a university's denial of funds to a religious organization amounted to viewpoint discrimination).

126. 347 U.S. 483 (1954).

127. U.S.C. §§ 2000e to e-17.

128. For a more detailed discussion of this point, see Martin H. Redish, *The Logic of Persecution: Free Expression and the McCarthy Era* 63–131 (2005).

129. *See Brandenburg v. Ohio*, 395 U.S. 444, 447–449 (1969) (per curiam).

130. In this context, it is important to emphasize that I am in no way suggesting that harassing or coercive speech, said to unwilling listeners, is protected by the First Amendment. For a discussion of my position on this issue, see Redish, *The Logic of Persecution, supra* note 128, at 123–126.

131. U.S. Const. amend. XIV, § 1, cl. 4. Though the Fourteenth Amendment's Equal Protection Clause does not apply to the federal government, the Supreme Court has held that the Fifth Amendment's Due Process Clause is properly construed to contain a prohibition on equal protection violations. *Bolling v. Sharpe*, 347 U.S. 497, 498–499 (1954).

132. U.S. Const. amend I. *See Police Dep't v. Mosley*, 408 U.S. 92, 94–98 (1972).

133. *N.Y. Times Co. v. Sullivan*, 376 U.S. 254, 271–272 (1964) (stating that judicial imposition of liability in libel suits may implicate First Amendment protection).

134. To avoid triggering potentially intractable complications involving the speech–conduct dichotomy, I refer here solely to obscene publications that do not

include photographic depictions of real individuals. I thus confine the discussion to pure narrative or artistic renderings.

135. For present purposes, to simplify the analysis the discussion refers only to obscene speech that does not involve the actual commission of illegal conduct. It is thus confined to literary and nonphotographic artistic expression.

136. *See*, for example, *Va. State Bd. of Pharmacy v. Va. Citizens Consumer Council, Inc.*, 425 U.S. 748, 781 (1976) (Rehnquist, J., dissenting) (believing that the Court's decision to extend First Amendment protection to commercial endeavors is troublesome); and Richard A. Posner, Free Speech in an Economic Perspective, 20 *Suffolk U. L. Rev.* 1, 22n43, 39–40 (1986) (stating that because commercial speech does not produce significant external benefits it should be afforded less constitutional protection).

137. *See*, for example, Robert H. Bork, Neutral Principles and Some First Amendment Problems, 47 *Ind. L. J.* 1, 20 (1971) ("Constitutional protection should be accorded only to speech that is explicitly political").

138. *See id.*

139. *See generally* Redish, The Value of Free Speech, *supra* note 37 (arguing that any expression, political or not, that enhances the self-realization value should be permitted full First Amendment protection).

140. *See* discussion *supra* at 107–114.

141. *See* discussion *supra* at 112–114.

142. 131 S. Ct. 2653 (2011).

143. *Id* at 2663.

144. *Id.* at 2665.

145. *Id.* at 2672.

146. *See*, for example, Ralph Nader, *Unsafe at Any Speed* 3–41 (1965).

147. Earlier in this chapter, I suggested that the Supreme Court has in practice, if not in name, extended something approaching full First Amendment protection to commercial speech. *See* discussion *supra* at 75. But it is only with respect to *truthful* commercial speech that this is the case. The protections of the "actual malice" test of *New York Times Co. v. Sullivan*, 376 U.S. 254, 279–280 (1964), are denied to commercial speech, while they are extended to false noncommercial speech. Also, as previously noted, a number of highly respected scholars have argued that, contrary to the view of the Court, commercial speech is entirely undeserving of First Amendment protection. *See* discussion *supra* at 85–104.

148. Bob Herbert, In America: Nike's Pyramid Scheme, *N.Y. Times*, June 10, 1996, at A17; Bob Herbert, In America: The Wrong Indonesian, *N.Y. Times*, Nov. 1, 1996, at A35; Bob Herbert, In America: Nike Blinks, *N.Y. Times*, May 21, 1998, at A33.

149. *Kasky v. Nike, Inc.*, 45 P.3d 243, 247 (Cal. 2003), *cert. granted*, 537 U.S. 1099 (2003), *and cert. dismissed as improvidently granted*, 539 U.S. 654 (2003).

150. *R.A.V. v. City of St. Paul*, 505 U.S. 377, 392 (1992) (plurality opinion). It might be suggested that a rational basis for distinguishing between Nike and its accusers is that Nike has special access to knowledge on the question and a significant degree of power and access for the expression of its views. But much the same could be said of one of its primary attacker, Bob Herbert of the *New York Times*. No one can doubt the *Times*'s power and access in the media world. And while of course Herbert cannot be assumed to have the same access to information about

Nike as Nike itself does, one can reasonably wonder why, if he lacks adequate information about Nike, he is making accusations in the first place. Moreover, under *Sullivan*'s actual malice test, Herbert cannot be held liable for product defamation even if he was grossly negligent in making the accusations. It is unclear why a lack of comparative access to information should insulate such grossly negligent behavior—except, of course, for the fact that we place a premium on free expression. It is a mystery why we would not provide equal breathing room, even for an individual or entity with presumably superior access. Moreover, to suggest that Nike's arguable superiority in access to information logically leads to using a standard tougher than actual malice misses the point. The issue, from the perspective of the chilling effect concern evinced in *Sullivan*, is not what Nike does or does not know but rather what Nike will be chilled from saying because of use of the stricter standard of liability. In any event, under the actual malice test, Nike's superior access to information would simply mean it would be easier to establish its knowledge of falsity.

Most importantly, in no other context of First Amendment analysis do we ever impose comparative gradations of protection on the basis of the relative power of the speaker or the speaker's access to information. Resort to this rationale to justify the outrageous disparity in protection in *Nike*, then, only goes to underscore the discriminatory treatment received by those speakers who advocate purchase of their product or service. In any event, *Consumer Reports* rarely lacks for either power or information access. Yet *Consumer Reports* is universally extended full First Amendment protection by courts and commentators.

151. One additional possibility is the argument, fashioned by Robert Post, that commercial speech, unlike noncommercial speech, fails to contribute to "public discourse." For reasons explored in detail in Chapter Three, however, this argument is unpersuasive.

152. *See* discussion *supra* at 97–103.

153. *See* discussion *supra* at 100.

154. For a more detailed consideration of this point, see Chapter Three, *supra*.

155. *Cf.* Redish, *The Logic of Persecution*, *supra* note 128, at 46–62; Blasi, The Pathological Perspective and the First Amendment, *supra* note 61, at 449–450 (espousing the view that the First Amendment should function at its most protective during times when intolerance of unorthodox ideas pervades the social and political climate).

156. *See* discussion *supra* at 103–104.

157. *See* discussion *supra* at 85–104.

158. *See*, for example, Carl Auerbach, The Communist Control Act of 1954: A Proposed Legal–Political Theory of Free Speech, 23 *U. Chi. L. Rev.* 173, 217–220 (1956) (arguing that the passage of the Communist Control Act of 1954 does not constitute an abandonment of democratic principles).

CHAPTER FIVE

Adapted from Martin H. Redish and Elana Nightingale Dawson, "Worse than the Disease": The Anti-Corruption Principle, Free Expression, and the Democratic Process, 20 *Wm. & Mary Bill Rts. J.* 1053 (2012).

1. *See Austin v. Michigan Chamber of Commerce*, 494 U.S. 652, 654 (1990) (finding constitutional a Michigan law that prohibited "corporations from using corporate treasury funds for independent expenditures in support of, or in opposition to, any candidate in elections for state office"); Burt Neuborne, Toward a Democracy-Centered Reading of the First Amendment, 93 *Nw. U. L. Rev.* 1055, 1056, 1070 (1999) (advocating an "egalitarian conception of democracy" where the "pervasive political inequality caused by massive wealth disparity" is limited); Frank J. Sorauf, Politics, Experience, and the First Amendment: The Case of American Campaign Finance, 94 *Colum. L. Rev.* 1348, 1360 (1994) (claiming that campaign finance reform is necessary when people believe that "[Political Action Committees] have 'bought' Congress" regardless of whether this belief is legitimate); David A. Strauss, Corruption, Equality, and Campaign Finance Reform, 94 *Colum. L. Rev.* 1369, 1370 (1994) (explaining that corruption in a system of campaign finance is a concern rooted in "inequality and the dangers of interest group politics"); and Zephyr Teachout, The Anti-Corruption Principle, 94 *Cornell L. Rev.* 341(2009).

2. *See* sources cited in note 1, *supra*.

3. Teachout, The Anti-Corruption Principle, *supra* note 1, at 347.

4. *Id.* at 374.

5. 130 S. Ct. 876 (2010).

6. *Id.* at 917.

7. *Id.* at 963–964 (Stevens, J., concurring in part and dissenting in part).

8. *Id.* at 961–962 (Stevens, J., concurring in part and dissenting in part).

9. *Id.* at 962 (Stevens, J., concurring in part and dissenting in part).

10. 494 U.S. 652, 654–655 (1990).

11. *Id.* at 660.

12. *Id.* at 679 (Scalia, J., dissenting).

13. *Id.* at 684 (Scalia, J., dissenting).

14. Teachout, The Anti-Corruption Principle, *supra* note 1, at 374.

15. *Id.*

16. *Id.* at 374.

17. *Id.* at 377–379.

18. *Id.* at 378.

19. U.S. Const. amend. I.

20. Teachout, The Anti-Corruption Principle, *supra* note 1, at 378 ("A virtuous citizen will not consider his own good as separate from the public good and would not strive to use government to pursue his own ends").

21. U.S. Const. amend. XIII (prohibiting slavery in the United States).

22. *See*, for example, U.S. Const. amend. XIV (restricting only state action); amend. V (restricting only the federal government).

23. *See Citizens United v. Fed. Election Comm'n*, 130 S.Ct. 876, 961–962 (2010); Burt Neuborne, One Dollar—One Vote: A Preface to Debating Campaign Finance Reform, 37 *Washburn L. J.* 1, 9 (1997); Strauss, Corruption, Equality, and Campaign Finance Reform, *supra* note 1, at 1382; and Teachout, The Anti-Corruption Principle, *supra* note 1, at 387.

24. *Id.* at 391; *see also* Neuborne, One Dollar—One Vote, *supra* note 23, at 9 (discussing the prevention of corruption in terms of "preventing unequal access to

government officials predicated on financial support"); and Strauss, Corruption, Equality, and Campaign Finance Reform, *supra* note 1, at 1382 (viewing corruption as "a problem because of inequality").

25. Teachout, The Anti-Corruption Principle, *supra* note 1, at 377–378, 386.

26. *Id.* at 378.

27. *See* discussion *infra* at xx.

28. U.S. Const. art. III, § 3, cl. 2 ("No Attainder of Treason shall work Corruption of Blood").

29. *See* discussion *infra* at 134–136.

30. *See* discussion *infra* at 136–141.

31. *See* discussion *infra* at 136–141.

32. *See* discussion *infra* at 139–140.

33. *See* discussion *infra* at 136–138.

34. *See* discussion *infra* at 156.

35. *See* discussion *infra* at 136–138.

36. *See* discussion *infra* at 136–149.

37. *See* discussion in Chapter Two *supra*.

38. *See generally* Chapter Two *supra*.

39. Martin H. Redish and Gary Lippman, Freedom of Expression and the Civic Republican Revival in Constitutional Theory: The Ominous Implications, 79 *Cal. L. Rev.* 267, 271 (1991).

40. *See* discussion *infra* at 126–133.

41. *See* discussion *infra* at 133–141.

42. *See* discussion *infra* at 141–149.

43. *Citizens United v. Fed. Election Comm'n,* 130 S.Ct. 876, 947–948, 963–964 (2010) (Stevens, J., concurring in part and dissenting in part).

44. *Fed. Election Comm'n v. Nat'l Conservative Political Action Comm.,* 470 U.S. 480, 496–497 (1985) ("preventing corruption or the appearance of corruption are the only legitimate and compelling government interests thus far identified for restricting campaign finances").

45. Teachout, The Anti-Corruption Principle, *supra* note 1, at 374.

46. *Id.*

47. U.S. Const., art. IV, § 2.

48. *Id.* at 375.

49. *Id.*

50. *Id.* at 378 ("Citizens must generally work for, and desire, the public good, at least in their political interactions").

51. *See* discussion *infra* at xx.

52. Teachout, The Anti-Corruption Principle, *supra* note 1, at 374.

53. *See* discussion *supra* at 123–125.

54. *Id.*

55. *Id.* at 376–377.

56. *Id.* at 374.

57. *Corruption*, Wikipedia, http://en.wikipedia.org/wiki/Corruption (last visited Oct. 2, 2011).

58. "Corruption" inquiry, Google, www.google.com (last visited Oct. 2, 2011).

59. Teachout, The Anti-Corruption Principle, *supra* note 1, at 377.
60. *Id.*
61. *Id.* at 378.
62. *Id.*
63. *Id.*
64. *Id.* at 379.
65. *Id.*
66. *See id.* at 378 ("This corruption of the citizen is possible in interactions with government or with politics. For a polity to work, citizens must not abuse the public trust in those interactions").
67. *Id.* at 379.
68. *Id.* at 387.
69. *Id.* at 388.
70. *Id.* at 389.
71. *Fed. Election Comm'n v. Wis. Right to Life, Inc.*, 551 U.S. 449, 479 (2007).
72. Teachout, The Anti-Corruption Principle, *supra* note 1, at 392.
73. *Id.* at 396.
74. *Id.* at 353.
75. *Id.*
76. *Id.*
77. *Id.*
78. *Id.* at 376.
79. *Id.* at 372n151.
80. *See* discussion *infra* at 134–139.
81. Teachout, The Anti-Corruption Principle, *supra* note 1, at 355.
82. *Id.* at 354.
83. *Id.* at 356.
84. *Id.*
85. *Id.*
86. *Id.*
87. *Id.* at 357.
88. *Id.*
89. *Id.* at 358.
90. *Id.* at 362.
91. *Id.* at 363.
92. *Id.*
93. *Id.*
94. *Id.*
95. *Id.* at 359.
96. *Id.* at 357.
97. *Id.* at 360.
98. *Id.* at 362.
99. *Id.* at 364.
100. U.S. Const. art. II, § 1, cl. 8.
101. Teachout, The Anti-Corruption Principle, *supra* note 1, 365.
102. *Id.* at 367.

103. *Id.* at 368.

104. *Id.* at 368–369.

105. *Id.* at 369. In Teachout's view, corruption exists when "integrity of the object of corruption is threatened by internal decay." *Id.* at 347. Beyond this broad, and somewhat circular definition, Teachout points to what she describes as modern concepts of corruption: "criminal bribery, inequality, drowned voices, a dispirited public, and a lack of integrity." *Id.* at 387. *See* discussion *supra* at 127–130.

106. *Id.* Teachout theorizes that the Framers felt that juries were less susceptible to corruption than judges, "who could regularly and predictably be bought." *Id.*

107. *Id.*

108. G. Edward White, *The Marshall Court and Cultural Change*, 1815–1835 at 7 (1988).

109. Teachout, The Anti-Corruption Principle, *supra* note 1, at 371.

110. *Id.*

111. *Id.*

112. *See* discussion *infra* at 146–148.

113. *See* Michael I. Myerson, *Liberty's Blueprint* 177 (2008) (Framers' primary concern was that elected officials "may forget their obligations to their constituents . . . "

114. U.S. Const. art. I, § 6, cl. 2.

115. *Id.* at § 9, cl. 8.

116. Teachout, The Anti-Corruption Principle, *supra* note 1, at 359.

117. *Id.* at 361.

118. Myerson, *Liberty's Blueprint, supra* note 113, at 176.

119. *Id.* at 177.

120. U.S. Const. art II, § 1, cl. 8.

121. *Id.* at § 1.

122. *Id.* at art. III, § 1.

123. *See* discussion *supra* at 130–131.

124. U.S. Const. amend. XIII, § 1 (prohibiting slavery).

125. For a discussion of this issue, see Martin H. Redish, Private Contingent Fee Lawyers and Public Power: Constitutional and Political Implications, 18 *S. Ct. Econ. Rev.* 77, 78–79 (2010).

126. Teachout, The Anti-Corruption Principle, *supra* note 1, at 346–354.

127. Martin S. Flaherty, History "Lite" in Modern American Constitutionalism, 95 *Colum. L. Rev.* 523, 578 (1995).

128. Gordon S. Wood, *The Creation of the American Republic, 1776–1787* at 612 (1998).

129. *Id.*

130. *Id.*

131. *See* Myerson, *Liberty's Blueprint, supra* note 113 at 171; 176–177.

132. James D. Savage, Corruption and Virtue at the Constitutional Convention, 56 *J. Politics* 174, 176 (1994).

133. Flaherty, History "Lite," *supra* note 127, at 578.

134. Calvin C. Jillson, *Constitutional Making: Conflict and Consensus in the Federal Convention of 1787* (1988).

135. *Id.* at 28.

136. *Id.* at 10.

137. *Id.* at 31.

138. *Id.* at 32.

139. *Id.* at 32–34.

140. *Id.* at 65.

141. *Id.* at 101.

142. *Id.* at 147–148.

143. *Id.* at 144–145.

144. Teachout, The Anti-Corruption Principle, *supra* note 1, at 375 (quoting Robert G. Natelson, The General Welfare Clause and the Public Trust: An Essay in Original Understanding, 52 *U. Kan. L. Rev.* 1, 48 [2003]).

145. *Id.* at 376 (quoting Laura S. Underkuffler, Captured by Evil: The Idea of Corruption in Law [Duke Law Sch. Legal Studies Research Series, Research Paper No. 83, 2005], available at http://ssrn.com/abstract=820249).

146. Jillson, *Constitutional Making, supra* note 134, at 18.

147. *Id.* at 22.

148. *Id.* (quoting Robert E. Shalhope, Republicanism and Early American Historiography, 29 *Wm. & Mary Q.* 40, 72).

149. Just a week before the Convention, George Mason wrote to his son saying, "Upon the great principles of it, I have reason to hope there will be great unanimity and less opposition, except from the little States, than was at first apprehended. The most prevalent idea in the principle states seems to be a total alteration of the present federal system. . . . It is easy to foresee that there will be much difficulty in organizing a government upon this great scale . . . yet with a proper degree of coolness liberty, and candor (very rare commodities by the bye), I doubt it may be effected." *Id.* (quoting *3 The Records of the Federal Convention of 1787*, at 23 [Max Farrand ed., 1911] [hereinafter *3 Convention Records*]).

150. *Id.* (quoting *3 Convention Records, supra* note 149, at 27).

151. *See* discussion *supra* at 131.

152. Teachout, The Anti-Corruption Principle, *supra* note 1, at 371–372, 375–376.

153. *Id.* at 372n151.

154. *See* discussion *infra* at 139.

155. *The Federalist No. 10*, at 171–173 (James Madison) (David Wootton, ed., 2003).

156. *Id.*

157. *Id.*

158. *Id.*

159. *Id.*

160. *See* discussion *supra* at 134–136.

161. *The Federalist No. 10* (James Madison), *supra* note 155, at 168.

162. Political scientist David Truman noted that "the antecedents of the modern trade organization go back on the local level at least to the guild organizations

of master craftsmen and traces of them can be found in very early American history." David Truman, *The Governmental Process* 75 (1951).

163. Daniel J. Tichenor and Richard A. Harris, Organized Interests in American Political Development, 114 *Pol. Sci. Q.* 587, 603 (2003).

164. E. Pendleton Herring, *Group Representation before Congress* 31 (1929).

165. *Id.*

166. *Id.* at 240.

167. Grant Jordan and William A. Maloney, *Democracy and Interest Groups* 2 (2007).

168. *Id.*

169. Tichenor and Harris, Organized Interests, *supra* note 163, at 589.

170. *Id.* at 598.

171. *Id.*

172. *Id.* at 599.

173. Herring, *Group Representation, supra* note 164, at 243.

174. *Id.* at 268.

175. *Id.* at 19, 21.

176. *Id.* at 240.

177. *Id.* at 23.

178. *Id.* at 30.

179. Allan J. Cigler and Burdett A. Loomis, Introduction: The Changing Nature of Group Politics, in *Interest Group Politics* 10 (Allan J. Cigler and Burdett A. Loomis, eds., 1983).

180. *Id.* at 11.

181. Ronald J. Hrebenar and Ruth K. Scott, *Interest Group Politics in America* 6 (1982).

182. *Id.* at 8.

183. *See*, for example, *Boy Scouts of America v. Dale*, 530 U.S. 640 (2000).

184. Gale Research, *Encyclopedia of Associations*, available at http://galenet .galegroup.com.turing.library.northwestern.edu/servlet/AU/form?origSearch= false&n=100&l=1&locID=northwestern&secondary=false&u=r&u=s.

185. *Id.*

186. Jane J. Mansbridge, *Beyond Adversary Democracy* 3 (1980). *See generally* Chapter Two, *supra.*

187. *Id.*

188. *Id.* at 18. *See generally* Chapter Two, *supra.*

189. *Id.* at 4.

190. *Id.* at 6.

191. *See* Chapter Two, *supra.*

192. *Id.*

193. Madison recognized as much, in a letter written in 1787, to Jefferson, stating: "In all civilized Societies, distinctions are various and unavoidable." Wood, *The Creation of the American Republic, supra* note 128, at 502.

194. Mansbridge, *supra* note 186, at 5.

195. Arthur L. Kalleberg and Larry M. Preston, Liberal Paradox: Self-Interest and Respect for Political Principles, 17 *Polity* 360, 360 (1984).

196. Wood, *The Creation of the American Republic, supra* note 128, at 612.

197. *See* discussion *supra* at 103–105.

198. Wood, *The Creation of the American Republic, supra* note 128, at 504.

199. *See* Chapter Two, *supra.*

200. Wood, *The Creation of the American Republic, supra* note 128, at 504 (quoting 2 *The Records of the Federal Convention of 1787,* at 204 [Max Farrand, ed., 1911]).

201. Teachout, The Anti-Corruption Principle, *supra* note 1, at 375.

202. *See,* for example, Texas v. Johnson, 491 U.S. 397, 414 (1989) ("If there is a bedrock principle underlying the First Amendment, it is that the government may not prohibit the expression of an idea simply because society finds the idea itself offensive or disagreeable").

203. *Id.* at 406.

204. *Id.*

205. *Id.* at 412.

206. *Id.* at 387.

207. Pub. L. No. 107-155, 116 Stat. 81 (codified in scattered sections of 2 and 47 U.S.C.).

208. *Citizens United v. Fed. Election Comm'n,* 130 S.Ct. 876, 888 (2010).

209. *Id.* at 887.

210. *Id.* at 886–887.

211. *Id.* at 888.

212. *Id.* at 917 (finding unconstitutional "2 U.S.C. § 441b's restrictions on corporate independent expenditures").

213. *Id.* at 899 ("We find no basis for the proposition that, in the context of political speech, the Government may impose restrictions on certain disfavored speakers. Both history and logic lead us to this conclusion").

214. *Id.* at 898.

215. *Id.* (quoting *Eu v. San Francisco County Democratic Central Comm.,* 489 U.S. 214, 223 (1989) [internal quotations omitted]).

216. *Id.*

217. Teachout, The Anti-Corruption Principle, *supra* note 1, at 391.

218. *Id.* at 393.

219. *Id.* at 392.

220. *Id.*

221. Strauss, Corruption, Equality, and Campaign Finance Reform, *supra* note 1, at 1370.

222. 424 U.S. 1 (1976).

223. Strauss, Corruption, Equality, and Campaign Finance Reform, *supra* note 1, at 1383.

224. *Id.* at 1385.

225. For a more detailed response to the argument that speech in a political campaign should be equated with the vote, *see* Martin H. Redish, *Money Talks: Speech, Economic Power and the Values of Democracy,* 136–139 (2001).

226. *Citizens United v. Fed. Election Comm'n,* 130 S.Ct. 876, 947–948, 963–964 (2010) (Stevens, J., concurring in part and dissenting in part).

CHAPTER SIX

1. *See*, for example, *Wooley v. Maynard*, 430 U.S. 705 (1977); and *West Virginia Bd. of Educ. v. Barnette*, 319 U.S. 624 (1943).

2. *See* discussion *infra* at 152–159.

3. *The Federalist Papers*, it should be recalled, were all written under assumed names.

4. *See*, for example, *Talley v. California*, 362 U.S. 60 (1960); and *McIntyre v. Ohio*, 514 U.S. 334 (1995); *see* discussion *infra* at 160–163.

5. *See generally* Chapters One and Two, *supra*.

6. *See generally* Chapters One and Two, *supra*.

7. *See Central Hudson Gas and Electric Corp. v. Public Service Commission of New York*, 447 U.S. 557, 563–564 (1980) (excluding all false commercial speech from the scope of First Amendment protection). *See* note 60, *infra*.

8. *See generally* Chapter Four, *supra*.

9. 376 U.S. 254 (1964). *See also Garrison v. Louisiana*, 379 U.S. 64 (1964); *Rosenbloom v. Metromedia*, 403 U.S. 29 (1971); and *Curtis Publishing Co. v. Butts*, 388 U.S. 130 (1967).

10. 376 U.S. at 279–280.

11. *United States v. Alvarez*, 132 S. Ct. 2537 (2012).

12. The one appellate decision that appears to have considered the issue in detail was in the Supreme Court of the State of Washington. State ex rel. *Public Disclosure Comm'n v. 119 Vote No! Committee*, 135 Wash.2d 618, 957 P.2d 691 (Washington 1998). There the court found that the First Amendment did protect conscious falsehoods in the electoral process outside of the defamation context. *See* discussion *infra* at 165–167.

13. *Buckley v. Valeo*, 424 U.S. 1, 71 (1976) (per curiam). The Court noted, however, that had the contributor demonstrated a "serious" threat to First Amendment interests and an "insubstantial" governmental interest, its conclusion might have been different.

14. *Id.* at 66–67.

15. It should be emphasized that this discussion intends to distinguish this *internal* First Amendment dilemma from a need to balance First Amendment interests against competing nonexpressive interests. In drawing the appropriate balance in the case of political fraud, it is no help to begin the balancing process with "a thumb on the scales" in favor of the free speech interest, since *both* interests are appropriately seen as First Amendment interests.

16. *See* cases cited in note 1, *supra*; discussion, *infra* at 160–161.

17. *See*, for example, *Shelton v. Tucker*, 364 U.S. 479 (1960).

18. *See* discussion *infra* at 157–160.

19. *See* discussion *infra* at 160–161.

20. *See* discussion *infra* at 164–171.

21. *See* discussion *infra* at 171–175.

22. Martin H. Redish, *Money Talks: Speech, Economic Power, and the Values of Democracy* 175 (2001).

23. *Id.*

24. *Id.*

25. *Id.*

26. *Id.* (footnote omitted).

27. *See* cases cited in note 1, *supra.*

28. *See* Chapter Three, *supra.*

29. Alexander Meiklejohn, *Political Freedom* 9 (1965).

30. Alexander Meiklejohn, The First Amendment Is an Absolute, 1961 *Sup. Ct. Rev.* 245.

31. Meiklejohn, *Political Freedom, supra* note 29, at 26.

32. *See generally* C. Edwin Baker, *Human Liberty and Freedom of Speech* (1989). Professor Baker's focus is on the liberty interest of the speaker. Thus, where the expression is not derived from the voluntary choice of the speaker (for example, where the expression comes from a corporation) Baker finds no value in the speech, despite the fact that listeners may well benefit as a result. *See* C. Edwin Baker, Realizing Self-Realization: Corporate Political Expenditures and Redish's The Value of Free Speech, 130 *U. Pa. L. Rev.* 646 (1982). I have been quite critical of his approach. *See*, for example, Martin H. Redish, Self-Realization, Democracy, and Freedom of Expression: A Reply to Professor Baker, 130 *U. Pa. L. Rev.* 678 (1982).

33. 395 U.S. 367 (1969).

34. *Id.* at 369.

35. *Id.* at 392.

36. *Id.* at 390. For a pioneering explanation of the First Amendment theory underlying the right of access, see Jerome A. Barron, Access to the Press—A New First Amendment Right, 80 *Harv. L. Rev.* 1641 (1967).

37. 418 U.S. 241 (1974).

38. *Cf.* Guido Calabresi and Philip Bobbitt, *Tragic Choices* (1978).

39. 362 U.S. 60 (1960).

40. *Id.* at 64.

41. *Id.*

42. 514 U.S. 334 (1995).

43. Id. at 341 (citing *Talley*).

44. Where forced expression requires the private speaker to parrot governmental positions that he does not accept, then the listeners are, of course, better off with total silence than with misleading private support for government positions. The fact remains, however, that as a categorical matter silence, in and of itself, cannot possibly advance the public discourse.

45. This is particularly true when the government seeks to compel the private individual or entity to reveal information that might be valuable to the populace. It is also true in the case of a forced provision of expressive access to other private individuals, as was the case in *Red Lion.* It is not the case, however, when the government seeks to force the private individual to reiterate government-held positions with which the speaker disagrees.

46. 357 U.S. 449, 460 (1958).

47. *Id.* at 462–463. The Court also stated that "it is not sufficient to answer, as the State does here, that whatever repressive effect compulsory disclosure of

names of petitioner's members may have upon participation by Alabama citizens in petitioner's activities follows not from state action but from private community pressures. The crucial factor is the interplay of governmental and private action, for it is only after the initial exertion of state power represented by the production order that private action takes hold." *Id.* at 463. *Cf. Shelton v. Tucker*, 364 U.S. 479 (1960) (upholding First Amendment right of schoolteachers to keep secret the list of organizations of which they are members).

48. There are a number of respected free speech scholars who have framed the First Amendment right exclusively in terms of a speaker's intent to contribute to public discourse. As a literal matter at least, private exchanges of political views would not seem to qualify under this description of the right of expression. However, as I have recently argued, to the extent the "public discourse" approach actually intended to exclude such private communications, it is fatally flawed. *See* Chapter Three.

49. *See* discussion *infra* at 173–175.

50. *See* discussion *infra* at 167–169.

51. 376 U.S. 254 (1964).

52. *Id.* at 271–272.

53. Absent First Amendment insulation, the Court reasoned, "would-be critics of official conduct may be deterred from voicing their criticism, even though it is believed to be true and even though it is in fact true, because of doubt whether it can be proved in court or fear of the expense of having to do so." *Id.* at 279.

54. Justices Black, Douglas, and Goldberg differed with the majority on not making the First Amendment protection against defamation actions absolute. Id. at 293 (Black, J., concurring) (joined by Douglas, J.), 297 (Goldberg, J., concurring) (joined by Douglas, J.).

55. *Id.* at 279–280. Note that the label is something of a confusing misnomer. "Malice," in the sense of evil intent, is by no means sufficient to bring defamatory speech within the exception. For example, a speaker could be motivated by the malicious goal of destroying his victim, yet nevertheless believe the truth of his allegations.

56. Note that the Court also recognized an exception for statements made with reckless disregard of their truth or falsity. However, in subsequent decisions the Court confined this exception narrowly to make it virtually identical to actual knowledge of falsity. *See St. Amant v. Thompson*, 390 U.S. 727 (1968). Note also that at the time of its decision, the *New York Times*'s First Amendment protection of false defamatory statements was confined to comments about public officials. However, in subsequent years the Court extended that protection to comments about public figures, as well. *Gertz v. Robert Welch, Inc.*, 418 U.S. 323 (1974).

57. The concurring opinions differed with this assessment on the grounds that even a well-meaning speaker might fear the burdens and risks involved in defending against the allegation of conscious falsity. 376 U.S. at 293 (Black, J., concurring). For present purposes, however, this discussion proceeds on the assumption of the correctness of the majority's conclusion.

58. The Court has also applied the *New York Times* doctrine in the context of so-called false light privacy. *Time, Inc. v. Hill*, 385 U.S. 374 (1967). However, this tort is strikingly similar to the defamation tort in relevant ways.

59. Retrieved from http//dictionary.law.com.

60. *Central Hudson Gas & Elec. Corp. v. Public Service Comm'n*, 447 U.S. 557, 563–564 (1980).

61. *Id.*

62. *See* discussion *supra* at 153.

63. The court in *Alvarez* dealt with a law criminalizing the consciously false claim that the speaker had been awarded a medal.

64. State ex rel. *Public Disclosure Comm'n v. 119 Vote No! Committee*, 135 Wash.2d 618, 957 P.2d 691 (Washington 1998).

65. R.C.W. 42.17.530.

66. The court, emphasizing the importance of political speech as part of the First Amendment's protection, concluded that the law "coerces silence." 957 P.2d at 627.

67. *Id.* at 628–629.

68. *Id.* at 624–625 (quoting *New York Times*, 376 U.S. at 271).

69. 957 P.2d at 626.

70. *Id.* at 627 (citation omitted).

71. *See generally* John Stuart Mill, *On Liberty* (1859).

72. *Abrams v. United States*, 250 U.S. 616, 630 (1919) (Holmes, J., dissenting) ("The ultimate good desired is better reached by free trade in ideas").

73. *Whitney v. California*, 274 U.S. 357, 375 (1927) (Brandeis, J., concurring) (advocating marketplace of ideas rationale for free expression).

74. As I wrote many years ago, "The 'marketplace-of-ideas' concept, in its use as a defense of free speech, has often been subjected to savage attack." Martin H. Redish, *Freedom of Expression: A Critical Analysis* 46 (1984).

75. Harry Wellington, On Freedom of Expression, 88 *Yale L. J.* 1105 (1979), 1130.

76. *Gertz v. Robert Welch, Inc.*, 418 U.S. 323, 339 (1974).

77. *See* discussion *supra* at 34–36.

78. *See generally* Chapter One, *supra*.

79. *See* Martin H. Redish, The Adversary System, Democratic Theory, and the Constitutional Role of Self-Interest: The Tobacco Wars, 1953–1971, 51 *DePaul L. Rev.* 359 (2001).

80. *See* discussion *supra* at 168.

81. *See generally* Martin H. Redish, *The Logic of Persecution: Free Expression and the McCarthy Era* (2005).

82. *See* discussion *supra* at 161–163.

83. *See* discussion *supra* at 163.

84. The same logic would apply when an alias is chosen but it is obviously and unambiguously an alias—for example, "Publius" as one of the authors of the *Federalist Papers*. Use of that name is, as a practical matter, the equivalent of doing nothing more than concealing the speaker's identity.

85. *Abrams v. United States*, 250 U.S. 616, 630 (1919) (Holmes, J., dissenting).

CHAPTER SEVEN

1. *See* Chapter One, *supra* at 2.

2. *See* Chapter Two, *supra* at 10–15.

3. See in particular the discussion in Chapter Five, *supra*, of the so-called anti-corruption principle, grounded in such an exclusionary principle of free speech protection.

4. *See* Chapter Two, *supra* at 15.

5. David Held, *Political Theory and the Modern State* 176 (1989).

6. Carole Pateman, *The Problem of Political Obligation: A Critique of Liberal Theory* 171 (1985).

7. Held, *Political Theory and the Modern State*, *supra* note 5, at 176.

8. *Id.* at 177.

9. *See* Martin H. Redish, *Money Talks: Speech, Economic Power, and the Values of Democracy* 147–195 (2001).

10. "It has been said that democracy is the worst form of Government except all those other forms that have been tried from time to time." Winston Churchill, Speech to the House of Commons (Nov. 11, 1947), reprinted in *The Oxford Dictionary of Quotations* 150 (3d ed., 1979).

11. Giovanni Sartori, *The Theory of Democracy Revisited* 286 (1987) (footnote omitted).

12. *See* Chapter Three, *supra*.

13. *Id.*

14. *See generally* Chapter Five, *supra*.

15. *See* Chapter Three, *supra* at 43–69.

16. *See* discussion *supra* at 60–62.

17. *See* discussion *supra* at 60–62.

18. *See* discussion *supra* at 2.

19. John Rawls, *A Theory of Justice* 136–142 (1971).

Index